The Complete Beg[inner's Guide to]
USING [EMAIL]
FOR THE FIRST TIME

For a complete list of Management Books 2000 titles,
visit our web-site on http://www.mb2000.com

The Complete Beginner's Guide to
USING EMAIL
FOR THE FIRST TIME

Bill Hall

author of
The Complete Beginner's Guide to
Using a Computer for the First Time
and (2003) The Complete Beginner's Guide
to Using a Digital Camera for the First Time

2000

First published in 2002 by Management Books 2000 Ltd
Forge House, Limes Road
Kemble, Cirencester
Gloucestershire, GL7 6AD, UK
Tel: 0044 (0) 1285 771441/2
Fax: 0044 (0) 1285 771055
E-mail: m.b.2000@virgin.net
Web: mb2000.com

Printed and bound in Great Britain by Biddles, Guildford

British Library Cataloguing in Publication Data is available
ISBN 1-85252-417-0

Contents

Acknowledgements   **9**

Introduction – the scope of this book   **10**

Conventions used in this book   **12**

Chapter 1 – Understanding Email   **13**
1.1   Opening remarks   13
1.2   The composition of an electronic letter   15
1.3   Sending an electronic letter   19
1.4   The addressing of an electronic letter   25
1.5   Attachments to an electronic letter   27
1.6   The journey and delivery of an electronic letter   29

Chapter 2 – Connecting to the Internet   **32**
2.1   Getting ready to connect   32
2.2   Beware of automatic disconnection   35
2.3   Starting Outlook Express   36
2.4   Manually checking for mail   46
2.5   More about the on-line connection   48
2.6   Closing Outlook Express and disconnecting   49
2.7   Alternative on-line connection methods   51

Chapter 3 – Sending and Receiving an email   **54**
3.1   Creating and sending an email   54
3.2   Receiving and reading an email   62
3.3   Saving and editing an email   64
3.4   A few points to consider   69

Chapter 4 – Sending and Receiving attachments   **73**
4.1   Sending an attachment   73
4.2   Receiving an attachment   80
4.3   Comments about attachments   84

Chapter 5 – Working off-line　　　　　　　　　　**88**
5.1　What is on-line and off-line?　　　　　　　　88
5.2　Using Outlook Express off-line disconnected　90
5.3　Switching from on-line to off-line disconnected　92
5.4　Switching back from off-line to on-line　　　95

Chapter 6 – Managing your Email addresses　　**98**
6.1　Adding contacts to the Windows Address Book　98
6.2　Sending using the Address Book　　　　　　103
6.3　Editing and deleting from the Address Book　106
6.4　Creating a group of addresses　　　　　　　109
6.5　Sending email to a group of addresses　　　113

Chapter 7 – Read Receipts, Replies and Forwarding　**116**
7.1　Has your email arrived at its destination?　　116
7.2　How do you know if email has been read?　　118
7.3　Replying to someone　　　　　　　　　　128
7.4　Forwarding to someone else　　　　　　　135

Chapter 8 – Managing Email　　　　　　　**141**
8.1　The need to manage　　　　　　　　　　141
8.2　Deleting unwanted email　　　　　　　　142
8.3　Filing to a new folder　　　　　　　　　145
8.4　Flagging an email　　　　　　　　　　149
8.5　Ordering the lists　　　　　　　　　　151
8.6　Searching for something　　　　　　　　153

Chapter 9 – Protecting against Viruses, Hackers and Spam　**158**
9.1　Avoid viruses and stay healthy　　　　　　158
9.2　I never knew they could do that!　　　　　162
9.3　Spam, spam and more spam　　　　　　　171

Chapter 10 – Using Webmail　　　　　　　**181**
10.1　Using Email anywhere in the world　　　　181
10.2　Using Webmail　　　　　　　　　　　182
10.3　How Webmail works　　　　　　　　　196
10.4　Be careful with your password　　　　　　199
10.5　Concluding remarks　　　　　　　　　200

Appendix I – The Internet – what is it?　　　**202**

Appendix II – Setting up a modem for use on a computer　**205**

Appendix III – Setting up an ISP account   **215**

Appendix IV – How to check that your modem and ISP account are ready to use   **238**

Appendix V – Showing sub-windows in Outlook Express   **244**

Appendix VI – Using different identities and accounts   **246**

Appendix VII – Setting up accounts for Dial-up connections   **263**

Index   **269**

Exercises:

In Ch 2:
Exercise 1 – Getting the email program running on-line   36
Exercise 2 – Manually checking for mail   46
Exercise 3 – Closing the email program and disconnecting   50

In Ch 3:
Exercise 4 – Creating your first email and sending it   55
Exercise 5 – Receiving and reading your first email   62
Exercise 6 – Creating and saving an email without sending   65
Exercise 7 – Retrieving, editing and then sending an email   67

In Ch 4:
Exercise 8 – Attaching an image file to an email and sending it   76
Exercise 9 – Receiving an email and detaching an attachment   80

In Ch5:
Exercise 10 – How to work off-line disconnected   92
Exercise 11 – How to get back on-line from startup   95

In Ch 6:
Exercise 12 – Adding contacts to the Windows Address Book   98
Exercise 13 – Sending an email using the Address Book   103
Exercise 14 – Editing an entry in the Address Book   106
Exercise 15 – Deleting an entry in the Address Book   108
Exercise 16 – Creating a group of addresses   109
Exercise 17 – Sending email to a group of addresses   113

In Ch 7:
Exercise 18 – Asking for a read receipt   119
Exercise 19 – Receiving the read receipt   125
Exercise 20 – Using the Reply function   129

Exercise 21 – Using the Forward function   135

In Ch 8:
Exercise 22 – Deleting an email   142
Exercise 23 – Re-filing an email to a new folder   146
Exercise 24 – Flagging an email   149
Exercise 25 – Ordering lists   152
Exercise 26 – Searching for an email   154

In Ch 9:
Exercise 27 – Checking the Windows XP Firewall   166
Exercise 28 – Adding to the Blocked Sender List   171
Exercise 29 – Creating a message rule   174

In Ch10:
Exercise 30 – Sending and receiving via Webmail   183
Exercise 31 – Sending and receiving attachments via Webmail 188
Exercise 32 – Detaching Webmail attachments   194

Trademarks

The following trademarks are acknowledged for the respective companies:

Adobe Systems Incorporated:	Adobe Acrobat
Intel Corporation:	Intel
Microsoft Corporation:	Windows XP
	Windows 98
	Outlook Express
	Internet Explorer
Symantec Corporation:	Norton AntiVirus
	Norton Personal Firewall
	Norton Internet Security
Tiscali UK Ltd:	Tiscali

Acknowledgements

I would dearly like to thank the following people for their valued contributions in making this book a reality...Dilys Birkett, Eileen Gowthorpe and Vic Reading, my trusty litmus-test team who have read each chapter as it was produced, and worked through all the exercises. It was hard work for them but their feedback has been just invaluable. David G North of Texas, USA, for his trust in receiving my email out of the blue and dignifying it with a reply. David's technical help as a company email administrator can now be shared with our entire readership. Annette Bontke, of Tiscali UK Ltd, for her patience in receiving my emails and keeping my spirits high with her replies. James Alexander, of Management Books 2000 Ltd, for his guidance in steering this book to its finished form, and his for patience too. And finally, again I must thank my wife Norma, who greatly deserves the credit for her faith and sharing the burdens of producing it.

Introduction

The scope of this book

This book has been specially written for an older audience of average ability. It is the second in the 'First Time' series of computer guides and its aim is to provide instructions on using electronic mail, or **email** as we now call it. It will be of particular value to people who may have no expert on hand to teach them, or those who prefer to learn by themselves at their own pace.

The book has a narrative style that is easy to read. It teaches by example using a number of practical exercises for you to follow on your own computer. Each step is carefully explained and illustrated so that you always know what to do next.

Doing things for yourself is a key feature of this book. Yes, you can ask other people to show you, but quite often they will not have the time to explain things in detail. Even if they do, unless you have an unusual memory, you can find that a day or two later you have forgotten most of what they said. By doing things for yourself, you get the confidence that you *can* sort it out yourself if need be. It makes you more independent and that has to be a good thing with a computer, for there is much to learn! And learning on your own can be just the job for older readers, for it means you don't have to be embarrassed or intimidated by the progress of others. If something does slip your memory, then this book will quickly remind you how you did it.

● The book starts from the point of first connecting to the Internet and sending or receiving your first simple emails. It then shows you how to attach and detach photos of your family, documents, and other computer files. You are also shown how to manage an address book containing all your email contact details, how to make groups of such contacts, and how you can email things to everyone in the whole group in just one go.

● In the later chapters of the book, you are shown how to get confirmation that your email has arrived, how to quickly reply to incoming email, and how to forward items on to show others. You will also see how to create your own folders, re-file your emails, and delete those you no longer want. There is also a chapter about the nuisance factors with email, such as computer viruses, hacking by others, and 'junk' email.

- Finally, the book shows you how you can use Webmail, which is a new way of using email. Webmail not only allows you to read your email from home but also while you are away on holiday, so that you don't lose touch with your friends or colleagues – even if you are travelling from one place to another.

Throughout, it is assumed that you are familiar with the basics of a computer such as using the mouse and keyboard. It is also assumed that you know how to start programs running, and that you know a little about computing terms such as computer 'files' and such like. If you find yourself in trouble with any of these basics, then you really need to read and study the companion guide called *Using a Computer for the First Time*. In this present book about using email, the same groundwork is not covered again but it will be taken as read that you have these things 'under your belt'. However, we will discuss in detail any new ideas or computing terms that have not been previously covered, so rest assured that any jargon we may need to introduce will not hold any fear for you.

This book will specifically discuss those computers that use the Microsoft email program 'Outlook Express' (versions 6 or 5.5) and the Windows XP or 98 operating systems. However, most of the ideas and instructions will be equally applicable to earlier and later versions of Outlook Express and Windows, even if there are minor variations in certain detail.

Take time to work your way through the chapters slowly and make sure you have understood them before moving to the next. Many people make the mistake of rushing to advanced things before they are really ready. This can be quite stressful and frustrating later on, particularly when you know that some task is possible, but cannot make it happen yourself.

Computers are without doubt complex tools to use properly. The problem usually is not that they are inherently difficult – it is more the sheer number of new things that you need to get to grips with. Many of these things are simple if taken step by step, but the need to remember each of these things and their sequences can be daunting to the beginner. The real secret for success is to **build your knowledge and skills slowly**. Don't try and learn too much in one go. Don't be afraid to read and re-read sections over again. You will be surprised at how much more you take in and remember the second time. Do follow the chapters by practising the exercises on your own computer as you go along. You will retain more of the information you learn in that way.

Conventions used in this book

Throughout this book, there are a number of practical exercises for readers to perform using their own computer systems. During these exercises, readers are asked to carry out certain actions with their mouse or keyboard. The following conventions have been adopted in describing these actions:

click This means swiftly press and release the normal left mouse button.

right-click This means swiftly press and release the right mouse button.

drag This means press the left mouse button and keep it pressed as you move the mouse pointer to a new position. Only release the left mouse button when you have reached the new position.

press Unless the text specifically refers to a keyboard key, this means position the mouse pointer over an 'on-screen' button and then press and release the left mouse button.

select This refers to a menu and means position the mouse pointer over the item to be selected, then press and release the normal left mouse button.

Notes

● email and Internet – in common with other books on computing subjects, we have adopted the convention of writing these two words as shown, 'email' without a capital initial or a hyphen, and 'Internet' with a capital initial.

● 'on-line' and 'off-line' are shown hyphenated for the sake of clarity, although some computer programs show them without hyphens.

● 'program' is the word for a computer system, but we would be happy for you to create a programme of study for yourself.

1

Understanding Email

1.1 Opening remarks

Welcome to email – even mightier than the pen!

To begin this teach-yourself guide on the subject, let me share with you a dilemma. In preparing this opening chapter, I have given much thought about how we should begin. Should we start with a practical exercise to prove that this is well within everybody's capability? Or should we start with the underlying theory, so that you understand what you see on the computer screen and what goes on behind it? To cater for the widest possible readership, this has not been an easy question to answer.

It can be argued that the best way would be to start simply with a practical exercise, to whet your appetite and amaze you with the power of this technology. We could then introduce some theory later, once you have been hooked and are eager to learn. However, there is a snag with this approach. When you are using email, even for the first time, you need to be able to access the Internet successfully in order to do so. Some of you may never have seen a modem before, and you may need to understand the principles in order to set up your computer system. This could well be a deciding factor in determining the way that you choose to progress.

If you know that your computer equipment has already been set up to access the Internet, then you at liberty to jump straight to the next chapter and 'get your hands dirty'. This first chapter is devoted to the theory of email and it is not essential to read it before you begin. Having said that, there are three reasons why you might want to read at least part of it, before you move on to the practical work:

- The first reason could be because your computer system is not yet ready to access the Internet. If you understand the theory, it can make it a lot easier to get it working properly.

- The second reason may be because then you will have a better grasp of why you are performing certain actions. As a result, you can get more benefit from the practical work, and thereby more from the overall service.

• The third reason may be because you are naturally curious as to how it all works!

The decision on how you get started is for you to make. It will be influenced not just by your circumstances, but probably your personality too. If you are not too interested in how something works – you just want to use it – then reading the theory sometime later would be the best plan for you. At the end of these opening remarks, move on to chapter 2, and maybe come back and read these pages afterwards, if you have a need and wish to. I have lumped all the theory together so you know where it is.

Email is very much in widespread use today. You hear about it everywhere from TV and radio stations to newspapers and magazines. The word derives from a contraction of 'electronic mail', and this indicates immediately that it is referring to some new and exciting form of mail delivery service. The older, established form of mail delivery that we all know and love is ordinary 'postal' mail, and because it has been around for well over 100 years or so, it is well used and understood by everyone. This is not the case with email, and in explaining the principles for you, it seems quite natural to try and make some direct comparisons between the two forms of service. We will therefore adopt this approach in the theory introduced in the later sections of this chapter.

One question often posed by 'first-timers' is will email one day replace postal mail completely? It would be easy to surmise, 'Yes, one day it is bound to do so', for today's meteoric growth in the use of email is certain to have a heavy influence. But I personally think that the two services will co-exist for quite some time, for although email can transport a variety of electronic 'items' very quickly from one place to another, it cannot yet do so for physical items. This may no longer be true of course, if the futuristic technique of Star-Trek 'Teletransportation' ever becomes a reality. Then the postal mail service could be in deep trouble! However, I don't think this is something that need worry us too much within our own lifetimes.

Throughout the rest of this chapter, the concepts and descriptions provided will necessarily be technically condensed. I openly admit now that I am going to massage strict accuracy a little bit for convenience. My aim is not to make you an expert in the technology, but to encourage an understanding of the principle of what is going on – so that you have a better overall grasp when you come to set it up and use it. Postal mail is so easily understood because you can to watch it in action with your very own eyes. Unfortunately, you cannot 'see' email in action in quite the same way, and this (like much of computer software) is where the seeds of most difficulties lie.

One problem with introducing theory is that it can become 'heavy going', especially if you haven't studied technical matters for some time. My advice is to go easy with this first chapter. If it gets a bit dry, then move quickly to chapter 2 where you get to do things. You can always come back and re-read this chapter later when your practical skills can complement your understanding of the theory.

1.2   The composition of an 'electronic letter'

When we use the word 'email' in a general sense, we are normally referring to the delivery service itself. When we talk about 'sending an email' we are normally talking about actually sending something via the delivery service, and this something will eventually appear at the remote end. We may think of 'an email' therefore as 'an electronic letter', and this is a useful concept to have in mind.

The true nature of an electronic letter, however, it is quite difficult to fully appreciate because, for the most part, it is invisible as it travels from the sender to the recipient. So, in order to gain a better understanding, let us first identify the features that make-up the everyday postal letter, and see where this might take us:

- A letter normally consists of one or more pieces of paper with lines of **words** scribbled upon them, conveying a message of some sort or other.
- A letter is also something that is sent by one person and received by another. This indicates that there is some element of **travel** involved. For protection along the journey, we group and place the pages of our completed message together inside an envelope, and we seal the contents of the envelope by sticking the flap down.
- A letter needs an **address** visible on the outside of the envelope. This must state clearly the name and location of the person to whom the letter is to be sent. If we are diligent, we also include our own return name and address.
- A letter finally requires that we pay some kind of fee, usually by sticking one or more stamps on the front, the value of which must be adequate to pay for the **delivery cost** by a third party.

If we have hold of an object possessing these features, then we might all agree that we have in our hands a 'letter'.

Now let us see if we can construct the electronic counterpart. We start by considering the first point from the above list – we need electronic paper with lines of electronic words scribbled upon it …

Coding and signalling – the words of the message
It really all begins with the concepts of **coding** and **signalling**. In sending an email, we are going to use the telephone system as the method of connecting our

own computer with others in the wider world. And the only things that pass down a telephone line are signals in the form of varying electrical voltages and currents. In order to send intelligible signals conveying our email information, we need to employ a standardised coding method for signalling, so that our electronic words have meaning when they arrive at the distant end.

The coding method of interest to us has an odd but very well established name. It is called ASCII (pronounced 'ass-key') and this is an abbreviation for 'American Standard Code for Information Interchange'. Whilst at first this phrase seems to be a bit of a mouthful, once you have thought about it, it seems to fit the bill. We need to 'interchange information' and what better way to do this than to use a 'standard code' - at least then it should be understood universally!

To illustrate how this coding works, I am going to offer you a small example. Let us have a look at how we might compose and code an email that asks a friend 'How are you?' Now this seemingly simple phrase has 9 letters, 2 spaces, and 1 question mark (the quotation marks are not part of the message). The ASCII coding method is effectively a numerical coding scheme, and for each letter, space or punctuation mark there is an equivalent code number in the range 0 to 127. I won't bore you with the details of all of them but just give a few of the ones that we might require – letter 'H' is represented by decimal number '72' (seventy two), 'o' by '111' (one hundred and eleven), 'w' by '119' (one hundred and nineteen), a 'space' by '32' (thirty two) and so it continues… When we have coded all 9 letters, 2 spaces and the question mark we will have produced a sequential string of decimal numbers as illustrated in this picture.

H	o	w		a	r	e		y	o	u	?
72	111	119	32	97	114	101	32	121	111	117	63

The sequence goes from left to right and has a total of 12 decimal numbers to represent the whole message. Providing we can send this sequential string as signals down the telephone line – again in the order left to right – then in theory when they get to the far end destination, they can be converted back again into the original message.

In terms of electronic words and paper, the previous picture now shows us what these are. Electronic words (including the spaces and punctuation) are just groups of numbers. Electronic paper however is something a bit stranger. It equates to the fact that these numbers are arranged in a fixed, sequential string. The order of the sequence (left to right in the picture) gives the string of numbers meaning and structure, just as paper lets you write words in the correct order. If we lose the order, then it would be the same as tearing up the physical paper for a postal letter – just imagine opening up a postal letter only to find a jumble of individual scraps inside!

Okay. The example is simple enough for sending a three-word message, but what about a whole page consisting of many lines? The answer is found in the use two more codes – codes '13' (thirteen) and '10' (ten). Code '13' means that the end of an electronic line has been reached, and code '10' means that a new line is now starting. By adding these two codes on to the end of the sequential string, we can send a second line of the message, and then a third, fourth … and so on. The next picture illustrates a message containing two lines.

H	o	w		a	r	e		y	o	u	?				I	'	m		O	K		
72	111	119	32	97	114	101	32	121	111	117	63	13	10	73	39	109	32	79	75	13	10

Now it is very fortunate for us that we don't have to do all this coding for ourselves. Our computer is a genius at doing such coding, so all we need do is type the message at our keyboard, and the required codes will be produced automatically.

But how, you might ask, do we type in the end of line code (code '13') and the new line code (code '10')? The answer is that they are both generated automatically by the magic ENTER key. One press of the ENTER key produces both of these codes together, one after the other, in the order shown. The action of the ENTER key is a legacy from the old typewriter days, where the 'carriage return lever' did both of these jobs for the typewriter, and leads us to a subtle learning point to remember. It is good practice to always end a message by leaving things so that you are on a new line when you finish. This then means that the two codes for 'end of line' and for 'a new line' will always be the last items included at the very end of the created string.

Okay. We can now compose a message consisting of multiple lines on a single page, but what about several pages? This point is a small one that distinguishes email from postal mail. Although the coding system does include a code for 'end of a page', in practice we don't use it. The reason why is that we don't usually need to do so, for we can make a single electronic page as long as we wish to, just by increasing the length of the string of codes. (In the Windows system, we would employ scroll bars down the side of the page to move it about from top to bottom). Practically, most email messages tend to be fairly short in length. If we want to send a long document, then there is a different way to do it, and we will come on to this later.

The automatic creation of the sequential string of codes for our electronic letter needs to be done in a very controlled and measured way, and the string needs to be stored somewhere in the computer memory, ready for sending down the phone line. This is where we need the help of a special computer program – an email program (sometimes called an email reader program). The email program we will be using throughout this book is called 'Outlook Express' and is normally a program that you will find included free within the standard range of programs bundled with Windows type computers.

If you have read the companion book in this series, *Using a Computer for the First Time*, then you may recall from section 8.2 that this idea of a long string of codes is also the way that information is generally stored in the object that we call a 'computer file'. Indeed, the string structure of a computer file and that for an email message is very similar. If any of our email messages need to be stored for any significant length of time then they will simply be copied into an appropriate file within the computer.

Okay. So now we have a better understanding of the first feature of an electronic letter – the formation of the message part. Let us now consider how we might create the envelope and the addressing.

Email header – the address and envelope

The way we form the envelope is to add to the basic message content by building further sequences of numerical codes that are 'wrapped around' the basic message string. This produces a new longer string that is structured into three parts. The first part is referred to as the **email header**. This is then followed by the message content, which we now refer to as the **email body**. And the final part is the **email tail**. Our next picture shows the parts joined together in three blocks. Remember that this is really one long sequential string, and the last code number of one part is immediately followed by the first code number of the next.

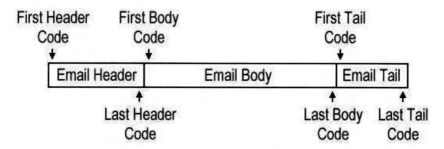

The header comes first. This contains the 'outer' pieces of information for the electronic letter, such as the name and address of where the email must be sent to, and whom it is from. Then comes the body, where the actual message content is placed (the codes for the 'How are you?' message), then comes the tail. In practice, the tail is very short compared to the lengths of the header and the body. It simply contains a small fixed length of codes to act as an 'end of envelope' marker, trapping the body inside.

If you want to make the analogy with a postal letter, the header and tail form the outer envelope for the email. The header part is effectively the face of the envelope where all the addresses are, and the tail is a bit like the flap of the envelope. Once the tail has been stuck on at the end, then the flap has then been 'licked' and 'sealed' - and the internal content of the email (that is to say the email body) is safely enclosed inside.

There is however, one major and important difference between this electronic letter and the postal counterpart. The electronic version usually has a lot more information written on the outside of the envelope – in the header part. One such piece of information is known as the subject title, and we shall meet this item later on when we create our first email.

Paying for it – the stamp

Finally, is there a direct equivalent of a 'stamp' anywhere? The answer is most definitely no, not on the envelope itself. There is certainly a charging mechanism but it's not part of either the formation or sending of the electronic letter. This lack of a 'stamp' has an important consequence as it means that the delivery cost is not chargeable 'per item' of mail as postal mail is. Later on, we will explore methods of paying for the email service and discuss the pros and cons of various alternative methods on offer.

1.3   Sending an 'electronic letter'

Okay. We can now appreciate that an email is just a long continuous string of numbers, starting with the first code number of the header and ending with the last code number of the tail. This is the complete 'sealed' electronic letter (envelope and all) and the actual message is held somewhere on the inside.

How do we send this electronic letter from one place to another? Take a look at this next diagram.

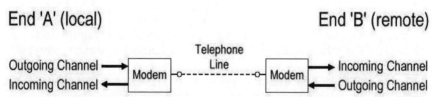

This diagram shows two locations, remote from each other (referred to as End 'A' and End 'B'), connected via a telephone line so that information can be exchanged between them. End 'A' is our own local end where we have our own computer equipment. End 'B' is the remote end where a third party company has some computer equipment of its own.

Now telephone lines, as we well know, carry voice information quite easily. But they were not originally designed for the electrical signals from computers. We therefore employ a device called a **modem** (pronounced 'mow-dem') in order to change the 'digital' electrical signals such as those from a computer into a form of 'analogue' voice signal that can travel down the phone line. When these signals arrive at the far end, they have to be changed back again to digital computer signals. This reverse type of action is carried out by a second modem.

Modems can either be internal or external to the computer processor unit. In chapter 2, we shall talk more about the physical characteristics of modems and how they are connected up to the telephone line. For the moment, we only need consider the theory of operation, and how this provides a mechanism that will allow us to send our electronic letter.

Before we are able to send any information via the phone line, we have to establish a **data connection** between End 'A' and End 'B'. This data connection when established will consist of two completely separate information channels so that information can independently flow in either direction. The diagram refers to each channel as either 'Outgoing' or 'Incoming' depending on the direction of information flow. The 'Outgoing' channel at one end is routed through the phone line to the 'Incoming' channel at the other end.

The procedure to establish a data connection is as follows. First our own computer at End 'A' will instruct our own modem to dial a special telephone number. A telephone call is thus made via the telephone line in the same way that a normal voice telephone call occurs. The call is answered automatically by the second modem at the far end, and this modem then sends a series of very strange 'scratchy hissing' noises back down the line to the modem at our local end. You can usually hear this whole process actually occur through a small loudspeaker contained inside the modem. After a period that may last anywhere from between five to fifty-five seconds, the 'scratchy hissing' noises will suddenly cease. At this point the data connection has become established.

Once the data connection has become established, the computer at the remote end can then send information through to your own computer, and vice versa. The very first pieces of information demanded by the third party company computer are usually two items known as your **'Username'** and your **'Password'**. These have to be responded to immediately by your own computer, and if they are correct and currently valid, then the connection between the two computers is firmly established and we say that you are now **on-line**. If the Username or Password is not correct or not valid, then the remote computer will instantly disconnect the telephone call, and you are thrown back to the position you were in when you first started.

This whole process of becoming on-line is described in much further detail in the next chapter (Chapter 2).

So now we are on-line but on-line to where? The answer to this seemingly innocuous question is on-line to the Internet – the new global network of millions and millions of computers that are all linked together! (If you are new to the Internet, you can find out more about it in Appendix I). The situation is now shown in the next diagram.

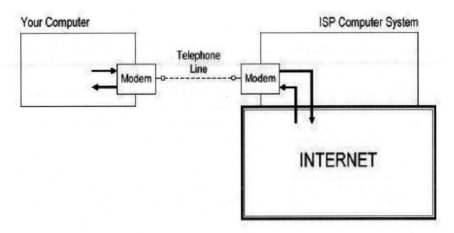

In the above diagram, I have shown the modem half inside your computer and half outside to signify that you may have either an internal or external modem. We also see that the remote end modem is similarly shown attached to an 'ISP Computer System'. ISP is an abbreviation for 'Internet Service Provider' and this term is used to refer to the third party company that has the direct access to the Internet. The service that they provide is usually a subscription service, and there are various different subscriptions schemes available from different ISP companies.

At this point in the procedure, we have a data connection from your computer direct into the Internet and we could use a number of different computer programs to access different services from the Internet. An interesting point is that we can also use these computer programs at the same time. For example, we will shortly be using the Outlook Express program to access the email service from the Internet, but we might also simultaneously use a program called Internet Explorer to look at pages from the 'World Wide Web' service. The data connection can handle several programs working at once and know which information is pertinent to which service or program that we are using. Exactly how it does this is beyond the scope of this book and a little deeper into the technicalities than perhaps a 'first-timer' needs to understand.

The only additional fact that I will mention here about the data connection is that there is a technique employed, in conjunction with the information channels through the modems, whereby errors that might crop up as information travels to and fro across the Internet are spotted and resolved. For those of you who would like to read more about it elsewhere, this technique is called TCP/IP (you pronounce it 'tee see pee eye pee'). We shall not have any need to consider it further. All we need to know is that when we receive information or send it, we can be fairly sure that it is error free (if it isn't then a message will pop up on screen somewhere to tell us different).

Now we are ready to see how our electronic letter is sent. We will also find out how such things are received.

In the previous section, we noted that we use the Outlook Express program as the means of creating the required sequential string of codes for our 'letter' in a controlled and measured way. Let us now look at how Outlook Express actually operates. This is shown in the next diagram.

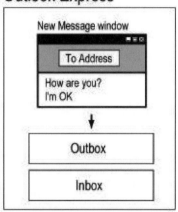

Here we can see the message being created in a **New Message** window, which is a form of work in progress area. The New Message window requires us first to insert the **'To' Address** of the person to whom we want to send the message, and then below it we write the message itself. When things are complete, we click on a special button to send it. This action of clicking the button automatically puts the message into an 'electronic envelope', that is to say, the Outlook Express program takes the message we have typed in (the body part) - adds to the front of it all the required addressing (the header part) - and finally tags on the end the 'end of envelope' marker (the tail part). The completed item is then dropped into a special box called the **Outbox folder**. This folder may contain several such 'letters' at the same time.

The letter will stay here in the Outbox folder until a further 'Delivery Trigger Action' is initiated. This trigger action may come from either Outlook Express itself automatically, or from ourselves manually by pressing the **Send/Receive** button (a special button within the program). When the trigger action happens, then an attempt will be made to send all of the letters waiting in the Outbox folder down the data connection to the Internet.

Also shown in the last diagram is a second special box called the **Inbox folder**. This folder, not surprisingly, is where any incoming mail is deposited inside the Outlook Express program ready for us to open and read. The trigger action that sends letters on their outward journey from the Outbox to the Internet will at the same time pick up any letters coming in from the Internet and put them inside the Inbox.

The **Delivery Trigger Action** is quite an important point to remember and we shall refer to it again later in a moment. Making a comparison with the ordinary postal mail system, it is equivalent to two things – first, ourselves walking down the street and dropping our outgoing letters into a post-box – and second, the postman walking down your garden path and dropping your incoming letters through your own letterbox. If the trigger action does not occur for some reason, then mail will neither be sent nor received.

Okay. Now we are in a position to show how the last two diagrams fit together and work co-operatively. We shall also add a new piece to the jigsaw – the mailboxes provided by the ISP Company themselves as part of the subscription service. Without these latter items, the whole system could not work properly.

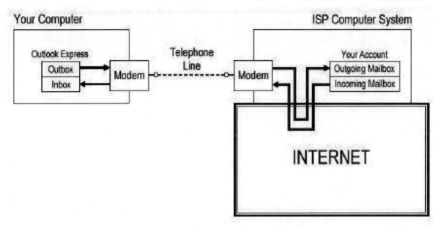

If we examine the left side of the diagram shown above, we can see that within your computer, the **Outlook Express folders** called **Outbox** and **Inbox** are simply connected to the data connection channels of the modem. On the other side of the diagram, inside the ISP computer system we that see that the data connection takes a strange 'double U-bend' path coming from the modem – dipping into the Internet and back out again – and then connecting to two mailboxes associated with 'your account' labelled **Outgoing Mailbox** and **Incoming Mailbox** respectively.

There are two important points to note about the 'double U-bend' connection:

● First, it represents a temporary connection to these mailboxes. For most of the time that you are on-line to the Internet, this connection will not exist. It is made at the instigation of the Delivery Trigger Action we mentioned earlier, and lasts only for the duration required to exchange mail between the ISP computer and your own computer. Once the exchange has completed then the connection is 'un-plugged'.

● Second, the connection has to be authorised before it is allowed. The authorisation requirement is a safety feature to prevent any other person who may be connected to the Internet from gaining unauthorised access to your ISP mailboxes. Authorisation is an automated check on the Username and Password you are using.

Later, in Chapter 3, when we send our first email, we will observe a message box on screen that displays a series of odd messages in rapid succession saying things such as 'Finding Host...' 'Connected' 'Authorising...' 'Sending...'

'Receiving...' 'Disconnecting...' The first three of these messages refers to what we have just been talking about – the formation of this 'double U-bend' connection, and the authorisation check that your Username and Password are the correct. The next two refer to mail being taken out of the **Outbox** (of your **Outlook Express**) and deposited into the **Outgoing Mailbox** (of your account with the ISP), followed by mail being taken from the **Incoming Mailbox** (of your account with the ISP) and deposited into the **Inbox** (of your **Outlook Express**). The last one refers to the 'double U-bend' disconnection and reflects the fact that it is a temporary connection, and it needs to be un-plugged once the mail transfer stages have been completed.

There is also a technical point worth mentioning here which crops up in Appendix III 'Setting up an ISP account'. Skip over this next paragraph if your ISP account has been set up already for you.

During the 'Sending...' phase of these latter two messages, the procedure for taking mail from the Outbox and depositing in the Outgoing Mailbox uses a set of rules called **SMTP**. During the 'Receiving...' phase, the procedure for taking mail from the Incoming Mailbox and depositing in the Inbox uses a different set of rules called **POP3**. I have no great wish to explain anything deeper about these two sets of rules, other than to say you may have to obtain some extra information known as the 'address of the mail server' in association with two sets of rules. The 'address of the mail server' is simply information that specifies where within the Internet your mailboxes can actually be found. There are two addresses in reality, one for the SMTP server, which is where the Outgoing Mailbox is located; and another for the POP3 server, which is where the Incoming Mailbox is located. These two addresses may be the same address, or they may be different. When you are setting up an account with an Internet Service Provider, you will be asked to enter this information. Normally such information is complete gobbledygook, but now you have some idea of what it is referring to!

Returning to our discussion about sending our electronic letter, we remember that it is the Delivery Trigger Action that initiates the exchange of mail information between the Outbox/Inbox boxes of Outlook Express and the corresponding Outgoing/Incoming Mailboxes of your account with the ISP computer system. This brings us to a very important function of the email tail part that is tagged on to the end of the letter. When the email tail has been successfully transferred, then and <u>then only</u> will the electronic letter be removed from the Outbox. If for any reason some form of hiccup occurs – for example, the telephone line gets abruptly disconnected in the middle of the transfer – then the email tail will not be received at the remote end, and the original copy of the electronic letter, in its entirety, will stay put in the Outbox. Should the hiccup be subsequently resolved – for example, you dial up the ISP computer system for a second time – then an attempt will be made to transfer the electronic letter again, in its entirety.

The same is true when receiving mail from the ISP computer. When the email tail of an incoming 'letter' is successfully transferred over the data connection, then the 'letter' will be deleted from the Incoming Mailbox. If for any reason this does not occur, then the mail is not deleted, and it will still be there waiting to be collected the next time that you dial up into the ISP computer.

There is one more point to be made concerning the Outbox. A successful transfer from the Outbox to the Outgoing Mailbox is also accompanied by a copy of the sent electronic letter being placed in the **Sent Items folder** of Outlook Express. This acts as a historical record for you of all the mail that has ever been sent.

1.4　The addressing of an 'electronic letter'

Email addresses take a particular unusual form. The written form generally looks like this...

Username@ComputerNetwork

There are two basic parts to the address separated by a special symbol called the 'at' symbol - @. We would read this address out as 'User name at Computer Network'. If this looks like more gobbledygook, then bear with me because there is a deliberate reason why I am not showing any spaces in the generalised form of the address.

The first part, 'Username', is the name of a person, and it may be a real name or a pseudonym. It can take several forms. Some examples are just one word or maybe two or more words that do not contain any spaces in between them. Other examples contain either two or more words separated by 'full stops' (.) or 'underscores' (_).

The second part, 'ComputerNetwork', is the address name of something that you can think of as an 'electronic street'. Electronic streets are really smaller sized networks – that is, much smaller than the whole Internet – that belong to and are controlled by ISP Companies. The form that this second part can take is slightly more standardised than the first Username part. It usually takes the form of two or more words or abbreviations separated only by full stops.

> Note – What is a small sized network? It's a group of computers joined together closely by a local cable so that they can interact as a local group. Each group is a small part of the much bigger network that we call the Internet.

Okay. Lets have a look at a few examples of email addresses and the different forms that you may come across...

John.Smith@abc.com
alanladd@oldpictures.co.uk
billy_the_kid@usa.com
johndoe23@aol.com

25

There are several features of email addresses that you need to be aware of. First, it matters not whether you use upper case (capital letters) or lower case (non-capital letters) in typing any part of the address (John.Smith@abc.com is treated just the same as joHn.smith@ABC.com). Second, never use spaces anywhere in the address. Third, if there are any funny symbols or numbers in the address, then you must type them exactly as they are shown.

Very often, there are several people with the same human names who wish to hold a mailbox account with the same ISP Company. Because their email addresses must be unique, there cannot be two people with the same address of 'John.Smith@abc.com'. To make them different, ISP administration will often suggest a number attached to the end of the 'Username' part. This is why you often see 'charliebrown98@abc.com' and 'charliebrown99@abc.com' as people's email addresses.

Now, although the second part, 'ComputerNetwork', is the address name of a group of computers, when it used together with the @ symbol, it inherently refers to a very specific computer within the group that performs the task of an 'electronic post office'. Thus, when we talk about an email address such as 'John.Smith@abc.com', we are really meaning 'John Smith at the electronic post office located on the abc.com smaller-sized computer network'. It is a strict rule that there can only be one such post office on this smaller sized network!

Let us briefly investigate what an electronic post office is ...

In the last section, we learnt that the ISP Computer system maintains a subscription account for you. As part of the account, two mailboxes were referred to – an Outgoing Mailbox, and an Incoming Mailbox. Now in reality, there is only one Outgoing Mailbox to serve everyone that has an account with the ISP. Effectively it is shared with all the other customers. The Incoming Mailbox is a box that holds only mail for just you – it is not shared. Therefore, the ISP Computer system must maintain a whole array of Incoming Mailboxes, one for every customer. Quite often, the ISP Company will provide you with more than one Incoming Mailbox for your account. In this way, you can pay only one subscription fee but have separate mailboxes for all the family. (If you are interested in knowing more about family mailboxes, take a look some time at Appendix VI). Taking the whole collection of mailboxes together, the ISP Company is effectively providing the function of a Post Office, so the computer equipment that performs this task is the 'electronic post office'.

Let us end this section by having a brief look at how email addresses are written on an 'electronic letter' in the 'header' part.

To enable email to be handled automatically by computers, there has to be a number of rules applied to the way that email addresses are included within the header. Fortunately for us, the Outlook Express program itself knows all about these rules so it can do this automatically for us, providing we give it the right addresses in the first place.

If we were able to apply a mythical 'magnifying glass' to translate the 'header' of an email into lines of text that we could observe, then we might see something like the following picture.

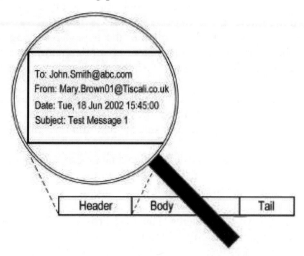

Remember that this header in reality is just a long sequential string of codes as before, with 'end of line' and 'new line' codes slotted into the string at the appropriate places.

Now the rules for composing the header are fairly straightforward. There are a number of recognised 'keywords' such as 'To' 'From' 'Date' and 'Subject' (plus a few more that we will not bother with) and these are immediately followed by a colon symbol (:). Anything following the colon symbol is treated as information about the keyword.

The boundary between the 'header' and the 'body' is simply a blank line. Anything after this boundary is treated as the first code for the 'body' part.

1.5   Attachments to an 'electronic letter'

One of the really useful features of email today is that not only can you send a written message, but you can also send other items as well. These items are treated as 'attachments' to the basic written message and later in chapter 4 we shall meet some practical exercises on how to both attach and detach these items.

The types of items we can attach are:

☑ Pictures (photos or other graphics)
☑ Video clips
☑ Audio clips
☑ Any other type of computer file

These items all exist as normal computer files before they are attached. As pointed out earlier, computer files themselves are simply long sequential string of codes, so they are ideally suited to accompany an email message on its journey through the Internet.

When the email arrives at its destination, the person receiving it can then 'detach' the attached item and save it to their computer as a normal computer file inside a normal folder. The file may then be used and manipulated in the ordinary way.

This idea of sending files via email is incredibly useful because of the speed at which it travels from one place to another. For example, a photograph taken with a modern digital camera can be taken in Australia one minute, and arrive in England two minutes later!

We are also not limited to making just one attachment, but can make several if we choose to do so. However, there are some practical points to consider when you decide to make attachments, and you need to consider whether it is better to send several items all at once in one big email, or maybe send several emails, each with its own attachments. There are pros and cons of each method, and again, we will discuss these in Chapter 4.

Okay. Let us now briefly consider the mechanics of how attachments are actually made to our emails so that we understand them better.

Earlier in this chapter we learnt that the basic structure of a simple 'electronic letter' consists of three parts – an email header part, an email body part and an email tail part. Now the way we form attachments to the 'letter' is to restructure the middle 'body' part. Instead of just having one single message within it, we sub-divide this into a number of individual sections. The first section may then be used to hold our original text message (the 'How are you? I'm OK' bit) and each subsequent section can then be used to contain the relevant attachment.

This technique of sub-dividing the body part up into a number of sections is an extension to the basic email delivery service as it was first invented. The set of rules governing how it should be done is referred to as MIME (Multipurpose Internet Mail Extensions – pronounced just as it looks 'mime'). One of the problems that used to occur fairly frequently to 'first timers' (not so much these days) was that they would receive an incoming MIME type of email, but be using an older type of email reader program that did not recognise this newer MIME format. This would cause utter confusion because what should have looked like a single message with a number of attachments, was displayed completely as one single message, looking like a load of gibberish!

We have no real need to delve into the detail of how these MIME rules are implemented in coding, save to say that a few additional 'keywords' are added to the email 'header' part. Outlook Express does this automatically for us if we specify attachments in the New Message window when we first create our basic message. If Outlook Express receives an incoming email with these new keywords in the header, then it knows to treat the 'body' in a particular way, so that the attachments can be separated out and presented as a list available for 'detachment' from the email at the user's wish. Note here that the detachment process is not automatic. It is up to the person receiving the email as to whether or not they want to make any such detachment.

There is one further point worth mentioning in connection with MIME. The rules not only allow for attachments, they also allow fancy styling and colouring to be added to a basic text message. This is done by changing the coding method from the standardised ASCII technique that we talked about earlier, to a more sophisticated one called **HTML** (pronounced 'aytch tee em el'). Again, we will not delve into the detail. We just need to appreciate that it is possible. One point to be particularly careful with is the ability, using new MIME features in Outlook Express, to embed pictures within the main text message instead of including them as an attachment. If the person receiving such an email does not use the same type of reader, set up with the same coding scheme, then there is a high likelihood that they will not be able to view the embedded picture. And because it is not a standard attachment, they cannot detach it either.

1.6 The journey and delivery of an 'electronic letter'

We have now reached the final section in this chapter and we shall end with a brief discussion concerning how our 'electronic letter' makes its journey across the Internet to reach its final destination. Our knowledge and understanding of email will then be deep enough to fully appreciate all the points that we shall learn about in the exercises covered in subsequent chapters.

Let us review what we have covered so far. We shall assume in this review that we are already 'on-line' to the Internet – that is to say, a telephone call has previously been established so that there is a data connection from your computer through your modem to another modem owned by a third party company (the Internet Service Provider):

- We know an 'electronic letter' begins its life by its creation using an email program such as Outlook Express. We use a New Message window to actually create it, and type the address of the intended recipient followed by details about the message itself. The message that we type at the keyboard creates a long sequential string of numbers held in the computer's memory, and it is this which forms the true information content that will become the 'body' part of the email.

- When we have finished our typing we then click on the Send button in the New Message window. This automatically puts the message into an 'envelope' by adding a header part in front of the message body and a tail part to the end. The header will contain all the address details required, together with a few extra pieces of information (such as subject title and date). The completed 'envelope' is then placed in the Outbox folder of the Outlook Express program, so it is still within your computer – it hasn't actually been sent yet. Let me say that again – the Send button does not actually send an email! It puts it into an envelope and drops the envelope into the Outbox ready to be sent.

- A 'Delivery Trigger Action' then occurs either automatically (caused by Outlook Express itself) or sometimes manually if we click on the Send/Receive button. This action initiates a procedure internal to the ISP. It is this procedure that actually does the sending! The procedure has several stages. First, an 'authorisation' check is made to ensure that you are entitled to be connected to these mailboxes. Second, the data connection from the ISP modem is connected (via the double-U bend) to the Outgoing and Incoming mailboxes associated with your account. Third, the 'electronic letter' sitting in the Outbox of your computer is then transferred to the Outgoing mailbox, and afterwards, if there are any letters sat waiting for you, they are transferred from the Incoming mailbox into the Inbox of your computer. And finally fourth, the double-U bend connection is disconnected.

This is as far as we have reached in the theory of operation; let us now very quickly complete the picture with a brief description of what happens next.

- Our 'electronic letter' is sitting in the Outgoing mailbox of the ISP computer. Because this is a shared mailbox with all the other customers of the ISP Company, then there is likely to be a big pile at peak times.

- The ISP computer is a very powerful computer and it has several programs all running at once. One of these programs is a mail delivery service. This program then systematically goes through each letter waiting in the Outgoing mailbox in turn and looks at the address (in the header part) to see where it needs to be sent. The ISP computer is permanently connected to the Internet (24 hrs a day when it is not being serviced!). It asks a question from a special group of Internet computers 'Can you tell me where the electronic street 'abc.com' is?' (Note – I use this example from the To address of 'John.Smith@abc.com' shown previously in the mythical magnifying glass diagram). Now this special group of Internet computers has a very elaborate street directory. It is so elaborate that it is not located just in one place, but extends across the whole world in a hierarchical pyramid type of structure. The ISP computer follows a trail through the hierarchy by asking a series of questions of different members of the group. Eventually, it will either have a satisfactory answer from the special group, or it will have a disappointing 'Sorry, nobody seems to know this 'street', anywhere in the world!'

- If the answer is disappointing, then the ISP computer will send you a note back (as another 'electronic letter' addressed to you) letting you know it cannot be delivered. If the answer is satisfactory, then the ISP computer will forward the original letter onward through the Internet to the 'electronic post office' at the 'electronic street' named 'abc.com'.

- Now here at the distant ISP computer system – that is, at the computer where the 'electronic post office' for 'abc.com' resides, another mail delivery service program is running 24 hours a day to sort the 'letter'. Providing that 'John.Smith' is a recognised customer of the distant ISP then the 'letter' will be dropped into his Incoming mailbox. There it will stay, until John Smith decides to go on-line and use his email program (which may or may not be Outlook Express) to retrieve it. John Smith will finally pick up the letter when the 'Delivery Trigger Action' takes place at his computer, for then it will be transferred into his Inbox folder. If the name 'John.Smith' is not a recognised customer, then the 'electronic letter' is usually dropped into the Incoming mailbox of the administrator person who looks after the ISP post office. This is generally a person who uses the pseudonym name 'postmaster'.

Now here is an interesting idea. If you are not sure of the exact name of the recipient for the letter, but you are confident that the street is 'abc.com', then you can always write to the 'postmaster@abc.com' and ask them if they can tell you the true electronic name of the person you are seeking (so that you can later write direct). They may of course decline to answer you, but you can always try for nothing!

We have followed the journey of our 'electronic letter' from one end to the other. We have had a good look at the whole process and now I think you will be able to understand what is going on with your own computer system when you see various things happening. Like the postal mail service, email is not infallible and there are several things that can go wrong. Normally, these occasions are not too frequent and generally, the email delivery service these days works surprisingly well. This is particularly true when you appreciate the true size of the system – it is absolutely vast, covering not just our own country but also every country in the world. And if we include the astronauts up in Space – sometimes out of it as well!

Now that you have a better understanding, throughout the remainder of the book we shall cease referring to the more cumbersome phrase 'electronic letter' and use the more widely accepted term 'email'. And enough now of all the theory – lets get into some practical exercises.

2

Connecting to the Internet

2.1 Getting ready to connect

The public email service is critically dependant on access to the Internet for its operation, and in the last chapter we discussed the theory that lies behind it. In this one we are going to cover the practical issues of making the connection from your computer, and reach the point where we are ready to send our first email. We will close this chapter by learning how to gracefully disconnect from the Internet.

Our discussion will centre on using a dial-up telephone type connection from home. There are alternative methods of connecting to the Internet and some of these are briefly described at the end of this chapter in section 2.7.

In order to be able to establish a dial-up connection to the Internet ready to use email, there are three important pre-requisites. These are:

- First, that your computer has been fitted with a modem, and the computer software is set up to use the modem.
- Second, that you are subscribing to an ISP (Internet Service Provider) Company and that the company has an account set up ready for you to go ahead and use.
- Third, that an email program such as Outlook Express has been set up to use your ISP account and to use the modem. (You can alternatively use the Webmail service, which does not use an email program – more of this in a moment).

For 'first-timers', it is better if you have someone with more experience set up your computer for you, particularly in respect of installing a modem. However, if you want to or need to do this by yourself, then Appendices II and III will give you further information about the modem and the ISP account respectively. If you are not already subscribing to an ISP Company, then Appendix III will help you do so. A CD is also included in the back of this book to make this easy for you to automatically set up a subscription. If you are uncertain whether the above pre-requisites have already been carried out for your computer, Appendix IV will give you further information telling you how you can make some simple checks.

Throughout the greater part of this book, we shall be using the email program Outlook Express in our discussion and exercises. This is a program included as standard within later versions of Windows-type computers. If you are using a different email program, then you will have to make your own interpretations and your program may differ in features from those we will cover.

You can use the email service without an email program by using something known as 'Webmail', which we discuss in chapter 10. The advantages and disadvantages of this method are described in sections 10.1 and 10.3. Until recently, I would have always recommended that you use the email program, Outlook Express, because there are many features available in it that were not available in Webmail. However, the position is changing rapidly and some 'first-timers' may now find that Webmail is perfectly sufficient for all their needs. If you want to use the Webmail service in preference to an email program running on your own computer, then I suggest that you read this chapter for information about making a dial-up connection into the Internet, but then jump forward to chapter 10. What do I personally use? I prefer to use Outlook Express from home – but I do use Webmail when I am travelling.

Okay. Before we attempt to connect to the Internet, we need to be sure that the modem cabling is correctly fitted, and it is best to do this before you power up the computer itself.

Note – In the following explanation, we shall describe various types of connectors. All of these connectors are also described in the companion guide 'Using a Computer for the First Time' and if these are unfamiliar to you, then you can find further help in section 1.4 of that book.

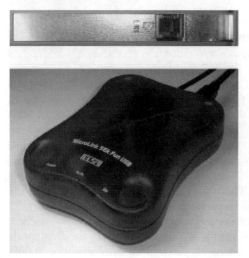

There are two types of modem in general use. One is an internal type that is fitted into a 'card slot' at the rear of the processor unit, and the other is an external type that comes as a stand-alone box. A typical internal modem (as viewed from the rear of the processor unit) is shown in the upper of these two pictures, and an external modem in the lower one.

The internal type of modem is the simplest to use. It obtains electrical power direct from the processor unit itself and consequently has no on/off switch.

Simply plug one end of the associated telephone cable into the modem socket at the rear of the processor box (the socket may be marked 'Line' meaning 'Telephone Line') and the other end into a standard telephone socket.

External modems are a bit more complex. These are sub divided into USB (Universal Serial Bus) and non-USB types. If it is a USB type, then normally it will not require an additional external power supply, because it obtains electrical power down the USB cable from the processor. If it is not this USB type, then normally it will need a power supply.

With a USB modem, in addition to connecting the telephone line cable, you have a second cable to connect. You need to plug the narrower 'B' end of a USB cable into the modem socket (shown on the left) and the other wider 'A' end of the cable (shown on the right) into any of the USB 'A' type sockets, found at the rear of the processor box. It does not matter which one because the computer will detect that the modem is present on one of them and automatically use that socket.

For non-USB modems, in addition to connecting the telephone line cable, you normally connect the modem to one of the Serial COM ports on the rear of the processor box using a serial port cable having either a 9-pin or a 25-pin 'D' style connector. Shown to the right is a typical 9-pin 'D' style cable connector. This connector will have holes to match up with the pins on the COM port itself.

Unlike the USB ports, the computer's Windows software will not automatically switch to the appropriate COM port, so here you need to be careful which one you plug the serial port cable into. Only one of them will have been correctly set up in software to use the modem (as part of the second of the pre-requisite conditions we mentioned earlier) and you need to know which one it was. Connect the other end of the serial port cable to the socket at the rear of the modem. Also, non-USB modems will usually have an external power supply. Plug this now into an appropriate mains outlet (and also into the modem if it is a detachable type power cable), and switch on. There may also be an on/off switch on the modem itself, so make sure that this too is switched on.

With all the appropriate modem cables and telephone line cables now attached, power up the computer and wait for it to reach the stage where the Desktop is displayed on the monitor. If you are using an external modem, then you should now be able to see some of the supervisory lights illuminated on its front panel.

Okay. At this stage all the preparations are complete for our first exercise, which is to start the **Outlook Express** program running and become connected to the Internet. Before we actually go ahead and do this, I should like to give a few words of advice about becoming disconnected from the Internet involuntarily. We shall do this in the next section.

2.2   Beware of automatic disconnection

When you become connected to the Internet so that you can exchange information with it, you are then said to be **on-line** (we discussed the theory of this in section 1.3). During this time, your telephone line will be engaged and so will one of the phone lines to the ISP Company. Both of them will remain engaged for the length of time that the telephone call remains established.

Exactly how this telephone call is paid for depends upon the type of account that you have subscribed to with the ISP Company. Appendix III describes setting up an ISP account and briefly mentions the different types of account that you may choose from. At one end of the range of choices is the 'Pay As You Go' type (where you pay local call charging on a time basis through your ordinary phone bill) and at the other end is the 'Anytime' type (where you pay a fixed fee per month and do not pay call charges on your phone bill).

If you choose the 'Anytime' type of account, then you will not be particularly concerned with the cost of the on-line call, and you may be inclined to leave your computer connected to the Internet, even when you are not using it. For short lengths of time this may not be a big issue, but for extended lengths of time it can have two undesirable consequences. The first is that your own phone line is tied up, and if someone is trying to ring you they cannot get through. The second is that the ISP phone line is tied up, and at peak times of Internet use this may mean that other people cannot get on-line when they want to. Now, some may argue that the ISP Company should install more phone lines to cater for these peak periods. Normally, it is in their interest to do so, but practically, there is a balance to be struck between peak time and off-peak time traffic. In our modern world, the utilisation of any resource should be done so efficiently to minimise the overall cost and cut down on waste.

To reduce inefficiency, the ISP Companies normally employ several techniques to handle the matter. One of these techniques is automatic disconnection. If the line remains engaged for certain lengths of time with no information passing in either direction, then the telephone call is automatically disconnected. Another technique is to disconnect the call after a protracted period of time in any event. If you are still using the line when the period end is reached, then you will experience disconnection and you have to dial back into the system to continue to use it.

Though automatic disconnection is more frequently experienced with the 'Anytime' type of account, it can also occur on the 'Pay As You Go' type as well, so all users need to be aware of it.

Being automatically disconnected from the Internet is not usually in itself a big calamity. More often than not it is just a small inconvenience. Generally, a message appears on screen to tell you that you are now disconnected, and you are normally presented with a button to click to take the option of reconnecting (your computer software can even be set up to do this automatically). However, at peak times of Internet usage it can sometimes prove a little difficult to get back on-line. This is because the ISP Company always has a finite number of telephone lines available for dial-up, and if they are very busy with other customers (for example around early evening when people have just finished their evening meal) then they can – and do – get over subscribed.

Throughout the remainder of this book you may find yourself part way through an exercise and, because you may be taking things slowly to read the exercise carefully, you may find that the automatic disconnection operates and cuts you off. Don't worry if this does happen. Just reconnect when you are presented with the opportunity to do so, and then continue the exercise. This may slightly upset the sequence of pictures presented for you to follow, but when you get back on-line you should be able to carry on where you left off.

2.3 Starting Outlook Express

Note – Certain key words such as 'click', 'right-click' etc. are given particular meanings throughout all exercises, and these are defined in the list of conventions at the beginning of this book.

Exercise 1 – Getting the email program running on-line

We begin this exercise by starting from the Desktop. This is the display showing many small icons that you first see on the monitor screen after you have powered it up. If your computer uses the Windows XP operating system, you may or may not be required to choose your own 'user' account and possibly enter a password, before you get to the Desktop. Earlier versions of Windows set up for home use usually power up to the Desktop display straight away.

On the Desktop, search through all the icons that you can see and look for the one that is labelled 'Outlook Express'. This picture shows a small part of a typical desktop and has the icon we are looking for in the top right-hand corner. The icon is of a stamped envelope wrapped in two blue arrows.

Now double-click on this icon to start the

program running – or if you prefer, right-click on the icon and then select 'Open' by clicking on it, if you find that easier to do.

Note – An alternative method for starting the program is with a single click on the smaller but similar looking icon located on the task bar at the very bottom of the screen. This icon can normally be found in a small group of three, just to the right of the Start button.

This one

Yet another method of starting is to click on the Start button and select (All) Programs, then select Outlook Express from the subsequent menu.

The program should now begin running, and the first thing you notice is a title message flash up fairly briefly showing 'Microsoft Outlook Express 6' (if you have Windows XP) or probably 'Microsoft Outlook Express 5' (if you have an earlier version of Windows).

If you then see a screen display appear that says 'Internet Connection Wizard', this is a sure fire sign that you do not have an ISP Company account set up on your computer ready for you to use (this was the third prerequisite we discussed in section 2.1). Press the Cancel button to exit from the 'Wizard' and read Appendix III thoroughly before going any further.

Note – Setting up your computer to be able to use an ISP service can be a little tricky. I recommend that 'first-timers' get the help of someone more experienced to do it for them, if possible. However, if you feel competent and wish to have a go yourself, then Appendices II and III will tell how to go about doing it.

What precisely happens after the title message has been displayed is difficult to generalise for everybody in all situations. There are in fact several slightly different variations of procedure that you might witness. Which one you actually experience depends on how your computer has been set up for you to use the Internet. I am going to try and cover one or two of the most common variations, but if your own situation is slightly different to my description then please accept my apologies in advance. All these variations do lead you to the eventual starting point that we need to reach in order to use the program for all our exercises.

One variation that I will quickly get out of the way is where several different users can all use the same email program but have their own individual email set up. With this variation, at this point in the procedure, you will be given a list of the available users. You then simply select the username you recognise as for your own use by clicking on the appropriate one and press the **OK** button. Then the start up procedure continues as normal.

More commonly, the computer is not set up for several users. With Windows

XP, even if there are several users, you will have already made the choice of user when you first powered the machine before you even got to the Desktop. Let us now discuss some of the more common variations of starting up that you might come across.

You might, for example, see something like this next screen appear…

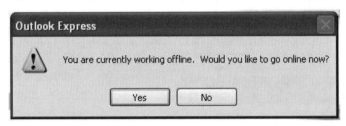

If you don't see this message, then don't worry about it. You only get to see this message if you were running the program **'off-line'** when you last closed it and stopped it running. (We will discuss what 'off-line' means in Chapter 5). If you do see it, simply click on the 'Yes' button because we want to go **'on-line'** at this moment.

The next screen you might see is a dialog box like the one in the following picture.

Note – There are different versions of the 'Connection' box that you may see, depending on the version of Windows that you are using and your settings. Don't be too concerned if yours is different. (Appendix VII has more information about how you can change some settings to see this dialog box.)

Now again, depending on how the computer is set up, your own computer may automatically begin to dial, or it may stop at this point stop and wait for you to do some action. Which of these two events happens depends on whether there is a 'tick' in the little **checkbox** labelled 'Connect Automatically' (see last picture). If the tick is there, then it will move on automatically.

Let us pause our discussion here for a moment and examine the dialog box shown in the last picture. There are some very important points about this box that you should understand in any event.

Notice that the **Connect to: box** in the picture shows 'Tiscali Intel Modem'. This is the name of some connection settings in my own personal computer. These settings tell the modem how to dial up and connect with the subscription account that I have with my ISP Company. The name of these settings for your own use will likely be different. The name should have some reference to your ISP Company. 'Tiscali', for example, is the name of the ISP Company that I am using. *The CD-ROM in the back of this book will allow you to join Tiscali if you so choose.*

When you are trying to connect your computer to the ISP's computer, the name of the settings that you see in this **Connect to: box** has to be the right one. If you only have one, then you having nothing more to worry about. But if someone has created more than one group of settings for your computer, then you may have a choice here to make from two or more possibilities. You would make your choice by clicking on the 'down arrow' at the right-hand side of the box. (For readers interested in the technical aspect, these settings are known either as 'Dial-up Networking' or 'Dial-up connection' settings).

The next two textboxes in the last picture refer to **User name:** and **Password:**. When your computer system was first set up to use an ISP subscription account then you will have been issued with two special things – the first is a 'User name' for the ISP account, and second is a 'Password' for the ISP account. Note that these two special things are not the same as the 'User name' and 'Password' for starting up the computer with Windows XP – if they happen to be the same then this is probably because someone has deliberately made them so.

The whole business of 'Usernames' can get very confusing. The fault lies with the companies because they use the term to mean different things at different times. In the **User name: box** here, you normally enter the full email address, not just the first part of it as we discussed in section 1.4. If you are making enquiries with your ISP Company, refer to it as the 'Dial-up Username' and you shouldn't go wrong.

Going back to the last picture, we had said that the dialog box shown may appear momentarily and then go on to the next stage, or it may stop and wait for us to take some action. If it is momentary, then the 'User name' and 'Password' text boxes will already be filled in for you, and after a short while this box will disappear. Let us now briefly say what to do if the dialog box is waiting for an action from you (you may skip over the next six paragraphs if it doesn't apply in your situation).

Examine the dialog box shown in the last picture and compare it with your own monitor display. Check that the wording in your text boxes for Connect to, User name and Password are filled out appropriately, according to the details for your own ISP account. These details are obviously your own connection settings name, Username and Password respectively. If you do need to modify the wording in the User name and Password text boxes, first position your mouse pointer tip inside the appropriate box and make a click. Then type the correct wording using the keyboard. Pay careful attention to the exact detail that you see in the boxes in respect of either 'dots' or the 'case' of the wording ('case' you may remember means either capital lettering or non-capitals – these are upper case and lower case, respectively).

In truth, it is only the Password that is critical about 'case', but even with the User name it is wise to copy the exact wording and spelling you have been supplied with. Take care also to watch out for spaces. If you put a space in where it should not be then the User name and Password will not be accepted by your ISP Company. Notice also that you don't get to see the 'actual' password that you type in. All you see are some large black 'dots' to indicate that something has been typed in to the box. This is a safety feature to avoid someone looking over your shoulder and copying your password. It is very much like using a high street Auto-Teller Cash Point machine when you are entering your PIN number.

When typing your Password, it is best to make sure the text box is completely clear of any large black 'dots' (by deleting them if need be with the Backspace key or the Delete key) before you then type in your own Password. Also, make absolutely sure that the Caps Lock indicator is not illuminated or you will be typing away in capital letters when you are not expecting to. This is a small indicator light (usually green) usually found in the top right-hand area of your keyboard. It is one of a group of three indicator lights, the others being Num Lock and Scroll Lock. The normal keyboard state is Num Lock indicator on (illuminated) and the other two off.

Caps Lock key   Caps Lock Indicator

Caps Lock (Capital letter locking) is a feature where any alphabetic key you press will be treated as a capital letter and not a non-capital one. If you have been used to a typewriter, then this is the same thing as 'SHIFT Lock'. When activated, it is just as though you had the SHIFT key permanently held down even though you are not touching it! However, the strange thing with a computer is that when Caps Lock is activated, then holding the SHIFT key down while pressing a letter key will make the key print a non-capital (lower case) letter!

I think this issue of capitals and non-capital lettering is one of the biggest causes of problems for 'first-timers' entering passwords! The Caps Lock feature is sometimes accidentally activated by inadvertently catching this key when you are looking to press the Shift key. If you need to, you can switch the Caps Lock indicator off by simply pressing the **Caps Lock key** once (this is to be found way over on the left-hand side of the keyboard, as shown in the last picture).

When you have finished checking over the dialog box, click on the **Connect** button in the dialog box to initiate a dial-up request to 'connect' with the Internet over the phone line.

Here we are at the same stage in the connecting procedure as for those readers where the dialog box appears momentarily and the sequence is automatic.

Various things now happen in quick succession. First, you should see the area underneath the Connect button change to show a series of messages about the progress of the connect request. It normally progresses by showing something like the next picture.

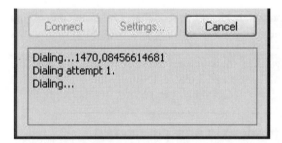

Here we observe that the computer is automatically dialling the telephone number '08456614681', which is the preset number for contacting the Tiscali ISP. (There is also a prefix of '1470,' that releases Caller ID). You may also be able to hear this dialling as a sequence of audible tones coming from the modem inside the computer. (You can usually adjust the loudness of these audible tones if you wish from the modem settings in 'Control Panel' - Appendix IV has some information about this).

As soon as the call is answered by the remote end, the modem then starts to make what can best be described as 'scratchy hissing' noises that can last anywhere from about five to fifty-five seconds. These hissing noises are a consequence of your own computer's modem trying to make a data connection with the modem belonging to the ISP Company at the distant end (as described in section 1.3). We call this process 'synchronisation' of the two modems.

If the two modems synchronise correctly – and they don't always do this on the first attempt – then the sounds disappear and you will see further status messages appear in the box below the Connect button as shown in the next picture.

If the synchronisation fails, then the modem will drop the line and then attempt to redial. You would observe this in the messaging as 'Dialing attempt 2' etc.

If you get to see the message that says 'Verifying user name and password' then this is a very good sign that things are working correctly, so do watch out for it.

The message 'Verifying user name and password' means most definitely that the two modems have fully synchronised and they are now at the stage where they can successfully exchange digital data between themselves. The message means that the remote ISP computer (the computer at the far end of the telephone line) is now checking out your ISP User name and Password to make sure that they are valid. You may remember from the theory in chapter 1 that the remote computer is a special computer owned by the ISP Company and it is your 'gateway' into the Internet. Your only way into the Internet is via such a remote computer.

Once the remote ISP computer has checked that the User name and Password are valid, then the next thing that will happen is that the dialog box will disappear completely.

If you are using Windows XP, then at the moment when you become connected, you even get a small message 'bubble' telling you so and at what speed the modems are working at – 46,600 bits per second in this example.

Click on the 'X' button to close the bubble and the message will disappear.

Let us just have a quick word about connection speed. Ideally, your modem will connect at somewhere around 45,000 bits per second, but it may be more and it can be substantially less. The key factors determining this connection speed are the type of modem you have, the quality of the phone line and the distance to your local telephone exchange. If you wish to test the quality of your line, some phone companies have a special telephone number that you may dial with an ordinary voice telephone to check it out. For example, in the UK on a

BT phone line, you can dial '17070' and use the 'Quiet Line test' option to listen and check if there are any crackles audible. If your modem connection speed is less than 28,800 then you should investigate why.

Okay. At this point your computer is on-line to the Internet, and your monitor is showing you the main working window of Outlook Express as shown in the next picture.

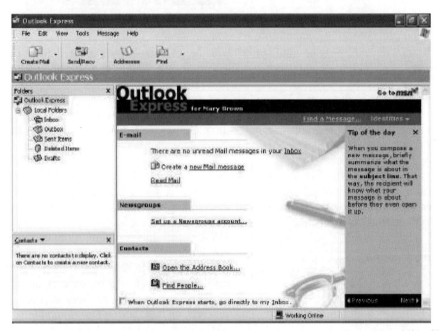

If the window for the email program does not fill your monitor screen completely, then click on the **Maximise** button (the middle one of the three in the very top right-hand corner) to make it do so. Also, for the remaining exercises in this book, you need to be able to see the two **sub-windows** called **Folders** and **Contacts** (shown on the left of the above picture). If you cannot see these sub-windows on your own screen then read Appendix V to learn how to make them appear on your screen.

Now that your computer is fully connected to the Internet, one of the first tasks that Outlook Express will automatically do for you is check to see if there is any mail waiting for you with the remote ISP computer (held in the **Incoming mailbox**). This automatic task is a consequence of the **Delivery Trigger Action** that we referred to before in section 1.3. Don't worry if you miss this next bit, but if you are quick enough to spot it in the bottom right-hand corner – just to the right of where it says 'Working Online' - you may observe the effects of this Delivery Trigger Action happening when a series of small messages flash up there. For example, you may see the wording 'Authorising' followed then by 'Checking mail...' The latter of these two is demonstrated in the following picture.

If there should be some mail, it will now be automatically extracted from the remote ISP computer and deposited into your own computer, being placed in the **Inbox folder** of the Outlook Express program.

When the automatic task is complete, then the program will be ready for you to use.

At this point, we have now completed the objective for our first exercise of getting the email program running on-line. Before we finish, we will check the **Inbox folder** and read any email that is in there. We need to do this to prepare for future exercises.

Look over at the **Folders sub-window** on the left side of the main program window and you should see the **Inbox folder**. If you cannot see it, then click with the mouse on the '+' symbol in the small square just to the left of 'Local Folders' to make it visible.

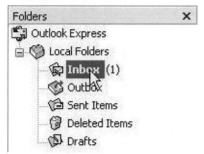

When the Inbox folder contains any mail that has not been read, you will see a number in brackets just to the right of it. This number is a counter of unread emails and in this picture, the (1) is indicating that there is one unread email. Move the tip of the mouse pointer over the Inbox folder and click on it...

The contents of the folder are now visible over on the right hand side of the screen, in the upper section. Here you can see all emails that have been received, as shown in the next picture.

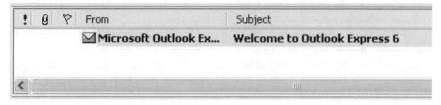

There are several columns in this upper section and later in the book we will discuss these in greater detail to learn all about them. We will refer to the line for each email listed in this section as a **Title line**. If you have several emails in the Inbox folder, they will appear with their Title lines listed one after the other in a vertical list. Normally the order of the list is that in which they were received, with the most recent at the bottom. However, be careful because this order can easily be upset by inadvertently clicking on the column headings. (If you do accidentally change the order then click on the **Received** column header to change it back again.)

If you look now at the left side of Title line in the last picture, you can see a little 'envelope' icon in the 'From' column, shown with the flap 'closed'. This signifies that the email has not been read. When the email has been read, the envelope flap will change to appear 'open' and normally this happens automatically about five seconds after the email has been selected.

To select any email and read its message content, the Title line in the upper section must be highlighted. If you have only one email in the folder then this will be highlighted and selected for you, but if there are several then you can select any email yourself by clicking on the appropriate Title line with the mouse pointer.

When an email Title line is selected, the message content of the email appears in the lower section, as shown in the next picture.

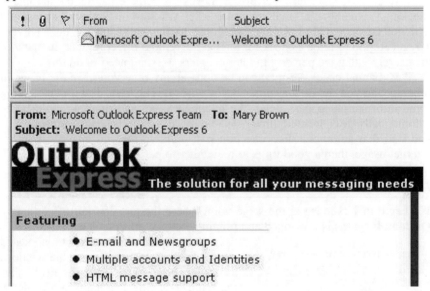

Here in the lower section, we see that this particular email is from the Microsoft Team, and is advertising the features of the email program itself – Outlook Express. Notice now in the upper section that the envelope icon on the Title line has changed its appearance. This email is now considered as read.

The view on your own monitor screen will probably seem a little different to the pictures we have just looked at, depending on whether you have received any more emails, and whether they have been read yet or not.

Scan down the list of your own emails now, and if you do have any unread then use the tip of the mouse pointer to click on each Title line in turn where the corresponding envelope flap is closed. You may need to use the vertical scroll-bar down the right in order see them all. Wait about five seconds on each one, until the flap appears open. As each flap changes to open, you may notice that the counter in brackets shown over in the Folders sub-window decreases by a value of one, until finally the counter disappears entirely as the last one is read.

Okay. All of your email received so far should now have been read and there should not be a counter visible in brackets against the Inbox folder icon. If you did not receive any new ones this time, then don't be too disappointed because in the next and subsequent chapters you most definitely will!

We have now reached the end of exercise 1.

2.4 Manually checking for mail

The exercise we shall now perform achieves the same effect as the automatic checking for mail that normally happens when you start up Outlook Express and first get connected on-line. We are going to manually initiate the Delivery Trigger Action to force a check for mail at the remote ISP computer. In many of the exercises that we perform in later chapters we shall need to do this.

This manual check for mail can be done at any time you have the program running, and you can do it as often as you wish. It is also a useful way of forcing some information to pass down the telephone line, and thereby avoid being automatically disconnected through inactivity, as we discussed in section 2.2. If you find that automatic disconnection is a problem for you at peak times of Internet usage, then a good tip is to remember to periodically do this.

Exercise 2 – Manually checking for mail

We begin this exercise at the same point where the last one left off – that is, **Outlook Express** is now open and running, and we are connected **on-line**.

Click on the **Send/Receive** button located on the Toolbar near the top of the window, as shown here. What happens next takes place fairly quickly. If it happens so quickly that you miss the detail, then don't be too concerned. You can click on the button again to repeat the action if you wish. A sample of what you may see is shown in the next picture.

Let us see if we can make sense out what is happening at this stage. First a message box pops up on screen saying 'Finding Host...'. The message then changes to 'Connected' 'Authorising...' 'Sending...' 'Receiving...' and 'Disconnecting...' all in rapid succession. If by co-incidence you do have any mail waiting for you, then the 'Receiving...' message stays showing a little longer, but chances are that they all happen in rapid fire, one after the other.

Relating this practical action back to the theory in section 1.3, what took place very quickly was the establishment of the 'double U-bend' connection that we talked about, and the subsequent stages of transferring any mail between your computer and the ISP's computer. You might like to have another read of section 1.3 and it will probably make more sense after this current chapter. The reason it happened very quickly now was because there was no mail to transfer. Later on, when you start to send and receive mail with your friends and acquaintances, it will take much longer. If someone sends you a big email, it will seem to take forever!

That is all there is to the procedure of manually checking for mail. You can do it anytime that you feel like it when you are connected on-line. If you should get automatically disconnected at some point, then performing this action will prompt the connection dialog box that we witnessed before in exercise 1 (the one titled 'Dial-up Connection'). This is a very quick and easy method to become re-connected without having to close down Outlook Express and start again from scratch.

Before we end this exercise there is something else that I would like to show you. Take a look at this picture. In particular, note the very small icon of two 'miniature monitor screens' located near the 'time' shown in the very bottom right-hand corner of the monitor display.

You should be able to see this icon on your own monitor screen at this instant, located on the task bar next to the 'time'. This icon confirms the fact that we are connected on-line to the ISP computer system.

The icon is also a very useful diagnostic item, and I should like you to pay particular attention to it while you perform the next action. Press the **Send/Receive** button one more time. Watch the tiny little screens of the icon flash a bright colour (light blue for Windows XP, light green for earlier versions of Windows).

Every time that data goes back and forth between your computer and the remote ISP computer, then this small miniature monitors icon changes its appearance slightly such that the two small monitor screens 'light up' in a different colour. When data is being sent from your computer to the remote ISP computer, then the 'front' small monitor flashes. When data is being received by your computer from the remote ISP computer, then the 'rear' small monitor flashes. If you have an external modem, you may also see indicator lights flashing on the modem front panel in sympathy with the small monitor screens.

Remembering the tip about avoiding automatic disconnection, every time you see either of these two small screens flash then the inactivity timer at the ISP computer will have been reset.

Exercise 2 is now complete.

2.5　More about the 'on-line' connection

Exercise 1 in section 2.3 demonstrated that we can make a connection to the Internet and get on-line by first starting the **Outlook Express** email program. 'First-timers' can be forgiven for thinking that these two are therefore always linked together. This is one convenient way of getting on-line, but there are other ways of doing so. We could, for example, run the program **Internet Explorer**, which is yet another program that uses the Internet to look at 'web pages'. After Internet Explorer starts running then we can make a connection to the Internet in the same way as we have done for email.

The true relationship between the on-line connection and programs such as Outlook Express and Internet Explorer is that they are really all separate items that can be function independently if you so wish. The fact that both programs can activate the on-line connection on starting up is just an arrangement that is provided for convenience. Similarly, when these programs close down, the fact that they offer you the opportunity to close the on-line connection is also an arrangement for convenience. Therefore, from a conceptual point of view, it is a good idea to think of each of these three things as separate 'programs' in their own right. The 'program' that creates the on-line connection is called **Dial-up Networking**. It is not a true user program in the normal sense, but it can be started and stopped independently from the other two programs. The relationship between these three programs is shown in the next diagram, and bear in mind that what is shown here is all happening within your computer.

When you have this mental picture of what is going on, then it is easier to understand and appreciate how they interact with each other. Whenever the other two programs wish to exchange information with the modem, then they always do this by activating this third item – the Dial-Up Networking 'program'. It is Dial-up Networking that actually provides the on-line connection.

In starting to run either of the Outlook Express or Internet Explorer programs, if the Dial-up Networking 'program' is already running, then there is no need to activate the on-line connection for a second time. Each program can sense that the connection already exists, and they can effectively share it. If either program senses that the connection does not exist when they start running, then they both have the ability to activate it.

If we use either the Outlook Express program or the Internet Explorer program 'on their own' - that is, without an on-line connection existing to the Internet, then we say that we are working 'off-line'. In chapter 5, we discuss this in further detail and see that there are in fact some benefits to be gained by working off-line at times. However, we know that eventually we will have to go on-line at some point in order to get our email transferred and delivered. For Outlook Express, it is the Send/Receive button that will take us from working off-line to getting back to working on-line.

2.6 Closing Outlook Express and disconnecting

From the discussion in the last section, we should now appreciate that the Outlook Express program and the on-line connection are two separate things. We learnt that when Outlook Express starts running that it can automatically create an on-line connection for us (using the Dial-up Networking 'program') - or at least prompt for one. So too when we close Outlook Express – it can prompt us to ask the question of do we want to stay connected on-line after the program has closed, or do we want to disconnect immediately. This feature is called Auto-disconnect.

As a final exercise for this chapter, we will now close down Outlook Express and see the Auto-disconnect feature in action.

Note – If by chance your computer does not show you the **Auto-disconnect** message in this next exercise, the reason is to do with the set up of 'Accounts' within Outlook Express. Appendix VII gives further information about changing the necessary settings, particularly the very last comment. If Auto-disconnect is not working on your computer, then don't worry because the next exercise tells you of an alternative method of disconnecting.

Exercise 3 – Closing the email program and disconnecting

We begin at the stage where we have just completed exercise 2. If you are not currently connected on-line then please re-connect now (you can click the **Send/Receive** button again to prompt for a re-connection if you need to).

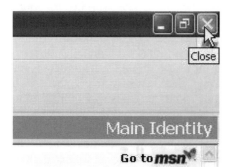

Click now on the **Close** button located at the top right-hand corner of the Outlook Express window as shown here.

After the window has disappeared, you should see the following Auto-disconnect message…

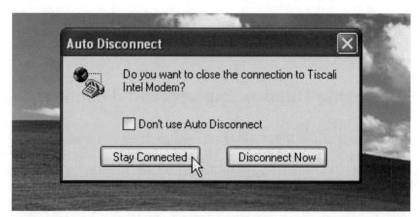

Note – If you don't see it, then skip the next two paragraphs to learn another method of disconnecting.

Normally at this point, you would click on the **Disconnect Now** button and that disconnects the on-line connection. However, I want to illustrate another point to you while we have the opportunity. I would like to demonstrate how you can close the on-line connection independently from the Auto-disconnect feature.

Click on the **Stay Connected** button, as shown in the above picture.

Observe now that Outlook Express has closed down altogether and you are back at the Desktop where you first began. However, if you look now to the **Miniature monitors icon** that we talked about in the section 2.4, you will see that this icon is still present in the bottom right-hand corner of your screen, in the **System tray** at the side of the 'Time' display. This confirms that we 'stayed connected'!

At this point, we are in precisely the situation that you might wish for if you wanted to use the on-line connection to the Internet for some other purpose. For example, if you wanted to browse through web pages with Internet Explorer, you can now start this alternative program running and use it straight away without having to wait for an Internet connection to be recreated. It is surprising how long the whole procedure of getting on-line can seem to take when you are in a hurry!

Now right-click on the miniature monitors icon and select the Disconnect option, as shown in the next picture.

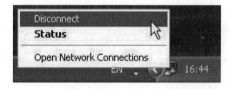

The icon will now be removed from the System Tray and the on-line connection to the Internet will be disconnected. If you have an external modem, you will also notice that some of the indicator lights that were illuminated now go off.

This last technique of closing the on-line connection with a right-click action on the icon is a useful one to remember, for if you don't close the connection when ending either the Outlook Express or Internet Explorer programs, then you can do so 'manually' afterwards at a much later time.

2.7   Alternative on-line connection methods

In this final section of this chapter, I want to briefly mention some of the other methods that you can use to get connected on-line to the Internet. The **Dial-up Networking** method using ordinary modems over a standard telephone line is just one of many. If you have no interest in these other methods then you can skip over this section without any loss of continuity.

ISDN
ISDN is an abbreviation for 'Integrated Services Digital Network'. It is a service that telephone companies can now offer to customers, providing that the quality

of the ordinary telephone line to their premises meets a certain standard. This is usually dependant on the physical distance between customers' premises and the local digital telephone exchange.

ISDN is more expensive in the UK than an ordinary (analogue) telephone line because it provides more service than just one telephone number over one physical pair of wires. You can be allocated two or more telephone numbers, depending on the level of service that you subscribe to, and effectively you get two independent telephone lines from just one physical line (they are called 'channels').

The great benefits of an ISDN connection over that of a normal (analogue) type modem connection are – it is much faster to connect, is about fifty per cent faster in speed, and is digital all the way from your computer to the remote ISP computer (the trunk telephone network itself is now completely digital). You can also connect to the Internet via one channel, while leaving the second channel free for ordinary voice telephone calls, or you can double up the overall speed of the connection by combining the two channels together. Be aware though that each channel is charged as a separate telephone call.

From a theory viewpoint, an ISDN connection is almost the same as using a conventional modem in that it is a dial-up type of connection. One difference is that you require a device called a Terminal Adapter in the place of an ordinary Modem.

Most ISP Companies can offer Internet service using ISDN these days.

ADSL (Broadband)

ADSL is an abbreviation for 'Asymmetric Digital Subscriber Line', but these days it is marketed under the more general name of Broadband.

Like ISDN, it is a digital service to your premises, but its fantastic advantage is that it is very high speed and it is 'always on' - that is, you do not have to dial-up each day via the normal telephone network to make the connection, so you effectively have instant access to the Internet. It is called 'Asymmetric' because the speed of sending data to you from the ISP Company is faster than the speed that you send data to them.

The speed is truly amazing when you have seen it in action. However, it is more expensive than even ISDN.

Mobile telephone

You can connect to the Internet using a mobile phone if you wish to. When first introduced, this method used to be considerably slower than using an ordinary (analogue) modem. This situation has recently improved with a service called GPRS, and will change again dramatically when the next generation of telephony arrives (the so-called 3G or third generation network).

To use a mobile telephone with an ordinary computer, you need a special form of modem. You can purchase a special telephone called a WAP (Wireless

Access Protocol) phone that has everything built into the phone, so that you do not need a separate computer. If you want to read email on the move, then this is the phone for you. But do remember that it will all change when the new 3G networks are built and come into service. The predicted date for these new networks is around 2004.

Office Local Area Network

If you work in a large office, your method of connecting to the Internet may well be via a network known as a LAN (Local Area Network). A LAN is a method of linking all the office desktop computers together with a cable that is completely separate from the normal telephone network.

The larger LAN installations do not normally use dial-up type connections to the Internet, but have a special (usually high speed digital) cable connecting the office or offices to an ISP Company. The speed capacity of such special cables can vary quite a lot, but usually they are significantly higher speed than home type dial-up connections. Some smaller LAN installations do still use dial-up connections via a modem.

Setting up your computer to use a LAN connection into the Internet is a specialist subject and would normally be undertaken by a qualified professional within the business that owns the office, or a contractor from an external company.

Whereas the operation of an email program such as Outlook Express can, and often does, work well in this type of office situation, there may be other complexities introduced. Instead of an account being directly subscribed from an ISP Company, more than likely in a large office environment, there will be other computers owned by the business that provide the function of the 'electronic post office' that we mentioned in chapter 1.

From a user's point of view, most of the information provided in this book on email will still be applicable. The only area that is likely to be different is the method of getting connected on-line. With a larger office LAN installation, this difference is usually associated with a generalised procedure for getting access to the LAN network itself. Once you are connected to the LAN, then you do not normally need to think of the Internet as being accessed via a remote connection – you simply consider that you are always connected to the Internet and let the qualified professional worry about the mechanism by which this is achieved.

Some offices permit public email service from the LAN, some do not. You may need to obtain special permission from your IT department in the business to have such public email access. One of the concerns in a business environment is the susceptibility to inadvertently acquiring a computer virus, but with appropriate virus checking software this risk can be managed.

3

Sending and Receiving an email

3.1   Creating and sending an email

In this section, we will undertake an exercise of creating and sending the very simplest form of email, which is just a single short message. Now, as a 'first-timer' you may not yet know of anyone else's email address to actually send it to so we are going to use a small trick. Whereas normally, we would create an email and send it to someone else, in this exercise we are going to create an email and send it to ourselves. We will just pretend that it is addressed to someone else!

Using this trick, not only will we experience the process of creating and sending the email, but we will also experience receiving and reading it, which we achieve in the exercise following this one. For practice, you can repeat both of these exercises as many times as you care to without having to worry that you might be getting on someone else's nerves by bombarding them with test emails.

The email will be created and sent in the standard way through the Internet network, just the same as if we were sending it to someone else. But if you should happen to make any mistakes in the process then you don't have to be embarrassed about them because no one else will ever know.

You may think of this idea of sending an email to yourself as analogous to throwing an Australian boomerang. You launch it into space and seconds later, if you have done it correctly, it will come magically whizzing back to you!

As a preliminary requirement for the exercise, you need to know precisely and in full the **email address** for yourself. This is the address that you will quote to other people if you want them to send email to you. By 'in full', I mean something like '**mary.brown01@tiscali.co.uk**' or '**john.smith@bigbusiness.com**'. It might be as well just to remind yourself of how we would say such addresses. For example, the first of these two would be pronounced as 'mary dot brown zero one at tiscali dot coe dot you kay'. This pronunciation is important because you may need to quote your own email address to someone, either in person or over the phone, and if you follow the accepted style, then they will easily understand you.

(Full addressing was covered in section 1.4 so re-visit this if you need a refresh). In concluding these preliminary remarks, I want to emphasise that the way I will show you how to achieve various actions is not the only way that they can be done. Microsoft, the program creators, usually provide for several ways of 'skinning the cat'. Therefore, don't be perplexed if you should discover yet another way to achieve the same actions and end result. In the final analysis, it is your choice of how you prefer to go about doing things. I will show you one way so that you can at least make progress. If you find it easier later on to do it differently, then that is entirely up to you.

Exercise 4 – Creating your first email and sending it

To begin this exercise, you need to repeat exercise 1 and reach the point where we have just opened the Outlook Express program and we are on-line – that is, we have a working data connection via the modem into the Internet.

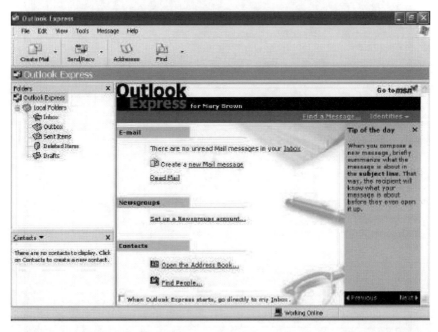

If the Outlook Express window does not fill your monitor screen completely, then click on the **maximise** button (the middle one of the three in the very top right hand corner) to make it do so. Also, if your monitor does not show the **'Folders'** and **'Contacts' sub-window** areas of the screen (as can be seen in the picture above), then follow the advice given in Appendix V to get them back again.

Click now on the toolbar button towards the top of the screen that says 'Create Mail', as in this picture (for those users of Outlook Express version 5, the button is worded 'New Mail' instead of 'Create Mail').

Almost instantly, up pops a new window that is the basic starting point for all new email messages. This new window is shown in the next picture.

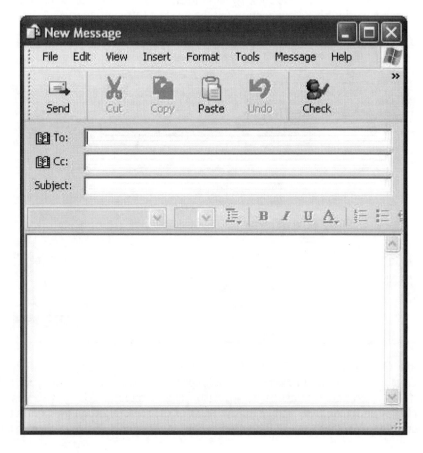

Note – If your **New Message window** also shows a **From: textbox**, it is because more than one 'mail account' has been set up for you within Outlook Express. Throughout all the exercises in the book, we work on the standard set-up where this is not the case. If you see a From: textbox, you need to make sure the appropriate account is selected within it.

Now I hope you will agree, this window is not too complex.

- First of all, consider the long white **textbox** that has the label **'To:'** marked on its left-hand side. In the picture above, you can see that there is a vertical line 'cursor' positioned just inside it. This white text box is where we will shortly write the full **email address** of the person that we wish to send the message to.

- Second, notice that the white text box immediately below it has the label **'Cc:'** instead. This abbreviation is a common office term meaning 'carbon copy'. Here, it signifies that we have a choice to send a complete copy of this email to yet another person, in addition to the 'To:' person. If we put someone else's email address in here, then the copy email will be sent automatically at the same time as the main email. This means you only have to write the message contents once, and the email will be sent to two different destinations.

- The third text box is the **'Subject:'** title box. When the email message eventually arrives at its destination, it is the wording that we put here inside this box that is first displayed to the reader, before they see the actual contents. Though not absolutely essential, it is always a good idea to put some words into the Subject title box, no matter how trivial they may be. If you don't, then the program will give you a warning message.

- The large white area in the lower half of the window is a fourth text box, and one that, because of its greater height, can show multiple lines of text. This is where we write the details of the message that we want to send – the actual message contents. Down the right-hand side of this fourth text box we see a vertical scroll bar in a faint 'greyed out' style. If our message contents prove to be larger than can be shown in the visible area, then this scroll bar will change to being not 'greyed out', and we will be able to scroll up and down in order to view the contents in their entirety.

Okay. We are ready to start filling out this window with the details for the 'test' email to be sent for our exercise.

In what follows, I am going to illustrate the example with an email address of '**mary.brown01@tiscali.co.uk**'. I do **not** want you to copy this literally, but to use your own full email address instead.

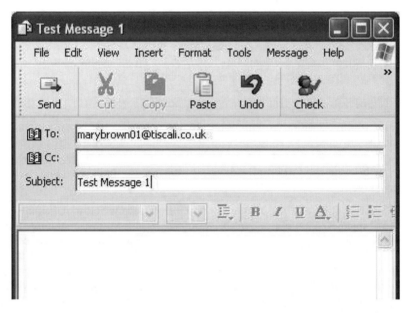

When the New Message window first pops up on your own monitor screen, you should see the black vertical line cursor flashing in the To: text box. This cursor indicates the position where any text entered at the keyboard will be placed. We say that the To: text box currently has the 'focus of attention'. Whatever you type goes straight into the text box that has the focus of attention – and not in any other text box.

If you accidentally lose the vertical line cursor from this textbox for any reason (that is, it does not flash inside this box), simply point your mouse pointer back inside the white area of the To: text box and click on it. The cursor will then return. When the pointer is over the textbox it changes its shape. If it is inside the area of the white text box, it changes from an arrow style pointer to a strange 'vertical line' with bits on the top and bottom (looking something like a tall 'I' symbol).

Okay. Go ahead now and type in your own full email address in the **To:** textbox. When you get to the end of typing it, don't be tempted to press the ENTER key or the box will change its size! If you do this accidentally, then press the BACKSPACE key once to rub it out again and the box will return to its normal size.

When you have finished typing, move the mouse pointer to point inside the white area of the **Subject:** text box and make a click. Notice that the flashing vertical cursor is now flashing inside this other text box. Then go ahead and type the subject title 'Test Message 1', just as I have illustrated in the last picture.

Okay. Move the mouse pointer inside the very large white 'contents' text box in the lower part of the window and click again. Observe that the flashing cursor jumps once more.

Now complete the creation of the email by typing the message as shown in the picture below (and remember to use your own name instead of 'Mary'!). Notice that I have placed a comma at the end of the first line. After that, I then pressed the ENTER key to get the cursor to go to the start of the next line. Then I pressed the ENTER key yet again to leave a blank line, before entering 'This is my... etc'.

Also notice at the very end of the message contents – after the last word 'Mary' - I have pressed the ENTER key one last time to take the cursor to the line below, as the very last thing that I typed. This is good practice. It means that if you decide to add any more text on at the end, you can position the cursor in the right place to do so. It's only a small point, but these are the ones that will make your work look more professional when you gather further knowledge and expertise.

Okay. We have now completed the email and we are ready to send it. Click now on the Send button at the top part of the message window...

A few things will happen fairly quickly now, ending with the email being sent. If you don't get to catch all of the action, you can repeat the exercise later.

The first thing that happens is that the message window closes, and the email that we have created is placed in a special area called the OutBox folder. This folder is shown in the next picture and is one of a list of folders that are visible in the Folders sub-window section of the main Outlook Express window.

Note – You may recall that we met the **Outbox folder** before in section 1.3 during the discussion of the theory of email. All email that we are sending out to the Internet will be placed in the Outbox folder before it is transmitted.

The number you can see in brackets to the right of the Outbox folder is the number of emails that are waiting in there ready to be sent. The picture to the left shows '(1)' and corresponds to what we have just created. Notice also in the picture that the lettering of the Outbox folder is shown bold. This indicates that there is something in there waiting to be sent.

Providing that you are on-line then the email will be sent out to the Internet almost immediately. This is the Delivery Trigger Action at work, and it is initiated automatically, but only if you are on-line.

If by chance you have been automatically disconnected, then the email will wait here in the Outbox folder indefinitely (in such a circumstance, click on the

Send/Receive button to prompt a reconnection and get back on-line).

After the email has been sent, you will then see the Outbox folder change back to its former state where there is no number shown in brackets to the right and the lettering returns to the normal non-bold appearance as shown left.

That is really all there is to sending a simple email. Later in the book we will learn how to send more complex emails, but even then the procedure for sending them will be much the same. The only difference we will probably notice is that it may take a bit longer to complete the sending process.

In the next exercise, we will look at how to receive the email that we have just sent, but before we do that, I want to show you a method of proving that the email has really been sent. Position the tip of the mouse pointer now on the Sent Items folder (visible just below the Outbox folder) and make a click action.

As soon as you have clicked, you will see the folder become highlighted (as shown here). Now look over to the window sections on the right-hand side of the screen. In the upper of the two sections, you will then see the Title line of the message that we have just sent. In the lower part below it, you will see the actual message contents.

The **Sent Items folder** is a historical record of all such outgoing messages, and the fact that our message is now appearing here means categorically that it has been sent. You will find this folder very valuable in the future if you need to remind yourself of old emails, and what you have said, to whom and when you said it!

Okay. We have reached the end of exercise 4. Don't break here if you can avoid it, but move swiftly to the next one.

3.2 Receiving and reading an email

Exercise 5 – Receiving and reading your first email

This exercise begins at the stage reached immediately after completing the last one.

Click now on the **Send/Receive** button as shown in the next picture. This initiates the **Delivery Trigger Action** manually. We do not have an email to send this time, but there should be one waiting for us to receive at the remote ISP computer.

The action now will happen very quickly, so you may not see all that I describe.

You should see a message box pop up and very rapidly it will display a series of messages that say something like 'Finding Host...' or 'Connected' followed by 'Receiving message 1 of 1...' and 'Disconnecting...' One of these is shown in the next picture.

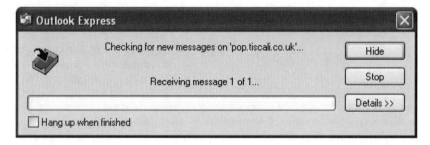

The action ends with any incoming email then being received down the telephone line into our computer, and subsequently into the **Inbox folder** of the **Outlook Express program**. What you should finally see in the Folders sub-section window is something like the next picture...

Notice now that the **Inbox folder** has a number in brackets associated with it, to the right-hand side. If there had been more that one incoming email, then this number would have increased accordingly.

Note – You may remember from exercise 1 in chapter 2 that the number in brackets is actually the total number of emails that have not yet been read. This displayed number reduces each time we read one.

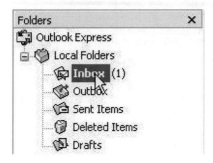

Okay. The final part of the exercise is to read the incoming email. Position the tip of the mouse pointer now on the **Inbox folder** and make a click action. As soon as you have done so then it becomes highlighted as shown in the picture on the left.

Look then over to the sections displayed on the right-hand side of the screen. In the upper section, you will see the **Title line** of the message that we have just received. The Title line shows whom the email is 'From', and its 'Subject' title. This is illustrated in the following picture.

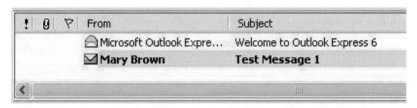

Notice that when you first see this Title line in the upper section, the envelope icon shows the flap closed.

Normally when you open the Inbox folder after receiving an email, the Title line of the latest received email is automatically highlighted and selected. If you now wait for about five seconds, the envelope will change appearance and the flap will open, as shown in the next picture.

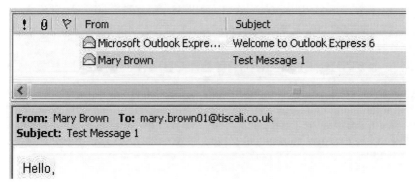

If you receive a few emails at the same time, you will need to click on the line of the one that you want to read, in order to read its particular message contents. Just occasionally, even when you receive just one, the highlighting may not automatically happen and you may have to click on it to read it.

> Note – When you see the Title line in the upper section, it corresponds to the email 'header' that we talked about in section 1.2, and the contents in the lower section correspond to the email 'body'.

Okay. Now look back to the left hand side where the folders sub-window is. Do you notice another change? You should see that the number in brackets at the right of the **Inbox folder** has disappeared. The number is only present where there are emails within the folder that have not been read. Later on, when you may have several emails in the Inbox folder at the same time, you will have a larger number in brackets, for example you might see it displayed as (4), and this value reduces by 1 for every instance where one of the email messages has been read.

Good. We have received and read the email that we sent in exercise 4.

Before we finish this current exercise, there is one further small point I would like to mention. The automatic change of status of an incoming email from being 'unread' to being 'read' is fine for short emails like the one in our exercise, but sometimes it can prove to be a bit inconvenient. For example, you may occasionally receive an email and see it change from 'unread' to 'read', but in truth you may not have time to read all of it – at the time that you actually receive it. This may be particularly if the email is a long one with many lines of text.

Though we will not bother with this now, you can change the status of an email back to 'unread' very simply with a right-click on its Title line. In the menu that then pops up, there is an option for you to select and mark it as 'unread' (and if you do then there is also another option to change it back to 'read' again!). If you want to read an email at a later time, then this can be a handy way to reverse the envelope icon picture back to having its flap closed. And you are reminded later on that it needs to be read.

This concludes exercise 5.

3.3 Saving and editing an email

Just occasionally, you may want to start writing an email but not have time to finish it there and then. The two exercises in this section show you how you can first begin creating an email, and then save it for completion at a later date – followed by how you subsequently pick up your saved work, finish it off, and then send it.

Exercise 6 – *Creating and saving an email without sending*

We begin the exercise with **Outlook Express** opened and on-line to the Internet.

Click now on the **Create Mail** button on the toolbar at the top of the screen (labelled **New mail** if you are using Outlook Express version 5).

Up then pops a New Message window…

Fill out the textboxes so that they look like the last picture (and remember again to put your own email address in the To: textbox instead of 'mary.brown01@tiscali.co.uk').

Okay. Now instead of sending this email, we are going to save it in the **Drafts folder**.

Be careful not to click on the Send button, but click instead on File from the Menu bar just above it, and select the Save option as in this picture.

A message box then pops up to tell you that 'the message' (meaning your email) has been saved in the Drafts folder as in the next picture.

Click on the **OK** button and the message box will disappear. Notice now though that the Drafts folder in the list of folders to the left has changed its appearance, and is shown in bold with a number in brackets '(1)' attached to the right.

This signifies that a copy of the email message is safely secured within the Drafts folder. If a calamity should strike your computer at this very instant (for example, a power failure) then all the work that you have done so far on this message will not be lost.

Thinking of your future work with email, you may find this ability to save a copy of your work – before you have sent it – extremely useful.

The **New Message window** will still be visible on screen, and if you wanted to you could continue working with it – by either adding or editing the text – then you could do so. However, I want to demonstrate how you can cease work altogether at this point and so we will not do any more in this exercise. Close the **New Message window** now by clicking on the **Close** button in the top right-hand corner and the window disappears.

We have reached the end of this exercise. We have now created and saved an email, but it has not yet been sent.

If you want to, you can now close the **Outlook Express** program and do something else, or leave it open and move immediately on to the next exercise.

Exercise 7 – Retrieving, editing and then sending an email

A pre-requisite for this exercise is that you have completed exercise 6. We begin at the stage where **Outlook Express** is open and you are on-line to the Internet.

In the **Folders sub-window** on the left side of the monitor screen, you should see that the **Drafts folder icon** is showing in bold with the number in brackets. Click on this icon and it will become highlighted, as illustrated here.

As soon as you have done this, you will see over on the right side of the screen that the upper section displays the Title line of the message that was saved in exercise 6, and the lower section displays the contents.

Now move the mouse pointer over to point inside the right upper section. Position the pointer tip so that it is over the **Title line** and then make a **right-click** action, as shown in the next picture.

67

From the pop-up menu that now appears, select the **Open option** with a click. Instantly, the **New Message window** then re-appears with a copy of the original message displayed inside.

Click now in the large white message textbox just below the line 'This is my second email'. Edit the message by typing a new line of text saying 'It has been saved and edited.' Press the ENTER key when you get to the end of the line, so that you maintain a blank line after it. Your work should now look something like this…

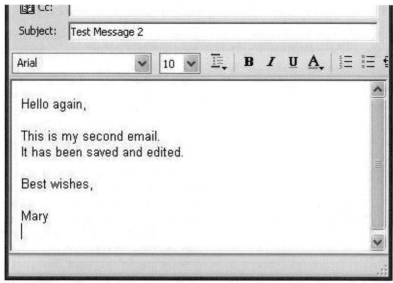

Now, at this point you have a choice. If you wish to save the email message back to the **Drafts folder** and keep it for a later date, then you can click on **File** again in the **Menu bar**, and take the **Save option** again. You may then close the window with the **Close** button in the top right-hand corner as you did before. Alternatively, you can choose now to send it – we will take this option.

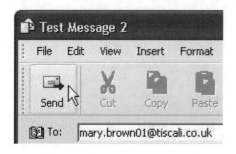

Click now on the Send button as illustrated here.

As soon as you have clicked, the **New Message window** closes. The edited version of the email is immediately placed in the **Outbox folder**, and at the same time the older copy in the **Drafts folder** is removed. Providing you are on-line at this moment, then the **Delivery Trigger**

Action will be automatically initiated, and the email will be sent over the Internet data connection in the normal way.

To finish off the exercise, we will receive this second email from the ISP computer. Click the **Send/receive** button once more…
 This should receive our second email and deposit it in the **Inbox folder**. Click on the **Inbox folder icon** and, in the right-hand upper section, you will see its **Title line**. Again, after about five seconds, the small envelope changes appearance to 'opened'.

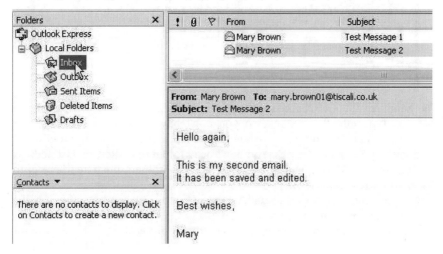

Exercise 7 is now concluded.

3.4   A few points to consider

From the exercises in this chapter, you now have the skills to be able to send and receive emails all over the world. Email is without doubt a very powerful tool and before we leave chapter 3, I want to briefly discuss some of the considerations that you should think about when you are using it.

First let us consider a few technical useful tips.

Though we don't do this in any of the exercises, you can copy your email to some other person – in addition to the intended recipient – simply by putting their email address in the **Cc: textbox**. That seems fairly obvious. What is not so obvious is that you can make a list of two or more people in either the **To: textbox** or the **Cc: textbox**. You do this simply by separating the email addresses with a semi-colon symbol (the ; symbol). Later on in chapter 6, we learn how to send to more than one person using a 'group', but that is for later.

To illustrate the point, this is how the Cc: textbox would look like if we were copying an email to several people...

The height of the **Cc: textbox** changes automatically to accommodate the list that you type into the textbox, so you don't have to press the ENTER key yourself to put more addresses on a new line. Notice that the semi-colon is only used to separate the addresses. You don't need to put one after the last address.

Remember that you can also use the same technique illustrated here in the **To: textbox** if you need to.

Now an important point to understand is that if you send a single email to more than one person, either by using To: and Cc: or by making a list in either one separated with semi-colons, then the email only gets transferred once into the Internet, and it is the job of the ISP computer system then to make duplicate email copies and deliver them to every addressee. The beauty of this is that the ISP computer does all the donkey-work of making the copies for you, so that you don't have to. Very importantly, in the next chapter where we get to attach other 'things' to the email, these 'things' are also copied by the ISP computer. It means that if you send a big email, you only send it once into the Internet, so the amount of time taken up sending it down the phone line is just the same as sending it to one person only!

When should you use the Cc: box instead of a list in the To: box?

Well, there must always be at least one person in the To: box. But to answer the question in a broader sense, my thoughts are that you should include people in the To: box for one of two reasons. The first reason is where you have actions that you want people to do for you. I would tend to put people in the Cc: box if I did not expect them to do anything as a result of me sending them an email (it was for their information only). The second reason I would put people in the To: box is if I was worried about making sure people feel they were being treated equally, or of the same importance. There is no significant technical difference between these two boxes that you would notice.

Now for a few philosophical considerations...

When you have mastered the first skills of creating simple emails, you quickly realise that the whole process of communicating this way can be so much easier than using postal mail. This is particularly true if you send email to friends and relatives overseas. In no time at all, you discover that the world has become a much smaller place.

The ease of communicating with email leads us to an important point to watch out for. The written word – even when scribbled very quickly in an email – is quite different to the spoken word because it does not convey any feeling or emotion direct from your body. Whereas in a telephone call, the tone of your voice adds to the overall content, in an email this information is absent. Something that you might say in a flippant manner by word of mouth can be accentuated or misunderstood in an email, and can be read with a degree of offence that was never intended. So be careful in your choice of words in an email. It is sometimes better to tone a phrase down a little so that it does not sound so strong when read by the recipient.

To try and avoid this problem of the lack of 'body language' in an email (the tone of voice, facial expression, a gesture of your arms and such like) some people have begun to include symbols mixed in with the words. A very common symbol you might see to indicate that something is being said in a very jocular manner is the so-called 'smiley face'. This symbol appears as :-) when written, that is three keystrokes of the keyboard – colon, dash and right curved bracket – are typed one after the other to try represent a smile (look at it with your head tilted to the left to get the idea!). I often use this trick myself to make sure that something meant to be funny is taken explicitly as such. I may even repeat it twice :-) :-) if I am trying to express joy or laughter in my 'voice'. The opposite symbol is :-(to express sadness! Some reference books on the topic will give you a whole host of symbols, which have been dubbed 'emoticons', but I draw the line at these two.

Another important point to remember when using email, particularly when sending it to the other side of the world, is the 'time shift' capability. By this I mean that you can write an email in the morning, and the recipient can read it at any time of the day, or possibly several days later. This has both good points and bad points.

A good point is that you are not being so demanding on the other person's time with email. For example, if you try making a telephone call to company employees, then you may not get through to them. They may either be in a meeting or away from their desk at that time, and not able to take your call. With an email, this does not matter, for they can always read their incoming email at a time less demanding and more convenient for them. You may indeed find that

71

email works to get you a response when several attempts at a telephone call will fail.

A bad point is that people can choose to ignore an email if they so desire. They can (and do!) invent a thousand excuses why they never received it. Some of these excuses might just be genuine. If someone is away on two weeks holiday, then sending him or her an email may not be very productive, and you may not find out for some while why not.

A final point about using email that I would like to stress is be wise and do not try and use email to vent your anger or emotion with another person. It is very unlikely to give you the result that you desire, and it is very likely to do the opposite.

4

Sending and Receiving Attachments

4.1   Sending an attachment

In the last chapter, we learnt how to send and receive emails in the form of simple written messages. Here in this chapter, we will take the capability of emails one stage further. We will learn how to add an **attachment** to the basic email message when sending it, or how to detach such an attachment from the message when it is received.

Section 1.5 of chapter 1 introduced the idea of attachments. They are items in addition to the basic message content. Practically, they may be photographs or pictures, audio or video clips, program files, or indeed any type of computer file we care to think of.

Photographs of the family are a very popular type of attachment these days. They can be taken either with a modern digital camera or scanned with a digital scanner. Some high street stores now offer a service whereby you give them an ordinary photographic film to be developed, and they will return the processed images as computer files on a CD-ROM. Once you have an image in digital form, it can easily be added to an email as an attachment. When the email arrives at the distant end, the recipient can detach the image attachment, and view or print the photograph.

You may add more than one attachment to the same basic email message, and they can be of mixed types. By this I mean that you can make one attachment a picture type and another attachment a document type, both to the same email. The receiver of such an email will then be able to detach these at the remote end, either individually or as a whole.

All attachments are files, and before we embark upon practical exercises to show you how to deal with attachments, it may be worthwhile just reminding ourselves about the idea of 'file types' and what this means. When you receive an attachment and detach it, you may need to know what 'type' of file it is, so that you know which program to use in order to work with it. Sometimes the computer helps out by automatically starting up the right program for you, but occasionally it gets it wrong – and that is when you need to understand about different file types.

> Note – Section 8.2 of the companion guide 'Using a Computer for the First Time' discusses 'file types' in much more detail.

A good analogy for understanding file types is to think about an apple and a pear. They are both types of fruit, but they are different types. So it is with computer files – they are all collectively known as files, just as all apples and pears are collectively known as fruit, but there are 'apple' file types and 'pear' file types.

To the computer, this idea of file type is very important because it is the way that it can tell the difference between a photograph file and a document file – they are both files but they are different file types. How does the computer recognise which file is which type? That's simple – they both have little bits of information added on to the end of their file names – and the computer just looks at these added bits and knows immediately what type of file it is. These 'bits' turn out to be alphabetic letters – usually three letters for Windows computers – with a dot symbol in front of them. An example would be '.gif' for a special form of picture file.

Normally, the computer's Windows software hides this added bit of information to end of the file name, so that you cannot see it. But it does indicate it by using different icons to represent the file types. If you see two data files in a folder with different icons, then you know that their file types are not the same, and very often the icons tell you which program to use with it.

When you get very experienced with your computer, you may start to recognise the file type just by looking at its icon. For example, a text file created with the 'Notepad' program contains pure text – that is text without any fancy layout. A 'Word' document type file, on the other hand, can contain a great deal of fancy layout. Here are two example data files from these two programs:

Shopping List   War and peace

The left picture is a pure text file created with 'Notepad' and the right picture is a 'Word' document file, created with 'Microsoft Word'. If you could see the complete file names including the added information for file type they would look like those below:

The relevance of all this is becomes more obvious when we start the next few exercises. In our first example exercise of making an attachment, I want to illustrate how to attach a picture type file. But unfortunately, the only picture type file that I know most definitely will be on everyone's computer,

Shopping List.txt   War and peace.doc

regardless of what other software they may have, is a file called 'Backgrnd.gif' (pronounced 'Background dot gif'). This file is contained in the 'Windows' folder of your normal hard drive (or C: drive). To fully understand the example attachment and detachment therefore, you need to understand what a 'dot gif' (.gif) file means, and you need to understand that it is a picture. Sadly, it is not a particularly interesting picture, but it is a picture nevertheless. In reality, it is a design pattern – as you will discover.

At this point, if you are not particularly interested in knowing more about file types, you can jump forward to the start of exercise 8. For those readers who may be exchanging more complex file types then here is a bit more information...

Note – If you want to make visible the file type for a file inside a folder, then you have a bit of clicking and selecting to do. For Windows 98 computers, you need to select the 'View' menu from the folder main menu – then take the last option of 'Folder Options...'. Then click on the 'View' tab – then click the checkbox to uncheck it labelled 'Hide file extensions for known file types'. Then click the 'Apply' button and then the 'OK' button. For Windows XP computers, you need to select 'Tools' first instead of 'View' then follow 'Folder Options...' as before for Windows 98 computers.

What are some of the common types that you will meet?

If you are dealing with photographs (or any graphic images), then there are three common ones:

- .bmp   pronounced as 'dot bee em pee'
- .gif   pronounced as 'dot gif'
- .jpg   pronounced as 'dot jay peg'.

There are others, but these are the most generalised types. The .bmp files are called **bitmaps** and they are the simplest form, but tend to be large file sizes. The other two are compressed files and are therefore much smaller. For email, it pays to use one of the compressed forms if you can because they will be transmitted faster. My own preference is to use .jpg files where possible.

If you are dealing with Microsoft Office files, then the common file types are:

- .doc   pronounced as 'dot dock'   (a Microsoft Word file)
- .xls   pronounced as 'dot ex el ess'   (a Microsoft Excel file)
- .mdb   pronounced as 'dot em dee bee'   (a Microsoft Access file)
- .ppt   pronounced as 'dot pee pee tee'   (a Microsoft PowerPoint file)

One other very common file type that you are almost sure to come across (as an email attachment) is a '.pdf' file type ('dot pee dee eff'). This is a data file created from a program known as 'Adobe Acrobat' and you need a special program called the 'Adobe Acrobat Reader' in order to read these files. This reader is a free program that you can either install from CD-ROMs that come with popular computing magazines, or you can download it yourself from the 'World Wide Web' service of the Internet.

There are literally thousands of different file types associated with other software program vendors and we could go on all day about them. However, let us leave this topic now and get started with the first exercise of this chapter.

Exercise 8 – Attaching an image file to an email and sending it

We begin at the point where **Outlook Express** is open and running, and we are on-line to the Internet.

Click on the **Create Mail** button as we did for exercises 4 and 6 (the New Mail button for users of Outlook version 5) and fill out the **New mail window** as shown in the next picture. Remember to use your own email address in the **To: textbox.**

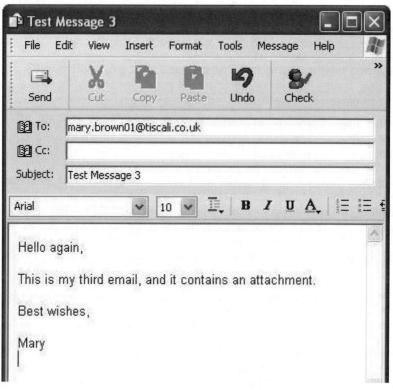

Okay. Now before we send this email, we will add the attachment file. Click now on **Insert** from the top **Menu bar**, and select the **File Attachment...** **option** as shown in the following picture.

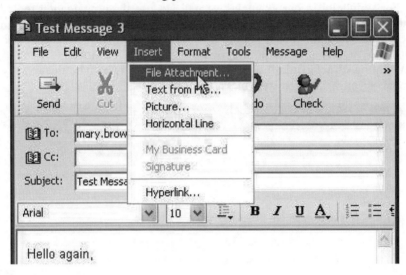

Now up pops an **Insert Attachment dialog box** (see the picture overleaf) where you specify the file that you wish to attach. When you have finished using it, you should be able to see the name of the file in the **File name: textbox**, and there are two ways that you can achieve this. Either you can select it by using the 'navigation' controls available such as the **Look in: box**, the folder icons below it and such like, or you can type the full '**pathname**' of the file directly into the **File name: textbox**. (If you know how to use a dialog box like this one, then skip over this next paragraph.)

When you work with a dialog box to look for a file, always make sure that the **Files of type: textbox** says 'All files'. To use the 'navigation' controls, you begin searching for your file by first choosing a starting point with the Look in: box. The 'down-pointing arrow' at the right-hand side of this box will give you a list of possible places to start from by clicking on it. Then select an item from the list (again with a click) to begin your search. This action immediately puts your selection into the Look in: box, and the sub-folders it contains then appear in the large white area below. When you have these sub-folders showing, you can either double-click on the appropriate one, or right-click and click '**Select**'. This in turn puts this folder into the **Look in: box**, and shows you more sub-folders and possibly files. You repeat this process of selecting an item, until finally you make a single click on the desired file for the attachment. This last click on your file will put its name in the **File name: textbox**. When using navigation controls, you should consider the folder structure as a type of 'inverted-tree'. Each level that you go down through has more sub-folders, until finally you get to the end of the 'branch', or you reach an intermediate level where your file is stored.

For simplicity in our example, we will not use these navigation tools but instead type the full filename (including its path) directly into the **File name:** **textbox**. Position the mouse pointer tip inside the text box and make a click, to put the 'focus' for the keyboard into the textbox. Then type **C:\Windows\Backgrnd.gif** as shown below (take care to type this exactly as shown or you will get an error message)...

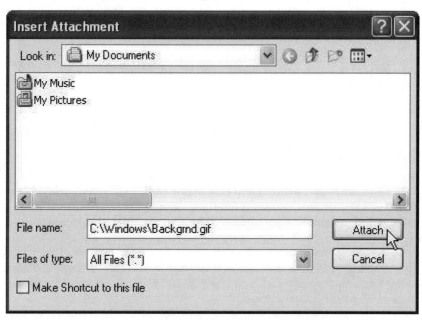

Click then on the **Attach** button to the right of the **File name textbox** as shown above. The dialog box will disappear, and the file will be automatically attached to the email, as shown in the next picture. Notice that we now see an extra textbox labelled Attach: under the Subject: textbox.

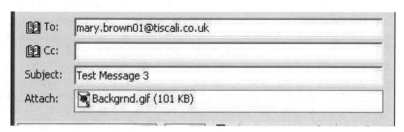

Note – In this exercise, we only wish to attach one file. In your future work, should you want to attach two or more files, then simply repeat the steps outlined previously, from the point of clicking Insert from the top Menu bar, until each file in turn has been attached. They will then appear as a series of files in the Attach: textbox. If you make a mistake and then wish to delete any attached file, then click on it within the Attach: textbox to highlight it and press the DELETE key. The corresponding attached file will then be removed from the email.

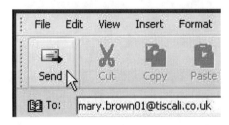

Now we are ready to send the email together with the attachment. Click on the **Send** button on the toolbar at the top as we have done before in previous exercises. The email is now placed in the Outbox folder. Providing you are on-line, the Delivery Trigger Action is automatically initiated and the email will be transmitted.

Because the attachment is a fairly large file, the transmission will take a few minutes to complete. You can watch the progress of sending the email and its attachment by observing the 'Sending mail...' status message in the bottom right-hand corner of your screen, and the miniature monitors icon appearing below it. These are shown on the left.

Eventually, the transmission will end, the **Outbox folder** will be empty, and the email with its attachment will have been sent to the ISP computer.

Now, before we finish the exercise, let us have a quick look at the historical folder containing a copy of all the items that we have sent. Click now on the **Sent Items** folder in the **Folders sub-window** at the left side of the screen. Then click on the title line wording 'Test Message 3' over in the upper section on the right side, as illustrated in the next picture.

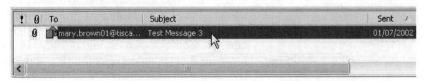

If you look closely at this title line, you can see a small **Paper Clip icon** to the left of the **To:** email address. This illustrates the fact that this email contains an attachment. Now inspect the contents of the email in the lower section...

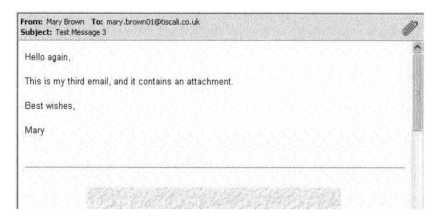

You can see that the appearance is slightly different than in previous exercises. After the email message text, there is a visible picture of the attachment separated from the text by a horizontal line. The size of the picture of the attachment is too big to fit within the lower section, and you will need to use the scroll bar down the right side in order to see the entire image. The image is simply a design pattern.

This brings us to the end of exercise 8. Don't break here if you can avoid it, but move swiftly to the next one.

4.2   Receiving an attachment

In this next exercise, we witness the reception of the email that we have just sent, and show how the attachment is detached from it and stored as a separate computer file. The exercise should be conducted immediately following the end of previous one.

Exercise 9 – Receiving an email and detaching an attachment

We begin at the point where **Outlook Express** is open and running, and we are on-line to the Internet.

Click now on the **Send/Receive** button as shown here. This initiates the **Delivery Trigger Action** manually. We do not have email to send, but there should be one waiting for us to receive at the remote ISP Computer containing an attachment.

The action now happens a little slower than we have witnessed in other exercises (exercise 5, for example). This is because the attachment to the email is very large in comparison to the basic email message text.

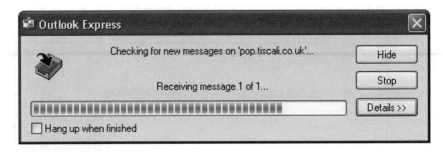

The action ends with an incoming email received into the Inbox folder as shown on the left.

Click on the Inbox folder as shown here, and then look over to the sections displayed on the right-hand side of the screen. Then click on the title line wording 'Test Message 3' in the upper section as shown below. Notice that there is a paper clip icon in the Title line, indicating that this email contains an attachment.

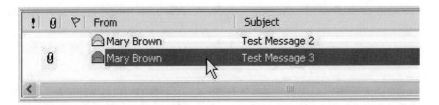

In the lower section, in the top right-hand corner, you can now see another **Paper Clip icon**. Position the mouse pointer over it, and click again as in this next picture.

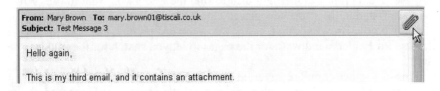

A menu then appears. Select the **Save Attachments...** option as shown on the left.

A **dialog box** then appears as shown in the next picture.

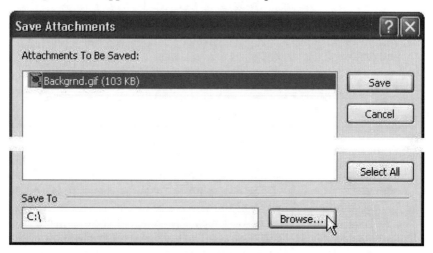

Okay. Let us pause a while and examine this dialog box. The first thing that we notice highlighted is the name of the attachment 'Backgrnd.gif'. We can also see its size as 103 Kilobytes – no wonder it took a bit longer to both send and receive!

> Note – If this email had two or more attachments, then they would be listed here one after the other.

Now the long white textbox at the bottom labelled '**Save To**' is where we specify the name of the folder that we want to save the attachment into (your own screen is likely to be slightly different to that shown). If you already know the precise name of the folder you wish to use, you can click in the textbox, delete the existing wording and type your new one in directly here. Alternatively, you can use the '**Browse...**' button just to the right of it to find the folder you want to use. When you have found it, the name gets placed automatically in the **Save To textbox**.

Click on the Browse button, as shown in the last picture, and then up pops a 'Browse for Folder' window (over the page) to let you search for the folder to be used...

This is a rather complex 'inverted tree' structure type of map. You can open and close folders or drives by clicking on the little square boxes marked '-' and '+' respectively. When you open a higher-level drive or folder (further left is considered higher up) then you see the sub-folders contained inside it. Go ahead now and pick the folder where you would like to save the attachment ('My Documents' or 'My Pictures' are the usual favourites). When you have selected your folder, click the OK button and the window will close.

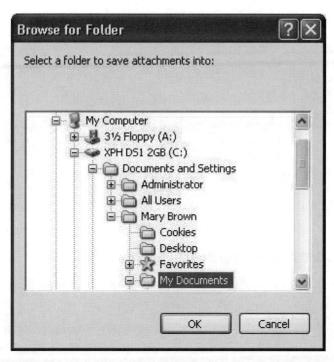

Now you will see your choice of folder written inside the long white **Save To** textbox. Then press the '**Save**' button as shown in this final picture.

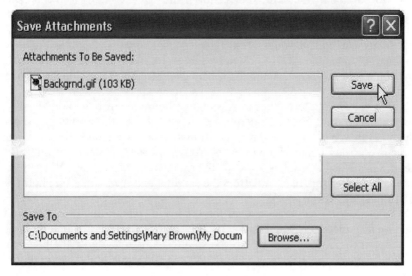

The attachment then will be saved and the dialog box closes. You are then back at the main window for Outlook Express, and the attachment has been detached.

Now here is a curious thing. We talk about 'detaching' an attachment from the email, but if you examine the monitor screen you will see that our received email 'Test Message 3' is exactly the same as it was before we went through the process of making the detachment. In fact if you wanted to, you could go through the process a second time, or even a third!

What we really mean by 'detaching' the attachment is that a copy of the attached file will be taken and saved in our specified folder. The email itself keeps the attachment more or less permanently. This has some very important consequences. If for any reason we should lose or damage the file that is saved away, then you can always come back again into Outlook Express and 'detach' the file once again.

This brings us to the end of exercise 9.

4.3   Comments about attachments

The sending and receiving of attachments is certainly one of the exciting enhancements to simple email messages. In this section, I should like to add a few general comments concerning them, to assist you in your future use.

One point that you need to watch concerning attachments is sizing, and the time taken to transmit the complete email. As we have witnessed in the exercises in this chapter, the speed of transmission is very much affected by size. If you send an email to a friend or relative that takes forever for them to receive, then they will not thank you for it. Worse still, if they are expecting to receive email from other people, and your email with a massive attachment arrives first, then they will not be able to receive the other emails until yours is out of the way. That really will endear you to them!

To give you some idea of how long things are likely to take, let us consider how you might go about calculating the time required for receiving an email and its attachment.

File sizes are quoted either in Kilobytes (thousands of bytes) or Megabytes (millions of bytes). For a modem operating at about 40,000 bits per second, which is fairly typical these days, it will take about 30 seconds (half a minute) to receive a file of size 100 Kilobytes. You can scale this up accordingly, so a file of size 1 Megabyte takes somewhere around 5 minutes. Okay? With this rule of thumb, how is this likely to affect the sending and receiving of a photograph of a grandchild, for example?

Modern digital cameras vary in the quality of picture they take. A typical good quality picture is often about 2.1 Megapixels (millions of pixels) in total pixel count (a pixel, by the way, is the smallest 'dot' making up the picture). If a digital camera was to output the picture as a file made up of every 'dot', and each dot had three colour components, then we would expect a file size of 3 times 2.1 Megabytes, or about 6 Megabytes total size. Wow, to send such a file as an email attachment would take about 30 minutes just to receive it! By the way, this type of picture is very similar to the file type that we know as 'bitmap' or .bmp that we referred to earlier in section 4.1.

Fortunately, digital cameras are quite complex electronic devices, and rather than output their photographs in this 'bitmap' style, they use a technique called file compression to 'squeeze' all of this information into a much smaller size file, often a .jpg ('jay peg') file type. With my own 2.1 Megapixel camera, my photographs are stored in my computer with file sizes that vary slightly, but typically are about 275 Kilobytes in size. If I sent one of these photographs as an attachment to an email, I would expect it to take a friend or relative about 80 seconds to receive it after dialling into their ISP computer. This is quite acceptable.

What about digital scanners? What sort of file do they produce and how big are they? Again, with my own A4 flatbed scanner, an A4 sheet of paper when scanned in colour at about 300 dots/inch gives me a .jpg file of approximately 1.4 Megabytes size. If I sent this file direct to a friend or relative, then we are talking around 7 minutes required to receive it. This is not something I would want to do to them without warning them first! There are ways of improving things. I could, for example, scan the A4 sheet of paper at a reduced resolution of say 75 dots/inch. It will depend of course on what I expect them to do with it. If it is for amusement, then perhaps a lower resolution will suffice, but if it is for printing as a quality poster to be displayed, then I might want to stick with my original 300 dots/inch.

Other things you can do to help the situation are tricks like breaking the picture into fragments and emailing the fragments separately. At least then, you can spread their transmission times, and give the person receiving them a breathing space before they receive the next one. When they have finally received all the fragments, these can be joined back together to complete the original file. For those readers who are interested, I am making available a computer program that can do both of these tasks – breaking up a file into a number of smaller files, and joining them back together again. The program allows you to specify the maximum size of the smaller fragment files, so that you have control over the transmission time for each one. (This program is also useful for copying a very large file onto a number of floppy disks, if you ever need to!). You can obtain this program by writing to the following address:

Bill Hall, P.O. Box 521, YORK, ENGLAND, YO19 6XZ

(Please enclose a cheque for £5 per copy – made payable to 'Bill Hall' - to cover software licence, administration costs, materials and return postage.)

Okay. What other considerations are there about attachments? One to think about is whether the recipient is also using Outlook Express. If they are, then a friendly act to do for them (when sending pictures) is to keep the overall resolution size of the attachment small enough, so that they can view it easily in the lower section of the main Outlook Express window. This avoids them having to open another program to view the complete picture. If you don't keep the size down, then you can easily 'overflow' the viewing area of the contents section. Let me show you want I mean with an example...

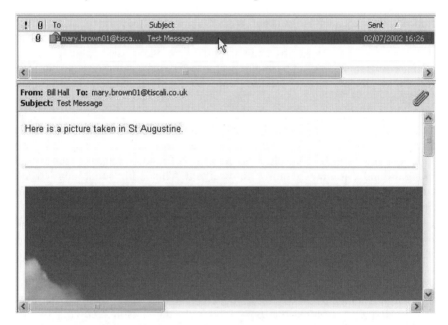

The above illustration shows an email that has been received in the Inbox folder with a picture attachment that is too large to view in the lower section. Notice that there are two scroll bars present, one vertical down the right side, one horizontal at the bottom. However, even using the scroll bars, it will be difficult to see the overall picture. The person receiving this email has either to detach the picture and print it out on a printer, or to use a graphics-editing program and to 'resize' the image so that it can be viewed.

Note – If you are using Windows XP, then you can use the 'Windows Picture and Fax Viewer' to see the picture, but the attachment will still need to be detached first.

Contrast the above situation with that shown in the next illustration. Here we have the same picture attached, but it has been 'resized' using a graphics-editing program by 33% in both the vertical and horizontal directions (that is – the 'aspect ratio' has been maintained). Though the picture is still only partially viewable, a simple drag with the mouse on the horizontal scroll bar will show you the overall 'view' of the picture without having to detach it.

If we compare the sizes of the two attachments in these illustrations, the first one is 300 Kilobytes and the second one is 50 Kilobytes. A benefit therefore of reducing the size is that the time required to receive the second attachment is very much quicker, and for casual viewing you should not notice any particular degradation of the picture quality.

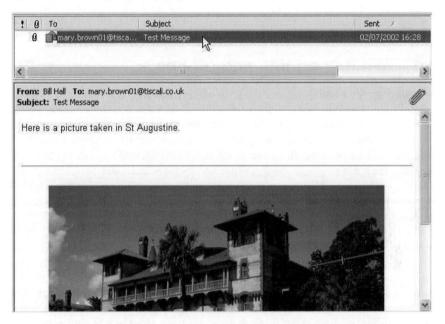

There are many a number of other techniques that you can use to help with sending attachments. However, they take us a little beyond the scope of this book so we will conclude the chapter, and our work with attachments.

5

Working Off-line

5.1   What is on-line and off-line?

In both chapters 1 and 2, we met the term **on-line** and in chapters 3 and 4 we were careful to always start our exercises from the on-line state. In this chapter, we will take a look at both being both **on-line** and **off-line**, and how to switch between them.

The technical terms on-line and off-line are curious expressions. Their original meanings came from the computer communications world, but more recently they have appeared in popular use by non-technical people as part of everyday language. Because they are used frequently within the Outlook Express program in their original specific meanings, it is important that we are careful to understand what these are.

First of all, what is the 'line' that these terms are referring to? If we understand that, then we are halfway there!

First-timers could be forgiven for thinking that this is the telephone line, and interpreting on-line to mean that the phone line is engaged whereas off-line means that the phone line is free. As we shall see shortly, that is near to the truth, but it is not quite the meaning that Outlook Express has in mind. To make sure that the program's messages don't confuse you, we need to dig a little deeper.

In section 2.5, we discussed the relationship between the on-line connection and programs such as Outlook Express and Internet Explorer, and we learnt that something called 'Dial-up Networking' behaves as a though it was another separate program effectively making the link between them. That relationship is shown again in this diagram.

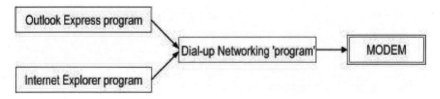

The modem is the device that physically makes the connection to the telephone line, and when a call has been established, the modem at our end of the line will establish a 'data connection' with a modem belonging to the ISP Company at the distant end. This gets to the heart of the meaning of the word 'line'. It is the data connection that is the real meaning of 'line'. This meaning encompasses several items – the telephone line, both modems at either end, and includes part of the software of the Dial-Up Networking program as well. It treats the whole thing as a unit – end to end – that is to say, from the Dial-Up Networking program at our end, through our modem, down the phone line, through the modem at the distant ISP end, and finally through the equivalent of the Dial-Up Networking program at the other end.

Now this leads us to the deeper meaning of on-line and off-line as employed by Outlook Express. Have a look at this next diagram.

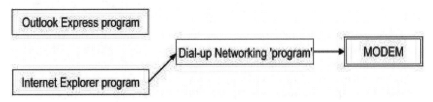

Here the Outlook Express program is shown not linked to Dial-Up Networking, but the Internet Explorer program still is. The phone line is still engaged upon a call to the ISP computer and the data connection still exists. But Outlook Express is not using it. Outlook Express is now said to be off-line. Careful inspection of the diagram indicates that Internet Explorer is still said to be on-line.

I think that you may now appreciate why the earlier interpretation – that a first-timer could be forgiven for thinking – is not quite the whole picture. It is the ability to use the Outlook Express program when it is not linked to Dial-Up Networking that is the true meaning of working with it off-line, as interpreted by the program and expressed in its messages to you.

Why would you want to work off-line? Well there are a few reasons, and not all of these are obvious. Here are one or two...

The Outlook Express program is a program that runs on your computer. It does not run on the ISP computer. The folders within the program, such as the Inbox and Sent Items folders, are held on your computer and in the theory of chapter 1, we explained what the relationship between these folders and the ISP computer really was. If you need to do some work with these folders, such as printing emails that you have already received, deleting old emails that you no longer want, or re-filing them to new folders, it is not essential that you are connected to the ISP computer in order to do so. If the phone line is busy – for example, if another family member is currently using it for a voice call – then you can still work with these folders in the off-line state.

Sometimes, even when you are on-line to the Internet, you may want to temporarily go off-line, but you may not want to lose the connection to the ISP computer. This is the very situation shown in the last picture. A good reason for temporarily going off-line is to make sure that you don't send off an email that you are in the middle of composing before you should or mean to do so. For example, if you have an important matter in hand, you may want to compose your email off-line and have a sincere think about it before you finally commit to sending it. If it is really important to you, the last thing you want to do is send it off and then wish that you had written something in a different way. Once the email has gone then you live with the consequences – as I'm sure that the Government spin-doctor who one day wanted to 'bury bad news' might agree!

So far we have only considered working from home. The original reason why Outlook Express operates on-line and off-line is to do with the alternative methods of connecting to the Internet, some of which were introduced in section 2.7. When you are working on your own, you only have yourself to consider. But if you work in a small office, you may be sharing a Dial-Up Internet connection with one or two others in the office. You may want to go off-line but the others may want to remain on-line.

Can you share one phone line connection to the Internet with others? Is this legitimate? Yes, it certainly is, for although I have shown two different programs working simultaneously into Dial-Up Networking, with the appropriate software there is no reason why these should not be two (or more) Outlook Express programs running on two different computers, but using one modem and effectively sharing the phone line. This is a common requirement within small office situations but could equally apply to mum and son, or dad and daughter at home – if they have their own computers! Users of Windows XP in particular may want to utilise a built-in facility called Internet Connection Sharing (ICS). However, this is taking us into the realms of networking which is beyond the scope of this book.

5.2 Using Outlook Express off-line disconnected

Now we know from the last section that Outlook Express can operate in either on-line or off-line states, but that in itself does not mean that the phone line connection is dropped. For clarity therefore, I am going to introduce the phrase off-line disconnected to mean the obvious – we choose to work with the program off-line and opt to disconnect the modem, which inherently frees up the telephone line.

In working off-line disconnected there are both advantages and disadvantages. If you are using a 'Pay As You Go' type of ISP subscription service, then one possible advantage is that you are not paying call charges when you are not connected. However, you have to be careful with this because it can work out to be more expensive on occasions. In the UK and some other countries, there is a minimum call charge for every time you make a call, and if you end up making several calls in a short space of time then it can work out cheaper to remain connected for a while. For example, if you collect your incoming email and then go off-line disconnected, you cannot send an immediate reply. Dialling up a second time to send your reply could be dearer on a 'Pay As You Go' account than staying on-line in the first place. Also, you cannot use the other services of the Internet without going back on-line again, and in a moment we shall see why you might want to do this in connection with email.

If you like using email and you enjoy services like the 'World Wide Web' then you should seriously consider subscribing to the 'Anytime' type of ISP account. There are a number of good deals about, especially if you want to use the Internet only during the daytime. With the 'Anytime' account, then you can switch between the off-line disconnected and on-line states as frequently as you wish without even thinking of the charging, and in the long run, it can prove to be much more economical (see Appendix III for a bit more information on this type of account).

One major reason why you might consider working off-line disconnected is to allow other incoming telephone calls to get through. If a relative or friend is trying to ring you then they get frustrated if your line is engaged for long lengths of time. Until recently, there was no alternative to this problem other than to have another separate phone line installed (or ISDN, or ADSL Broadband). However, the situation may change with the introduction of the very latest type of modem known as a V.92 modem. This modem type can be used in conjunction with the telephone feature known as 'Call-Waiting' in order to 'put the modem on hold' and allow you to take the incoming call without disconnecting from the Internet! At the time of writing, the major ISP companies have not yet adopted using V.92, but that situation may develop in the future.

While we are on the subject of 'Call-Waiting', if you have this feature enabled on your phone line, and you are using any modem other than a V.92 modem as just described – which is probably the majority of readers – then you should disable the feature before you connect to the Internet for the duration of the call. This is because it can cause disruption to normal modem operation if the call waiting signal arrives. You can disable Call-Waiting by dialling a code (often '#43#') from a voice telephone before you start, and then dial another code (often '*43#') from a telephone, to turn it back on again, when you have finished.

Now to the illustration of using email and other Internet services that I mentioned earlier. Sometimes you may receive an incoming email from a friend, telling you about an interesting 'web site' that they have just discovered. If you then wish to have a look at it for yourself, you need to be on-line in order to do so. Normally, such references to web sites within an email are displayed underlined in a different colour (often blue) and look something like this next picture...

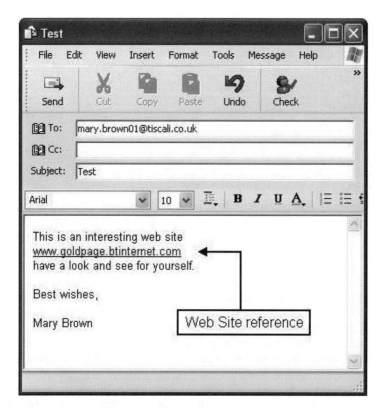

If you simply click with your mouse pointer on this underlined text, then the Internet Explorer program is automatically started for you, and it will display the web page in question immediately, without your having to go through the process of finding it yourself. If you are working on-line then this is usually quite quick. If you are off-line disconnected then it can be painfully slow.

You can put such web site references into emails that you send to your own friends very easily too. Just type the 'www' wording bit into your text, exactly as it looks, and the reference will automatically be created when you type something else after it (you might like to try this for yourself sometime and see).

5.3   Switching from on-line to off-line disconnected

Exercise 10 – How to work off-line disconnected

We begin at the point where **Outlook Express** is open and running, and we are on-line to the Internet. If the Outlook Express window is not maximised to fill the whole screen, then click on the **maximise** button, which is the middle one of the three in the top right-hand corner.

Now let us first take a look at the bottom right-hand corner of the window. We should see something like this next picture.

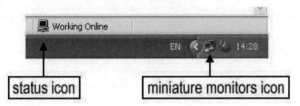

Here are two things that I want you to notice, and to keep your eye on throughout the exercise. First, there is a **status icon** labelled 'Working Online' on the grey status bar, and second, the **miniature monitors** icon is visible in the system tray area near the time display.

When we move to the **off-line** state, these will change. If we move to off-line but remain connected, then only the **status icon** changes (the miniature monitors icon is just the same). If we move to **off-line disconnected** then they both change (the miniature monitors icon disappears).

From the menu bar at the top of the window, click on **File** and from the drop down menu select the **Work Offline** option, as shown here.

This will cause a message box to pop up like the following...

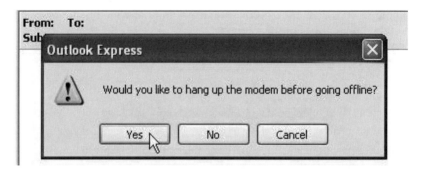

Okay. Just pause for a moment to consider this last message. This clearly shows the point we discussed in section 5.1. Going **off-line** within **Outlook Express** does not necessarily mean 'losing the phone connection'. If we should click on the **No** button here, then not hanging up the modem means the phone connection will remain ongoing, even though the program will be off-line.

> Note – The expression 'hanging up the modem' is drawing on the analogy of a telephone instrument. The modem is being treated as though it had a handset to put back onto some mythical switch-hooks to end the call and free the line.

Click on the **Yes** button – this will make the message box disappear – but keep an eye on the **miniature monitors** icon in the system tray just to the left of the time display. After a few seconds, the icon will vanish indicating that the modem has 'hung up' the phone call. From this moment onwards, the telephone line is free to accept an incoming call.

Now you should be back looking at the main Outlook Express window. Notice in the bottom right-hand corner of the window that the status icon on the grey status bar is now labelled 'Working Offline', as in this next picture.

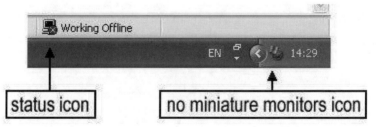

We are now working with Outlook Express in the **off-line disconnected** state.

We can still use the email program for as much and as long as we want to. We can create new emails, or we can read ones that we have previously received when we were last on-line. The choice is ours to make, and there is no need to be concerned from here on that the phone line is engaged.

At this point, if we wanted to go back on-line without closing Outlook Express then we only need click on the **Send/Receive** button located on the tool bar, and follow screen instructions from there onwards. We will not do that now because in the next exercise, I want to demonstrate how you also start up the program from the off-line disconnected state.

Click on the **Close** button in the top right-hand corner of the Outlook Express window and you will return to the desktop.

This concludes exercise 10. Don't break here if you can avoid it, but move swiftly on to the next one.

5.4   Switching back from off-line to on-line

Exercise 11 – How to get back on-line from start-up

Following immediately on from the last exercise, start the Outlook Express program running. As soon as the program begins to run, because we previously closed the program down in the off-line state, you will see a message box appear, as in this next picture.

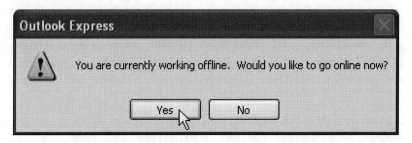

We have seen this message box once before. If you look back to exercise 1 in section 2.3, you will see that we have discussed this right at the very outset of our practical work. This message box appears only because we closed the program down previously in the off-line state.

If for any reason you wished to continue working off-line then you would click on the **No** button, and you would be able to carry on where you left off at the end of exercise 10. However, we want at this point to observe how to get back on-line so click now on the **Yes** button, and you will see a dialog box appear as in the following picture.

When you see this pop up on your monitor, the **Connect automatically check box** may or may not be cleared. If it is ticked, then the automatic dialling procedure will continue and you have nothing more to do. If it is cleared, you should check first that the details shown are correct, then press the Connect button. (The other Save password check box determines whether your password is remembered from previous occasions, or not as the case may be. For users of Windows 98, there was a problem recognised by many users where the 'Save password' feature stopped working properly. You may want to research the solutions suggested by others on the Internet. Trying searching on 'save password bug').

Note – If the 'Connect automatically check box' has previously been ticked and you press the Cancel button during the automatic dialling procedure, then you will find it is cleared when you next attempt to go on-line.

Before we move on to the next stage, I recommend that you move the tip of the mouse pointer over both check boxes and click to set both of the 'tick marks' (as shown in the last picture). Then click on the Connect button and the procedure for getting the 'Dial-Up networking' program operational begins running. This will make it faster for you to get on-line in the future.

When the modem goes into action, you will see the familiar dialling messages appear, as in the next picture.

After a wait of between fifteen and fifty seconds, the modems synchronise again and you are back on-line...

Click on the 'X' button to close the bubble and the message will disappear. Notice that the **miniature modems icon** is now back in the system tray next to the time display.

Okay. This is the familiar on-line state that you have experienced many times now. The Delivery Trigger Action will operate automatically once you are connected, so if by chance there is any incoming mail waiting for you with the ISP then you will see this received into your **Inbox folder**.

You are now at liberty to use Outlook Express as you choose to do. The phone line will be engaged now until you either you close down the program (and disconnect it with the **Auto Disconnect** feature), or you repeat the actions to go **off-line disconnected** as per exercise 10.

Click now on the **Close** button for the Outlook Express window, and disconnect using **Auto Disconnect**.

This concludes exercise 11.

6

Managing Your Email Addresses

6.1 Adding contacts to the Windows Address Book

One of the useful programs that is available as standard on every Windows type computer is the Windows Address Book. This is a very comprehensive program that can store a variety of different pieces of information about personal contacts that you may want to add to it. You can run and use this program on its own from the desktop by clicking on the Start button, then select (All) Programs, then Accessories, and then Address Book.

Now a very handy feature found inside Outlook Express is that it makes the Windows Address Book directly accessible from within it, so that you can use the book without having to run the program separately.

In addition to having the usual contact details of postal addresses and telephone numbers, the Windows Address Book can save email addresses for all of the people listed. You can then create an email for a chosen person by selecting them from the list in the address book, and let the computer enter his or her lengthy email address automatically for you. This helps avoid making simple typing mistakes, which is a common problem for many users. You can also create groups of people from the listed individual contact entries. Then you can create a single email, and with one action, send it to all of the people in the group. Such a feature is useful for club newsletters, invitations and such like.

In this chapter, we will undertake a number of exercises designed to show you how to get the best from this integrated feature of the address book.

Exercise 12 – *Adding contacts to the Windows Address Book*

We begin this exercise with **Outlook Express** open and its window maximised, but there is no need to be on-line. In the last chapter, we learnt how to operate either in the on-line state or the off-line state, and the choice is now yours. For the purpose of the exercises it does not matter which state you work within.

In the lower left corner of the **Outlook Express** window, below the **Folder sub-window**, you should be able to see the **Contacts sub-window** as shown in the following picture.

If you cannot see this sub-window then chances are that someone has closed it previously by clicking on the little 'X' shown on the grey title bar. In this circumstance, you should follow the instructions in Appendix V, so that it becomes visible again.

Now, with your own computer, you may or may not already have contacts listed inside the sub-window, depending on whether someone has used this feature beforehand (or the Address Book program on its own). Don't be concerned if your own situation does not show a blank list like that of the last picture.

Position the tip of the mouse pointer over the wording '**Contacts**' and then click. Notice that a drop down menu appears. Select the first option '**New Contact...**' as shown here.

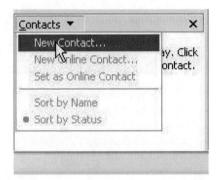

Up then pops a new window titled **Properties**, as in the next illustration overleaf. The textboxes shown there are suitably labelled, so there is no need to describe them individually. You should notice that the flashing vertical line cursor is first located in the **First: textbox**, and therefore whatever we type next at the keyboard will be entered here.

Let me make one quick point before we proceed with the exercise. Of all the six textboxes associated with the contact name, it is only the **Display: textbox** where it is essential that some text at least be entered. Any of the other five can be left empty if you wish. Now you will soon witness that this Display: textbox is slightly unusual in that typing into some of the others will automatically make some entry into this one (and vice versa).

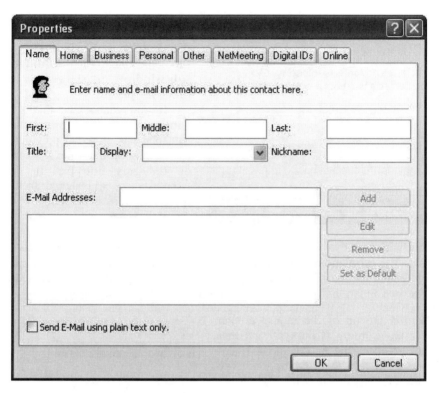

Proceeding now with the exercise, type the following information into the appropriate textboxes as shown in the next picture. This time I want you to use the exact name and email address shown here rather than your own details (we will create another entry for your own details shortly).

When you have finished entering the text 'Mary' in the **First: textbox**, you can move the flashing vertical cursor to the **Last: textbox** in one of two ways. The method use in previous exercises was to re-position the mouse pointer and then make a click, but I now want to illustrate what I think is an easier and faster method, because you do not need to take your hands away from the keyboard and fiddle with the mouse. Press the **TAB key** once and watch the flashing cursor move to the **Middle: textbox** then press it again to see it move to the **Last: textbox**.

If you are not sure where the TAB key is, then here it is in this next picture just to the left of the Q key...

TAB key

Okay. When you have completed the text 'Brown' in the **Last: textbox**, you will notice that the **Display: textbox** becomes filled automatically. Press the TAB key four times to take the cursor to the **E-Mail Addresses: textbox**. Now enter the email address 'mary.brown01@tiscali.co.uk' (not your own address this time).

> Note – This use of the TAB key, to quickly move from one textbox to another, is helpful in many other situations where there are several items of information that need to be entered. If you overshoot and want to go backwards, hold down the SHIFT key first and keep it held while you then press the TAB key.

With all the required text now entered, move the mouse pointer across and click on the **Add** button. The screen should now look something like the picture overleaf.

Notice first that a new little envelope icon has appeared in the larger white textbox, and the email address is displayed with the phrase '(Default E-Mail)' added to it. Notice second that the **E-Mail Addresses: textbox** above it has now been cleared of text, and the flashing cursor is now ready waiting for a further possible email address to be entered. This is because some contacts that you come across may have more than one email account with possibly different ISP companies. Why would they do this? Well one may be a personal email address and the other could be a business email address.

If you wanted to, you could at this point enter another email address (for this same contact) and press the **Add** button again. The additional email address would then be listed in the larger white text box, but it would not be tagged as '(Default E-Mail)'. If a contact has several email addresses, only one of them is

going to be nominated as the default one, and this term means that this is the one that will normally be selected for sending email to – unless you change it. If you did want to change it, then you would simply click to highlight the new default line, then press the **Set as Default** button.

If for any reason you want to remove an email address, then you simply click to highlight it, and then press the **Remove** button. You might need to do this if either you spot that you have made a typing mistake on entering it, or if the contact person should notify you in the future that they have changed it.

Okay. We could discuss much more about the **Properties window**. I will leave this for you to explore in the future at your leisure. You might, for instance, like to try clicking later on one of the other 'tabs' ('Home' 'Business' 'Personal' and such like). For the moment, let us continue with the exercise. Click now on the **OK** button in the bottom right of the window to make all the information we have entered a permanent entry in the **Windows Address Book**. Remember also that the information we have just entered here will be available in the future by running the Address Book program on its own, as mentioned earlier in the very beginning of this section.

After clicking the **OK** button, your monitor screen should show something

like this picture. If there were any
contact entries in the book before
starting the exercise, then this last new
entry could be off the screen (they are
listed alphabetically). In which case,
you may need to use a drag action on a
scroll bar that then appears down the
right side of the sub-window to make it
visible.

We now have this 'Mary Brown' entry in the contact list. If by chance you
know more than one person with the same name (yet another 'Mary Brown')
then you may later repeat the exercise to enter the second one. The Address
Book will allow you to create two entries with the same name, so you will have
to use a trick of your own to distinguish between them. My normal method is to
add something in brackets to their 'Lastname'. This then becomes visible in the
listing display text that appears in the sub-window. Be very careful though!
These names will appear in the email that they receive from you (as we shall see
in a later exercise) and if you label someone will a less than polite comment –
for example, 'Mary Brown (misery guts)' - then you might have a very red face
after they read an email you might send them!

Okay. Now I want you to repeat the process of adding a contact over again,
but this time use your own name and email address instead of the 'Mary Brown'
example. When you have finished, you will have two contacts (at least) listed –
one will be your own, and the other will be 'Mary Brown'.

This concludes exercise 12.

6.2   Sending using the Address Book

The next exercise requires that exercise 12 has been completed previously, but
does not have to follow on immediately afterwards.

Exercise 13 – Sending an email using the Address Book

We begin with **Outlook Express** open and its window maximised. As with the
last exercise, you can start work either in the on-line or off-line state. The
Contacts sub-window needs to be visible before you begin. If for any reason it
is not then read Appendix V to make it so.

In this present exercise, I am giving you an opportunity and a choice to
make. Up until this point, you have always used your own email address in the
worked example, but now I want to give you the opportunity to send a real email
to someone other than yourself. The purpose of the exercise is to send an email
using the address book, and you have two entries (at least) in the Address Book

that you can choose from to send this email to. Your choice therefore is to decide which of the two you are going to use. However, please read this next important note before you make your decision.

Note – The 'Mary Brown' contact is a real email address and in choosing this option for the exercise, I am inviting you to send an email to myself as the author. In receiving this email, I hope to be able to gather feedback directly from you, which may be used for statistical purposes, to make revisions to the text in future editions of this book, or to the ideas and text of other books in the 'First Time' series. Your email address will not be disclosed to others, or used for any purpose other than those now stated. If you do not wish to send such an email, then choose the alternative contact for the exercise, which is your own email address.

Please also note that if you do send an email to 'Mary Brown', I am unable to promise a response in return so do not be offended if you hear nothing further. I will endeavour to read as many as time permits, and to take your comments on board.

Okay. Let us now get the exercise under way. Move the tip of the mouse pointer over the contact name 'Mary Brown' (or your own contact name as the alternative) and make a **right-click**. A menu will then appear. Select the **Send E-Mail option**, as shown on the left.

After the selection, a New Message window pops up....

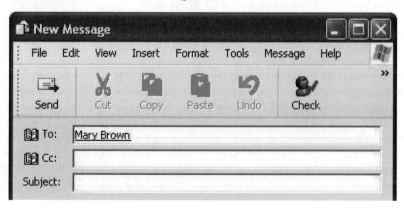

The first thing you will notice is that the **To: textbox** is already filled out for you, and the name is underlined. The underlining is indicating to you that this name has come from the Address Book. The form of the name is just as it appears in the address book, and this form will be transmitted along with the email.

Complete the rest of the email in a similar manner to that shown here.

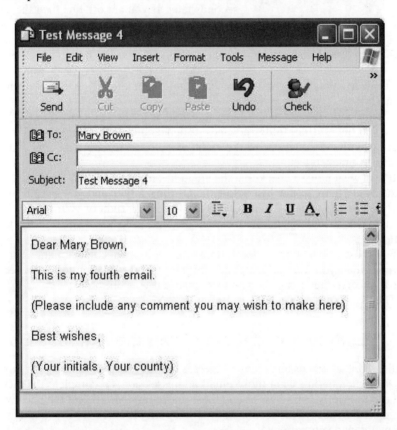

In the message content section, the parts shown in brackets are purely optional. If you would like to make any comment about this book, or about any other book in the 'First Time' series, then please do so. If you do not want to make any comment then please do not feel under any obligation to do so. I will be happy to receive your email in any event.

In the last line of the message content, it would be helpful for me to know just your initials and your county. I do strongly advise you not to include your name or address. Email that is transmitted as a simple message over the Internet may be read by a third party without either your knowledge or mine, and there are unfortunately some unscrupulous people about.

When you have completed the email, click on the **Send** button in the usual way.

The email will now be placed in the **Outbox folder**. If you are on-line at this moment, then the email will be automatically sent a few seconds later. If you are off-line then the email will simply wait in your Outbox folder until you are next on-line. In this latter case, click now on the **Send/Receive** button to establish a connection to the Internet (and follow any further instructions to actually connect), and the email will then be sent in the normal way.

Finally, after the email has been transmitted to the ISP computer, you will notice that the **Outbox folder** changes its appearance from being shown in bold lettering with '(1)' shown on the right of it, back to being normal with no number in brackets.

If you wish now to check that the email has in fact been sent correctly, click on the **Sent Items folder** just below the **Outbox folder** and you should see the title line 'Test Message 4' in the upper section on the right of your screen. Click again on this title line, and the message contents are shown again in the lower section.

For those readers who decided to use their own contact name for this exercise, then you may need to click on the Send/Receive button for a second time to receive the email that you have just sent yourself.

This concludes exercise 13.

6.3   Editing and deleting from the Address Book

Adding contact names and email addresses to the Address Book is a very useful way of remembering what those email addresses are. To complete the picture, we need to briefly learn how to edit these entries and also delete the ones we no longer wish to keep. This section has two very simple exercises illustrating these two maintenance functions.

Exercise 14 – Editing an entry in the Address Book

We begin with **Outlook Express** open and its window maximised. As with the last exercise, you can start work either in the on-line or off-line state. The **Contacts sub-window** needs to be visible before you begin. If for any reason it is not then read Appendix V to make it so.

Right-click on the contact name 'Mary Brown' in the **Contacts sub-window**, and select the **Properties** option, as shown below.

Up then pops the **Properties** window for this contact. Move the tip of the mouse pointer over the **Name tab** and click...

Then you will see all the Name textboxes that were visible when you first created this contact. On opening the Name tab, the First Name textbox will have the 'focus' and the word 'Mary' will be highlighted.

Now you may remember from past work that whenever text in a textbox is highlighted, then any keyboard key that you press will replace all of the highlighted text in one keystroke. Now type the word 'Margaret' in the **First: textbox** and you will notice that the **Display: textbox** magically alters accordingly, as shown in the next picture overleaf.

If you wished to edit any other details for this contact, you can obviously do so at this moment too, simply by clicking in the textbox and then using the keyboard keys. Even the email address can be edited – however this is done in a slightly different way. We shall not bother to alter the email address now, but the method to do it is to click on it first to highlight it, and then press the Edit button. You are then able to make any changes to the email address that you care to.

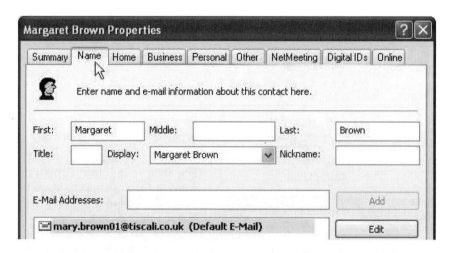

When you have finished all of your editing work, click then on the **OK** button at the bottom of the window and all the changes made will be saved to the **Address Book**'s main file. The **Properties** window will then disappear, and you will notice in the **Contacts sub-window** that your change to the First name is now also reflected here as shown here.

This concludes exercise 14.

Exercise 15 – Deleting an entry in the Address Book

We begin with **Outlook Express** open and its window maximised. As with the last exercise, you can start work either in the on-line or off-line state. The **Contacts sub-window** needs to be visible before you begin. If for any reason it is not then read Appendix V to make it so. This is a very simple exercise indeed.

If you have completed the previous exercise then you should have a contact name in the Contacts sub-window labelled 'Margaret Brown'. If you didn't complete the previous exercise, then it should still be labelled 'Mary Brown'. Right-click on the appropriate contact name to be deleted and then select the **Delete** option as illustrated here.

A confirmation message then appears...

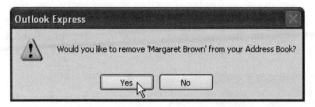

Simply press the Yes button and the contact will then be deleted.
This concludes exercise 15.

6.4   Creating a group of addresses

Creating a 'group' of email addresses allows you to send email automatically to all the individual email addresses that make up the group. This can save you a lot of time and hard work compared to emailing contacts individually.

The group is created initially from existing contact names in the Address Book, and is given its own 'group' name. It is then stored in the Address Book so that you can use it any time that you want to. You use the group name in much the same way as you would a contact name by specifying it in the **To: textbox** of a created email.

By removing the need to type in many individual email addresses, groups not only save time but can help you avoid making errors through typing mistakes.

Exercise 16 – Creating a group of addresses

We begin with **Outlook Express** open and its window maximised. As with previous exercises, you can start work either in the on-line or off-line state. The Contacts sub-window needs to be visible before you begin. If for any reason it is not then read Appendix V to make it so.

To make a group, we are going to need a number of contact names entered in the Address Book. Many readers may not have these yet so for the purposes of this and the next exercise, we shall first make two dummy entries that have the same email address as your own. Using the method given in exercise 12, create two new contact names having the following details:

1)	First name:	Amy
	Last name:	Andrews
	Email address:	(use your own email address)
2)	First name:	Brian
	Last name:	Beever
	Email address:	(use your own email address)

At this point, in total, you should have at least three contact names in the address book – the two you have just entered and your own entry (created as part of exercise 12). If you have not made a contact name for yourself then do so now.

Okay. First click on the **Addresses** button on the tool bar of Outlook Express, as shown in this next picture.

This pops up the **Address Book window**. From the menu bar, click **File** and select the **New Group...** option, as in the second picture.

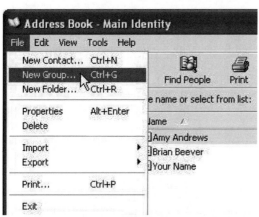

This action pops up a new **Properties** window for specifying group details.

Type the group name 'Bowls Team' in the **Group Name: textbox**, then click on the **Select Members** button...

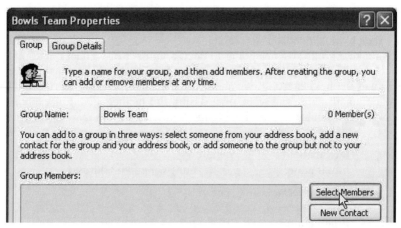

Now we see the **Select Group Members window**. From this window we are going to pick all of the contact names that we want to be in the group. First click on the entry 'Amy Andrews', as shown in the next picture.

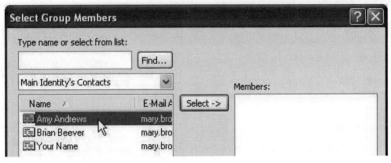

And then click on the Select button...

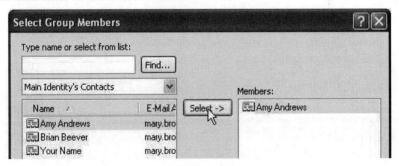

Notice that when you have done so, the contact name that you first clicked upon ('Amy Andrews') now appears in the **Members: listbox**, as seen above.

Repeat the action of clicking on the contact name at the left-hand side, followed by pressing the **Select** button in the centre, until you have all three contact names in the **Members: listbox** as shown below.

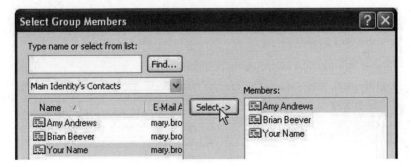

Okay. Now we have selected all of the members for our 'Bowls Team' group so we close the window using the **OK** button at the bottom of the window. This then returns us to the **Bowls Team properties window** as shown in the following picture.

Click the OK button in this window (as above), and this then returns you to the Address Book window. Close this one using the Close button ('X') in the top right-hand corner...

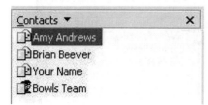

And you are back to the main **Outlook Express window**. Your **Contacts sub-window** should now look like the picture on the left. Notice that we have a new entry in the contact names list called 'Bowls Team'.

This concludes exercise 16.

6.5   Sending email to a group of addresses

Exercise 17 – Sending email to a group of addresses

This exercise requires that exercise 16 has been completed previously, but does not have to follow on immediately afterwards.

We begin with **Outlook Express** open and its window maximised. As with previous exercises, you can start work either in the on-line or off-line state. The **Contacts sub-window** needs to be visible before you begin. If for any reason it is not then read Appendix V to make it so.

Move the tip of the mouse pointer over the contact group name 'Bowls Team' and make a **right-click**. A menu will then appear. Select the **Send E-Mail** option, as shown here.

After the selection, a New Message window pops up with the To: textbox already filled out for you. Complete the rest of the email, as shown in the picture below.

Put your own first name at the end of the message contents section, after 'Best wishes'.

When you have completed the email, press the **Send** button as shown in the picture overleaf.

The email will now be placed in the **Outbox folder**. If you are on-line at this moment, then the email will be automatically sent a few seconds later. If you are off-line then the email will simply wait in your Outbox folder until you are next on-line. In this latter case, click now on the **Send/Receive** button to establish a connection to the Internet (and follow further instructions to actually connect), and the email will then be sent in the normal way.

After the email has been transmitted to the ISP computer, you will notice that the Outbox folder changes its appearance from being shown in bold lettering with '(1)' shown on the right of it, back to being normal with no number in brackets.

Finally, to check that the email has in fact been sent correctly, click on the **Sent Items folder** just below the Outbox folder and you should see the title line 'Test Message 5' in the upper section on the right of your screen, as in the next picture. Click again on this title line, and the message contents are shown again in the lower section.

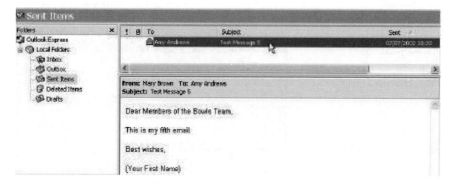

Notice that the name shown on the title line is 'Amy Andrews', who is the first person in the 'Bowls Team' group. Unfortunately, in this exercise, because we are not using different email addresses, the computer has spotted that the other members of the group have the same email address as 'Amy Andrews' so they are not all shown individually in the title line. Well, it is only an exercise! When you send email to your own real groups you will find that they are listed.

For those readers who were on-line for the start of this exercise, then you may need to click on the **Send/Receive** button for a second time to receive the email that you have just sent and clear the **Incoming mailbox**. If you were off-line for the start of this exercise, then you will probably have received the email already. This depends to some extent on the way that your ISP Company is set up, and how and in what order it checks the mailboxes for your account.

This concludes exercise 17 and the chapter.

7

Read Receipts, Replies and Forwarding

7.1 Has your email arrived at its destination?

We introduced the email delivery service in chapter 1 by making a comparison with postal mail. In considering the question 'Has your email arrived at its destination?' I am reminded of the words of Elvis and his popular lyric 'Return to Sender, address unknown, no such number, no such zone!' Were he with us today, what would he sing about email!

Email is similar to postal mail, in this respect – if you make a mistake writing the address, then the chances of it reaching its desired destination are considerably diminished. When you send an email with a mistake in the address, what happens next depends on several factors and the consequences of making a mistake can have implications that you didn't bargain for.

It is so easy to make a typing mistake. This is one important reason why you should use the Address Book introduced in the last chapter, to manage your email addresses for you. Provided that you have it written correctly in the address book, you can create an email directly from it and be sure that the address will not contain a mistake. We demonstrated this procedure in exercise 13.

What can happen if you get it wrong? Well, much depends on where the mistake exists within the full address. We learnt from our discussion of addresses in section 1.4 that all email addresses take the form of:

Username@ComputerNetwork

If the error is in the 'Username' part, then the email will actually travel across the Internet to the electronic post office at the specified computer network – that is to say, it will get delivered to somewhere. Usually, an email that has an error in the 'Username' part will be delivered to a special mailbox that is sorted by an administrator at the specified electronic post office known as the postmaster. The postmaster may employ an automatic system to send you a response telling you that the mail failed, or he/she may sift through it manually and – as with postal mail – try to second-guess what the correct address should have been. There is therefore an outside chance that your email will find its way to the intended destination, but it is not guaranteed.

This raises an important implication that you should be aware of. It is quite possible that the administrator will read your email in attempting to determine the correct address, so never send anything that you would be too embarrassed to admit to, or anything that is confidential and has not been suitably 'encrypted'. Encryption is the process of disguising the message content and is beyond the scope of this book.

If the addressing error is in the 'ComputerNetwork' part of the address, there can be two possible outcomes. It may be that the error accidentally spells a genuine address of some other computer network and so gets forwarded (probably ending up with the postmaster as an unknown person at that post office), or the computer of your ISP Company will decide that it is not a real computer network address and then send you back a response telling you so.

Okay. So far we have talked about mistakes in the email address, and we now have some idea what the outcome of sending badly addressed email may be, but what about an email that is correctly addressed – how can you be sure that it has reached the intended destination?

As with postal mail, there is no absolute guarantee that your email will arrive at the electronic post office that it was sent to. Generally speaking, the email delivery service works very well – in fact remarkably well considering its size – but there are some circumstances where it can get irretrievably lost. These circumstances are usually to do with congestion from the amount of Internet information being sent.

If for some reason, a particular part of the Internet becomes overloaded with information, there are normal safeguard mechanisms to try and prevent email from becoming lost. But if the congestion is such that this part of the Internet cannot fully recover, then the administrators may decide – in the interests of all the users as a whole – to cut their losses and restart a number of computers with 'empty' mailboxes. You can consequently lose email in this way. Sometimes the administrators will save a whole pile of emails for delayed delivery. In which case there may be a second attempt at delivering them when things quieten down a bit. But that is at their discretion, and if they decide to 'waste bin' a pile of emails – and yours happens to be one of them – then I'm afraid there will be nothing you can do about it, and you may never even know that it happened.

So what can you do to improve upon matters? Well, as with many things in life, a positive response is often better than a negative one, and you can ask the intended recipient of your email to write back to you and let you know that they have received your message. Now they could do this using an ordinary email, or even use the Reply function type of email (discussed later in section 7.3). But there is provision for a feature of the email delivery service that compares with

'Recorded Delivery' of postal mail. This feature is called **Read Receipts** and is the topic of the next section.

7.2 How do you know if email has been read?

If you are using version 5 of Outlook Express then you will need to check at this point that you have version 5.01, or a later version. For versions earlier than 5.01, the feature known as Read Receipts will not be available for you. Certainly, if you are working with Windows XP then you will not have a problem.

How can you check the version number? This is fairly easy to do. With the **Outlook Express** program running, click on **Help** from the menu bar at the top of the main window, and select the '**About Microsoft Outlook Express**' option. Up pops a dialog box, and directly under the fancy logo writing you should see a group of four numbers separated by 'dots' looking like this:

5.50.4133.2400

The leftmost two numbers are the version number. In our example above, the version is 5.50, which is generally referred to as 'version five point five'.

Read Receipts are a way of attempting to confirm that your email has arrived at its intended destination, and has been opened by someone. They cannot guarantee that whoever opens the email genuinely reads it, for I'm afraid it's another case of 'you can take a horse to the trough and show it the water...!'

The way that the feature works is this. First you need to adjust an internal setting within the **Outlook Express** program, to ask for a **Read Receipt**. You can do this just for one email that you are sending, or you can do it for all emails that you send. When you have made this setting adjustment, then the email that you create has a 'receipt request' automatically inserted into the email header. You send the email in the normal way. On arriving at the intended recipient's computer, it goes into their **Inbox folder** in the normal way and sits there waiting to be read. As soon as the email is opened, then a small message box pops up on their monitor screen to notify them that your email is requesting a receipt (this is the standard set-up for Outlook Express, but it can be changed to always receipt without notifying, or to never send receipts). They then have the opportunity to agree to the request, or to decline it. If they agree, then a **Read Receipt email** is placed into their **Outbox folder** and if they are on-line it will be sent back for you to receive. If they decline, then nothing further happens.

When the **Read Receipt email** arrives back in your own **Inbox folder**, it will look to you rather like a normal incoming email, only the Subject part of the Title line will indicate that it is a Read Receipt, so that you know to treat it as such. There may in fact be further information available in the message content part of the returning email, but this can vary a great deal on the software that the recipient is using.

The next two exercises are designed to show you how the feature works.

Exercise 18 – Asking for a read receipt

For this exercise, it is better to be on-line at the beginning, so start **Outlook Express** running, and if you were previously off-line then click to go on-line when asked. Also maximise the main window if need be, and check that the **Folders** and **Contacts sub-windows** are visible (from previous exercises, you should know what to do by now if they are not).

Move the tip of the mouse pointer to click on **Tools** from the menu bar, and then select **Options...** as shown in the following picture.

You will then see a fairly large dialog box pop up, as shown in the picture over the page.

Click now on the **Receipts tab** as demonstrated above, and you can then see the controls for adjusting the program settings as illustrated in the following picture.

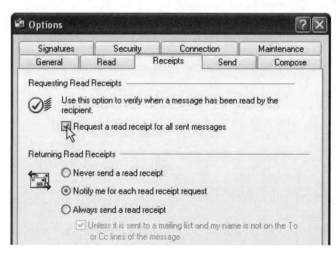

Now just taking a moment to have a look at these, we will deal with the first section shortly, but lower down in the middle you can see the controls for 'Returning Read Receipts'. This is the area that I mentioned earlier where the recipient can alter how their program will respond on getting a Read Receipt request. If your friends are always sending you a request and you get fed-up with the message box popping up asking you if you want to send them a receipt, then you can adjust this setting according to how you would like the automatic response to be.

Incidentally, a group of controls like these that are small circles with one of them having a 'dot' in the middle are known as 'radio buttons'. They are so-called because they behave like the old radio sets where you could change the wave-band selection by pushing down on one of them, and whichever one was previously selected would pop up again. To alter this setting in the future, just click with the tip of the mouse pointer in the middle of the circle representing your selection, and click the **Apply** button at the bottom. For our purposes now, we will leave the setting at the standard one of 'Notify me for each read receipt request'.

Okay. Looking back at the upper section, you can see a square check box that is labelled 'Request a read receipt for all sent messages'. It will not be ticked now, so click in the centre of the square with the tip of the mouse pointer, and the 'tick' symbol will appear (as shown in the last picture). When you have done that, move the mouse down to the bottom of the dialog box and press the **Apply** button, as shown in the following picture.

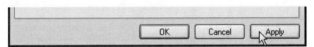

Finish by then clicking on the **OK** button and the dialog box will disappear. And you are then back at the main window of Outlook Express.

From this moment on, every email created will automatically have a **Read Receipt request** included in the email header.

Let us now create an email and send it to ourselves as we have done several times previously. We can see what happens at the recipient end. We will finish the exercise by agreeing to the request and that sends the Read Receipt back to the original email creator.

Click on the Create Mail button (New Mail button for version 5)...

And we see then the familiar **New Message window**. Fill out the details for the new email as shown, but do make sure that you <u>use your own email address</u> in the **To: textbox**.

Okay. Now just to show you something special to liven up this email, we are going to add a fancy background to it.

Click on **Format** from the menu bar in this window, and select the **Apply Stationery** option, as shown in this next picture.

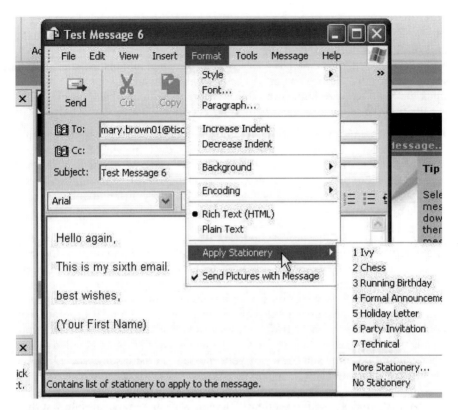

Then slide the mouse pointer over to the right and click on 'Ivy' (if you cannot see 'Ivy' for some reason, pick the first one that you can see). Suddenly, the series of menus disappear, and the appearance of your email is transformed as seen in the following picture.

Now the email is ready to be sent. Click on the **Send** button. The window disappears and the email is placed in the **Outbox folder**. Providing that you are still on-line (as at the start of the exercise), the 'Delivery Trigger Action' will automatically send this email to your ISP Company and into the Internet. Within a few seconds, the Outbox folder will be empty. (If you are not currently on-line, click the Send/Receive button and follow instructions to get back on-line).

We will pause for a moment here to reflect upon what we have done so far:

- First we adjusted the settings for the Outlook Express program so that a Read Receipt request would be included with every new email created.
- Then we created a new email called 'Test Message 6'. To make this email appear more fancy than a simple black and white, text-only style, we 'applied Stationery' to it. This gave the email a very different appearance!
- Then we sent the email to the Internet in the normal way.

Before we move to the next action, let me add a caution about the use of 'Stationery' within emails, and this also applies to fancy styling of any kind (that is, using different fonts, using coloured text, and such like). The ability for others to receive and read these 'fancy' emails depends on the use of the set of rules called **MIME** (see section 1.5 for a refresh on this subject). Some people will not be using the same email program that you are, and their program may not be able to 'understand' MIME rules. Consequently, when they receive your email, they may get a display on screen that looks like pure gobbledygook! There should be some semblance of your message in there somewhere, but the majority of the contents will appear nonsense.

If you want to send an email that is using only pure simple text (in the manner that we described in section 1.2), then you can remove all fancy styling from the message contents altogether, and you do it in the following way. If you look at the last picture but one, you can see above the **Apply Stationery option** that there are two other options grouped together called **Rich Text (HTML)** and **Plain Text.** These are mutually exclusive. The normal setting is for Rich Text (HTML) and this is the option that allows you to have fancy styling, stationery etc. But if in composing an email, you select the other Plain Text option from **Format** on the main menu, then all the 'fancy' elements will be removed from the message contents entirely. (Try this sometime and see what happens). By the way, selecting the Plain Text option should be just for that one email. The next one you send will be back to standard.

Okay. Let us move on to see what happens when the email is received. Click now on the **Send/Receive** button on the toolbar at the top of the main **Outlook Express window...**

This initiates the 'Delivery Trigger Action' and should pick up the email that we last sent, providing that you did correctly address it to your own email address. After a few seconds, there should be an incoming email waiting for you to read in the **Inbox folder**.

Click on the **Inbox folder** on the left to highlight it, and then click on the Title line 'Test Message 6' in the upper section over on the right. This is the act of opening the email to read it, and the consequence of this is that the **Read Receipt request** included in the email header now activates itself. This causes a message box to pop up on the monitor screen, as shown in the next picture.

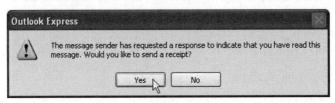

Now keep an eye on the Outbox folder while you click on the **Yes** button of this message box. Immediately that you make the click, the message box disappears and something automatically gets placed into the **Outbox folder**. Because you are still on-line, after a few seconds this something then gets sent automatically to the ISP computer and into the Internet, and the Outbox folder will be empty again. This something was the Read Receipt itself, being sent back to the originator of the email telling them that the email has just been opened and read.

We will conclude exercise 18 at this point. If you can avoid breaking here, move swiftly to the next exercise where you will see what the Read Receipt actually looks like when it arrives back with the email originator.

Exercise 19 – Receiving the read receipt

This exercise should follow on immediately from the previous one. You should still be on-line at this point. The situation we are now about to witness is the **Read Receipt** arriving back with the originator of the email.

Click now on the **Send/Receive** button on the toolbar at the top of the main **Outlook Express window...**

This initiates the 'Delivery Trigger Action' to pickup any incoming mail that may be waiting at the ISP computer. After a few seconds, you should see something arrive and be placed in the Inbox folder.

Click on the **Inbox folder** over on the left side to highlight it, then click on the Title line 'Read: Test Message 6' in the upper section over on the right. You should then see something looking like the following picture.

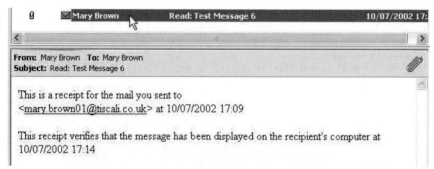

This new email that has just arrived is the actual Read Receipt requested as part of sending the original email. If you look at the details of the message content in the lower section, you can see details about the original email:

- to whom it was sent and at what time and date
- followed by the time and date when the recipient opened it.

You may also notice that the **paper clip icon** is showing on the left in the upper section Title line, and also over on the right in the lower section header. This indicates there is also an attachment to this Read Receipt. For curiosity, we will have a look at this attachment, but it will not mean much to us.

Click on the large **paper clip** button on the right in the lower section header, and select the first option, as shown in the next picture.

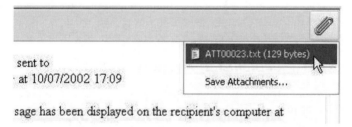

Then a new window opens and displays the content of the attachment...

As I said, it does not mean much to us! Close the new window using the Close button in the top right-hand corner.

This concludes exercise 19.

Before we leave this section on read receipts, you may remember that we adjusted the settings for Outlook Express such that every email that you now send will include a request for a read receipt automatically. For the remaining exercises, it is better that we change this setting back to its original setting, or the additional read receipts will distract us from the key learning points.

Move the tip of the mouse pointer to click on **Tools** from the menu bar, and then select **Options...** as shown in the following picture.

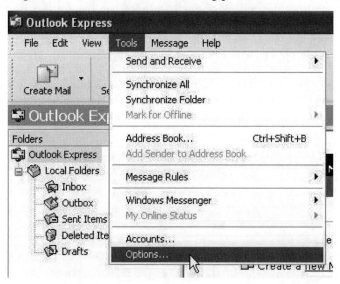

Click now on the **Receipts tab**. You can then see the controls for adjusting the program settings as illustrated in the next picture.

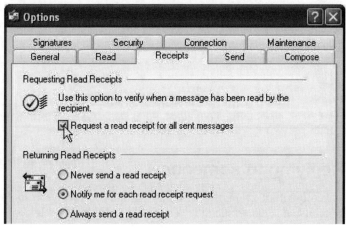

Click again on the **check box** labelled 'Request a read receipt for all sent messages' and the existing tick symbol will disappear. Then move the mouse pointer to the bottom of the **Options** window and press the **Apply** button to make this new setting permanent. Finish off by pressing the **OK** button to close the window. The setting has now been restored so that read receipts are not automatically requested for all emails sent.

Finally, how should you request a **Read Receipt** for just one single email? This is done from the **New Message window** when the email is being created. After you have completed the email, before you click on the **Send** button, first click on **Tools** and then click on the **Request Read Receipt** option. This act of clicking on the option makes the 'tick symbol' appear at the left side of it, but the silly thing is that it also closes the menu so that you cannot see it has been set! If you click on Tools for a second time (as shown in the following picture) you see then that it was set. However, do not select the Request Read receipt for a second time or it will clear it again. Click anywhere in the message contents area to make the drop down menu disappear.

This completes our work with read receipts.

7.3   Replying to someone

One of the really smart properties of email is that you receive it in electronic form, and because it is electronic, it is very easily and very quickly copied. What we are about to witness in this section is the use of a function known as '**Reply**' which gets the benefit of this easy and quick copying property.

Instead of replying to an email that we receive from a friend by creating a new and totally separate email, we are going to reply by first making a copy of their email message contents, and then we are going to add just a few comments of our own, and pop these in at the beginning of the reply. This is really a form of 'annotating' their email. If we compare this idea with postal mail, it is as though we took their letter and copied it in a photocopier, then marked up the copy with our own comments and sent it back.

The benefit of doing this is that both parties – the originator and the recipient – can understand that they are referring to the same subject matter, without having to manually search back through our work and remember what was originally said. Furthermore, if the originator sends the email to a group of people, and they each in turn respond with a reply copied to the entire group, then everyone will be able to view all the answers – and maybe noting different responses to the same question from different members of the group. Everybody gets to know everything!

For example, imagine that person 'A' creates an email asking a lot of questions and sends this to person 'B'. Person 'B' can then start to give some answers to these questions by making a direct reference to each original question, and include that original question in the email containing the answer. Person 'B' sends a Reply email back to person 'A', and it is obvious from just reading it which answer corresponds to which question, and what that question actually was. From a historical point of view, any other person 'C' receiving the reply can both understand the question and the answer in one simple act of reading. They do not have to match up two separate emails, one containing the questions, and the other containing the answers.

Let us now examine this Reply function with a practical exercise.

Note – At this point in the book I want to simplify the exercises slightly. Instead of describing every event and illustrating every event with a picture, I would like to simplify the narrative by taking certain actions as being self-evident. For those events which we have done several times over now, I will request that you carry the event out without going into every single detail. If you find yourself running into trouble, just have a look back at some of the exercises that we have done previously and see how you accomplished the task before. I promise not to jump too far ahead of the game!

Exercise 20 – Using the Reply function

Begin this exercise with **Outlook Express** running and on-line. Make sure that the **Folders** and **Contacts sub-windows** are visible as before.

Click on the **Create Mail** button, and fill out the details for the email as shown in the next picture. Remember to use your own email address in the **To: textbox**.

The email shown above is going to act as the 'original message' in this exercise. It is very typical of the sort of thing that we might send to a friend when we want to ask for some information.

Recheck that <u>you have used your own email address</u> in the **To: textbox**. Then click on the **Send** button, and the email will be placed in the **Outbox folder**. Because we are on-line, it will only be a few seconds before the email is automatically sent to the ISP computer, and the Outbox folder will be empty again.

Now we will pretend that we are the 'friend' to whom this email has been sent. Click on the **Send/Receive** button on the toolbar of the main Outlook Express window, and shortly the email will arrive in the **Inbox folder**. Click on the Inbox folder, and then click on the Title line 'Test Message 7' in the upper section window on the right side of the monitor screen, as shown in the next picture.

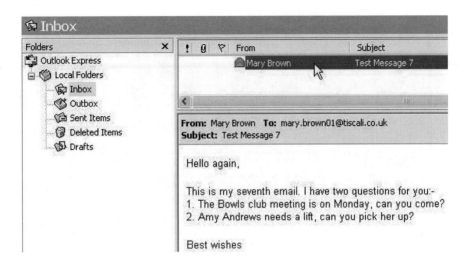

This received email looks much the same as others we have sent in earlier exercises. The only difference is that there is a bit more text in the message contents section because we have asked two questions.

Now acting as the 'friend' who received the email, you are going to make a reply, but instead of creating a completely separate new email to send your answers in, we are going to use the Reply function illustrated in the following picture.

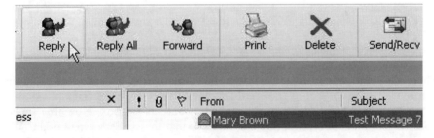

You may just want to note to yourself that there is another tool button, to the right of the one we will use, called 'Reply All'. If the email was originally sent to several people, then using this button will generate a reply to all of the people listed in the original email. The Reply button we are using only sends our reply to the sender of the email.

Click now on the Reply button, which is visible and active (it was 'greyed out' before') on the toolbar at the top of the main window. You will then see a new message window pop up that is a bit different to those that we have seen before...

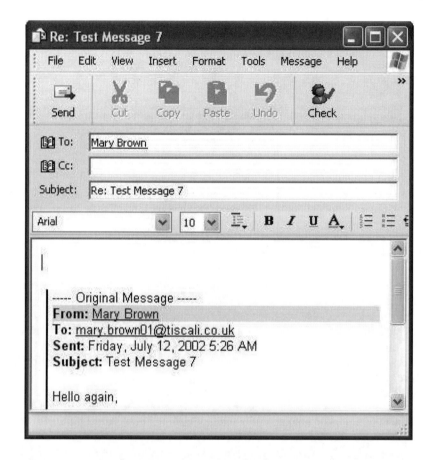

There are some interesting points about this window that are worth mentioning before we use it. First of all, notice that a complete copy of the original email is automatically entered for us in the message contents textbox. Now that saved your fingers a bit of typing! Second, observe that the sender's email address is automatically inserted into the To: textbox for us, so we don't have to worry about getting the right email address for the reply. Third, notice that the Subject: textbox is automatically filled out for us with the prefix 'Re:' inserted for us (you might also spot that the actual window title at the very top has the same wording). And fourth, observe that the 'flashing cursor' is positioned at the beginning of the message contents, ahead of the original message text, ready and waiting for us to type our response at the keyboard.

Okay. Before you start typing your response, just move the tip of the mouse pointer and click on the '**Maximise**' button for the new message window...

This will make it easier to see more of what you type.

Now I want you to type the following response, starting with the 'Dear Captain' bit, as shown in the next picture.

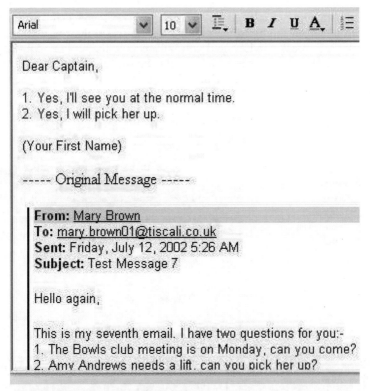

When you have finished typing your response, just reflect a moment on the words we have used. I think it is easy to see that, because the original message is part of the reply, you can get away with saying the minimal amount needed. Any third party looking at this response would know immediately what you were referring to.

Okay. Now click on the **Send** button…

Providing that you are still on-line, then the message window disappears, and the reply email is placed into the **Outbox folder**. Within a few seconds, the reply will be sent to your ISP computer and into the Internet, and the Outbox folder will be empty again.

 If you are observant, you may have noticed that a subtle change occurred to the 'envelope' icon in the Title line of 'Test Message 7'. It has now acquired a small little arrow symbol pointing to the left like this... This now indicates to you that you have created a reply for this incoming email.

Now we are going to pretend that we are ourselves again as the originator of first email. Click on the **Send/Receive** button on the toolbar at the top of the main Outlook Express window, and you will receive the reply email into your **Inbox folder**. When it arrives, click on the Inbox folder over on the left to highlight it, then click on the Title line 'Re: Test Message 7' over to the right in the upper section, as shown below.

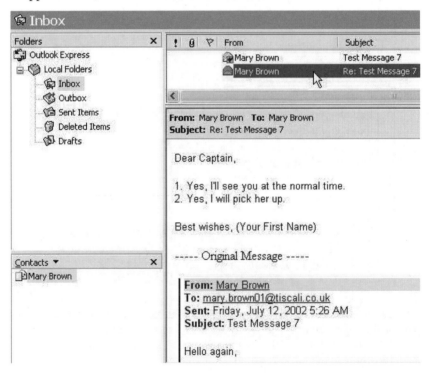

Now you see the message content for the reply in the lower section. You can see the original email message that you sent, and the annotated remarks that go with it, from the recipient. This concludes exercise 20.

Before we leave this section on the Reply function, there is one point that I would like to add. In making the copy of the original email and placing this into the message contents of the reply, the Reply function for Outlook Express only makes a copy of the message contents part. Any attachments are not normally included in the reply. Some other email reader programs may not do this, and it can be very irritating to receive a reply to one of your own original emails, and endure receiving your own attachment back again as well!

7.4 Forwarding to someone else

The **Forward** function works in a very similar way to the **Reply** function. The key difference is that instead of automatically filling in the **To: textbox** for you with the sender's email address, the Forward function will leave this blank for you to put in a forwarding email address.

Just as the Reply function makes a copy of the original email for you to annotate, so does the Forward function. However, the Forward function will copy any attachments as well. (The recipient will not have had a copy of them!)

Exercise 21 – Using the Forward function

Begin this exercise with **Outlook Express** running and on-line. Make sure that the **Folders** and **Contacts sub-windows** are visible as before.

Click on the **Create Mail** button, and fill out the details for the email as shown in the next picture. Remember to <u>use your own email address</u> in the **To: textbox.**

The email shown above is going to act as the 'original message' in this exercise. It is typical of the sort of thing that we might send to a friend giving them information that they may not have.

Recheck that you have used your own email address in the **To: textbox**. Then click on the **Send** button, and the email will be placed in the **Outbox folder**. Because we are on-line, it will only be a few seconds before the email is automatically sent to the ISP computer, and the Outbox folder will be empty again.

Now again, we will pretend that we are the person to whom this email has been sent. Click on the **Send/Receive** button on the toolbar of the main Outlook Express window, and shortly the email will arrive in the Inbox folder. Click on the Inbox folder, and then click on the Title line 'Test Message 8' in the upper section window on the right side of the monitor screen, as shown in the next picture.

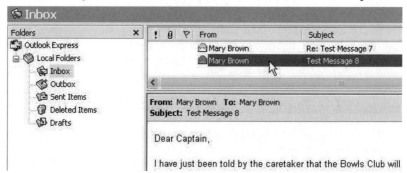

This received email looks much the same as others we have sent.

Now, acting as the person who received the email, you are going to forward this information onward to others, and add a question of your own. To do this, we shall use the **Forward** function that works in a very similar way to the **Reply** function. Click now on the **Forward** button on the toolbar of the main window, as shown in the following picture.

You will then see a new message window pop up that has a copy of the original message already in the message contents section. This time the To: textbox will be blank and the flashing cursor will be located here, ready for you to type the email address of the person (or persons) that you wish to forward to. This is illustrated in the next picture.

Go ahead and type in your own email address in this **To: textbox**.

Now when you have done that, before we add a few comments of our own into the message contents section, I want to demonstrate to you an additional feature that you can use for any email you create – be it an original email, or a reply, or a forwarded type. The feature is known as the Priority setting and has three levels:

- High   - Normal   - Low

In all the exercises that you have done to date, the priority setting assigned to email that you have created was the 'normal' setting by default. Not surprisingly this has no obvious effect that we can notice, or we would have spotted it by now! Now to demonstrate the feature, we are going to set the priority of our 'forwarded' email to 'High'. Move the tip of the mouse pointer over **Message** on the menu bar of the new message window and click, then select the **Set Priority option** and carefully slide the mouse pointer over to the right to select the **High** option, as shown in the following picture.

As soon as you have clicked to make the **High** selection, the menus disappear, but something new appears just above the **To: textbox**. This is a new **Priority label** with an icon of a red exclamation mark (see the next picture). The fact that we see this label means that additional information will be added to the email header, to indicate that the sender wishes this email to be treated as high priority.

Note – Changing the Priority of an email is only for that one email. Other emails you create afterwards will be 'Normal' priority, unless you specifically change them individually.

Now re-position the tip of the mouse pointer into the area of the message contents section and place it at the beginning, just above where it says 'Original Message', as shown in the next picture. Notice again how the mouse pointer symbol changes from an arrow to this 'I' shape. Make a click action to change the focus and the flashing cursor will now start flashing in this new spot.

Okay. We are ready to insert the additional comments for the forwarded email. Type out the wording as shown in the following picture...

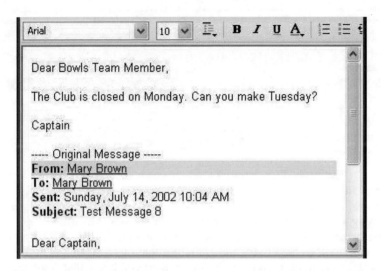

When you have finished, just reflect a moment on the words we have used. I think it is easy to see that, because the original message is part of the forwarded email, there is no need to explain in detail why there is a change of events. This will be obvious to whoever reads this forwarded email, by reading the original message.

> Note – in this exercise we are forwarding to a single person in the To: textbox, but we could have just as easily used a 'group' from the Windows Address Book, which we learnt about in section 6.4.

Okay. Now click on the **Send** button. Providing that you are still on-line then the message window disappears, and the forwarded email is placed into the **Outbox folder**. Within a few seconds, the email will be sent to your ISP computer and into the Internet, and the Outbox folder will become empty again.

 If you are observant, you may have noticed that a subtle change occurred to the 'envelope' icon in the Title line of 'Test Message 8'. It has now acquired a small arrow symbol pointing to the right like this... This now indicates to you that you have forwarded this incoming email.

Now we are going to pretend that we are the person to whom the email has been forwarded.

Click on the **Send/Receive** button on the toolbar at the top of the main Outlook Express window, and you will receive the forwarded email into your Inbox folder. When it arrives, click on the Inbox folder over on the left to highlight it. Notice that an exclamation mark now appears on the Title line for 'Fw: Test Message 8' over to the right in the upper section, as shown in the next picture.

You may now read the message contents for the forwarded email, and you also see the original message contents, as first received by the forwarding person.

Setting the email priority to 'High' does not affect the email, nor does it materially affect its transmission through the Internet. It is simply a way for the sender to mark the email to try and grab the attention of the recipient. If you see a High Priority email in your Inbox folder, then you know that someone wants you to read this as soon as you get the opportunity. Also, setting the priority to 'Low' will not affect it either. This is just the sender's way of saying, read this when you are not too busy.

Finally, after reading the forwarded message, you can decide what the next action should be. If this was a real situation, you might want to click upon the **Reply** button to answer the question.

Close also the main **Outlook Express** window and disconnect with **Autodisconnect**.

This concludes exercise 21.

8

Managing Email

8.1   The need to manage

After you have opened an account with an Internet Service Provider, it is natural to be keen to use the email delivery service. When you have learnt some of the basics as outlined in earlier chapters then you soon begin to send and receive with ease.

In the beginning, your **Inbox folder** is empty and as new emails arrive it starts filling up. Now for quite some time this is not at all a problem, for it is simple enough to scroll back and forth through the Inbox folder to remind yourself of what people have sent you. However, without realising it, this slowly builds up, and after a while it takes just that little bit longer to scroll backwards to find that email you are looking for. Then one day it catches you out. You know that someone sent you an email fairly recently and mentioned something quite important, but trying to find it becomes almost impossible. Despite your frantic efforts in scrolling back and forth, you just don't seem able to come across it. This is the moment when you realise that you need to start 'managing' your email, and certainly you need to throw away a whole pile of 'junk emails' that are cluttering up the folder.

If you work as part of a team in an office, then managing your email becomes even more important. Each person will probably have his or her own individual email account and the problem of storage size for the Inbox and Sent Items folders becomes magnified by the number of accounts. Very often these accounts are held on a centralised computer Hard Drive and an administrator deliberately limits the total storage space that they can occupy. Should you reach the size limit on your allocated storage then you are faced with no alternative but to delete some of the old emails, in order to make room for the arrival of new ones.

In this chapter, we are going to have a look at the various ways of managing email. Most of the tips and tricks we will investigate are really simple once you know how to do them. We start by learning how to delete an email, and finish by performing a search, looking for a particular word that you remember is buried somewhere in the message contents of one specific email.

8.2 Deleting unwanted email

Exercise 22 – Deleting an email

We begin this exercise with **Outlook Express** open and running. You can operate either on-line or off-line. The choice is yours. Make sure that the **Folders** and **Contacts sub-windows** are visible as before.

Click first on the **Inbox folder** over on the left side of the screen to highlight it. You should then be able to see the last emails that you received in the upper section of the main window, over on the right. Carefully move the tip of the mouse pointer over the top button of the small scroll bar in the upper section, as shown in the following picture.

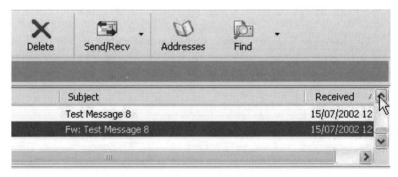

Now click to scroll backwards until you see the Title line of the very first email that we sent called 'Test Message 1', as shown in the next picture.

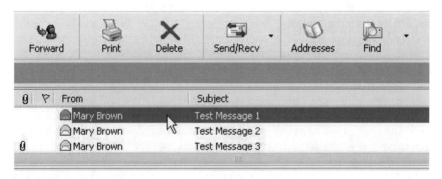

Click on this line to highlight it as shown above. We will now delete this email, and there are two ways that we can do it. For the exercise, I want you to use the second way.

The first way is to right click with the mouse when you are pointing on the Title line, and then to select the Delete option from the menu as shown in the following picture.

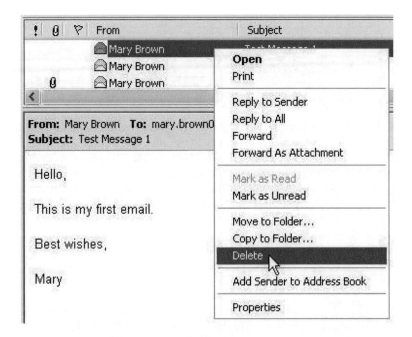

The second, and my preferred, way is to check again that it is highlighted then simply press the '**Delete key**' on the keyboard. Go ahead and do this now – check that 'Test Message 1' is highlighted, and then press the 'Delete key' on the keyboard (as shown in the next picture).

The reason why I prefer this method is that you have more time to think, 'Do I really want to delete this particular email?' When the menu is not cluttering your view, you also have a better chance to make sure that you have the correct one highlighted, and it really is the one you want to delete.

When it has been deleted, the upper section on your monitor screen will look like something like this…

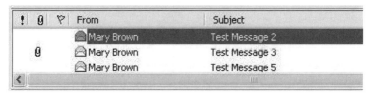

Okay. Now you can see that it has gone. But what if you made a mistake? Can you bring it back again? The answer is 'Yes' and next we will see how.

Click on the **Deleted Items folder** over on the left of the screen (in the Folders sub-window), and you will see that a copy of the 'deleted email' has now been placed there. Carefully re-position the mouse pointer on the Title line 'Test Message 1'. Then right-click and select the **Move to Folder...** option, as illustrated in the following picture.

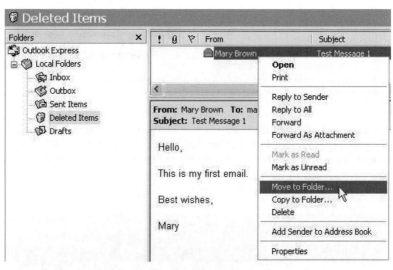

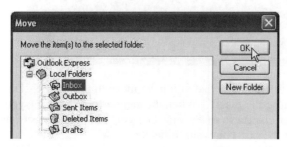

A new Move window then pops up like this one...

If your own monitor screen does not show the 'Local Folders' icon opened, listing the other folders below it, then simply click once on the tiny square box marked '+' (or double-click on the 'Local Folders' label – either will work) to see them.

Okay. Now click on the one marked **Inbox** as shown above, then click on the **OK** button. The **Move** window closes and the Title line 'Test Message 1' that was showing now disappears.

Not surprisingly, the email has moved back to the **Inbox folder**. Click again on the Inbox folder over on the left and then use the scroll bar again in the upper section of the main window to scroll backwards through the emails. When you reach the start, you will see that the once deleted 'Test Message 1' email has been restored back to where it was at the start of the exercise.

This concludes exercise 22.

Before we leave the topic of deleting emails, you should be aware that there is a method of permanently deleting them such that you cannot get them back again. Click again on the Deleted Items folder to highlight it. Then with the mouse pointer still positioned over it, make a right-click. The second option in the menu that appears is called 'Empty 'Deleted Items' folder' and is probably shown 'greyed out' on your monitor screen (it will be so if there are no items in the folder). If we had selected this option in the last exercise instead of moving the 'deleted email' back to the Inbox folder, then it would have removed the email altogether.

8.3   Filing to a new folder

Whenever I think of filing, I am always reminded of the 'Douglas Bader' method as portrayed in the film 'Reach for the sky'. Bader has just arrived back in the Air Force after taking months learning to walk on his artificial legs. He is taking over from some unfortunate squadron leader who has 'bought it' and is keen to get flying again as soon as possible. He walks into his new office to find a huge pile of papers stacked high on his desk. His assistant informs him that the first task must be to consider all of the papers and file them accordingly. Bader takes a good look at the pile and thinks for a moment. Then he picks them all up and drops them smartly into the wastepaper basket. Rubbing his hands to dust them off, he turns to his assistant and says 'Well that's the filing done. Now let's see what the next task is!'

As part of the management of email, filing into folders can maintain order to your information. If you don't pay regular attention to this issue, then one day you may be forced to use the 'Bader' method of filing!

When you first begin to use **Outlook Express**, you are presented with the five standard folders in the **Local Folders** section, but you are not limited to use only these. You can create folders of your own should you wish to, and use them in a similar way to the standard ones.

One strategy of working with folders is to keep the number of emails held in the **Inbox** folder to as small a number as possible. You would do this by periodically working your way through it and making decisions. Starting with the oldest email, you would decide, 'Do I re-file this? Or do I delete it?' If you decide to re-file it, then you may need to create a new folder to give it a proper home, and we will see how to do this in this next exercise.

Exercise 23 – Re-filing an email to a new folder

We begin this exercise with **Outlook Express** open and running. You can operate either on-line or off-line. Make sure that the **Folders** and **Contacts sub-windows** are visible as before.

Move the tip of the mouse pointer over the **Local Folders** icon, which is just above the Inbox folder on the left of your screen. Make a right-click, and from the menu that appears select the **New Folder...** option, as shown here.

This causes a new **Create Folder** window to pop up...

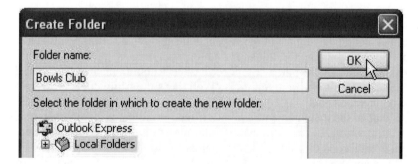

The flashing cursor will be located in the **Folder name: textbox,** ready for you to type at the keyboard. Go ahead and type the name 'Bowls Club', as illustrated above. Then press the **OK** button on the right.

Now we can see that a new folder has appeared in the Local Folders list with the name that we have given to it, as seen in the following picture.

If you wish to, you can create sub-folders within this new folder. First you would right-click the tip of the mouse pointer over the new folder, then select the **New Folder...** option again. This is a very similar 'tree structure' mechanism to that used for general folders on the Hard Disk.

If in the future you wish to remove any folder, just place the mouse pointer over it and right-click. Then select the Delete option.

Okay. We now have the new folder called 'Bowls Club' to work with. Next we shall transfer one of the emails from the Inbox folder into it.

Click first on the **Inbox folder** over on the left side of the screen to highlight it. You should then be able to see the last emails that you received in the upper section of the main window, over on the right. Carefully move the tip of the mouse pointer over the top button of the small scroll bar in the upper section, as we did before in the last exercise...

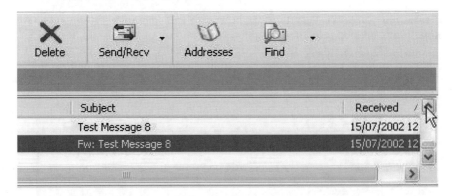

Repeated click, in order to scroll backwards, until you can see the email titled 'Test Message 5' appear. Position the mouse pointer over this Title line and right-click to show the drop down menu. Then select the **Move to Folder...** option, as shown in the next picture.

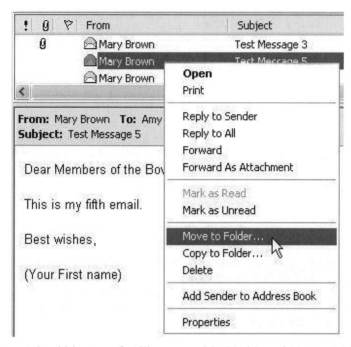

I think you should be very familiar now with this idea of 'right-clicking' over something and then selecting an option for an action of what to do. It is the fact that the right-click selects the item first that is really telling the computer 'It is this item highlighted and not any other that I want this action to happen to'.

As soon as you have selected the **Move to Folder...** option then a **Move** window pops up...

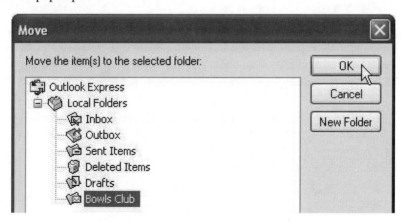

If your own monitor screen is not showing the complete list of folders, then click on the small square marked '+' to show them.

Now click on the **Bowls Club Folder** to select the target destination for the 'Move' and then click the **OK** button. As soon as you have done, then the transfer out of the Inbox folder and into the Bowls Club folder occurs.

You should notice that the email is not now showing in the upper section (for the Inbox folder). Check out that the transfer has successfully taken place by now clicking on the **Bowls Club folder** away to the left of the screen...

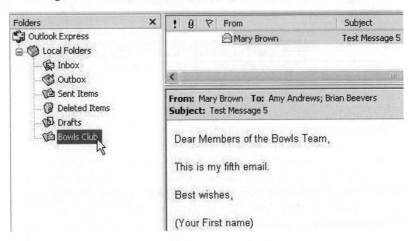

And there it is.

This concludes exercise 23.

8.4   Flagging an email

Often when you are working with folders, you may want to temporarily mark one particular email, so that you remind yourself that you have some work to do concerning it. You may not want to do the work immediately, but you do not want to forget about it. The solution to this is to 'set a flag' on the Title line of the email, then when you are next routinely managing your email, it will remind you that there is something special about this particular one that needs attention.

This next exercise is very simple.

Exercise 24 – Flagging an email

We begin this exercise with **Outlook Express** open and running. You can operate either on-line or off-line. Make sure that the **Folders** and **Contacts sub-windows** are visible as before.

Click first on the **Inbox folder** over on the left side of the screen to highlight it. You should then be able to see emails that you have received in the upper section of the main window, over on the right. Carefully move the tip of the mouse pointer over the top button of the small scroll bar in the upper section, and in similar manner to the last two exercises, click to scroll backwards until you can see the email with the subject Title line 'Test Message 2'.

Click on the Title line to highlight it, as shown in the following picture.

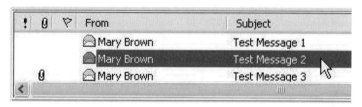

Now there are two methods that you can use to 'flag' this message. I want you to use the second method, but I will show you the alternative first.

If you click on **Message** on the menu bar at the top of the main window, then a drop down menu appears. Providing that the message was first highlighted, you can then select the **Flag Message** option. If the message was not first highlighted then the option is 'greyed out', so do remember that you must click on the email to tell Outlook Express which one to flag. This method of 'flagging' is illustrated in the next picture.

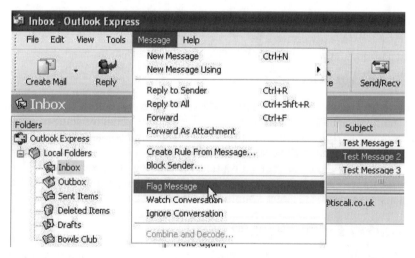

The method that we are going to use to flag the email is quicker but perhaps a little trickier. Carefully position the tip of the mouse pointer just a little to the left of the Title line 'Test Message 2' and also to the left of the envelope icon.

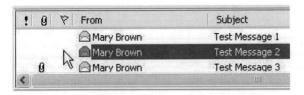

You need the tip to be actually positioned in the column space that has a little grey flag icon as the header, as shown here.

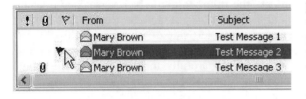

Now make a click action without moving the mouse pointer. If you do this in the correct place, then you will suddenly see a red flag icon appear like this...

That is the second method finished.

Now click with the mouse for yet another time in this same spot (over the red flag itself if you want). You then see that the email become 'un-flagged' again. It's a toggle type of action – click once to set the flag, click again to clear it. Click yet one last time so that the red flag is showing. We will leave it like this so that we can use it in the exercise for the next section.

This concludes exercise 24.

8.5 Ordering the lists

In all our work to date, the emails in the **Inbox folder**, and also in the **Sent Items** folder, have always appeared in a 'natural' order based upon date and time of receipt. In the last exercise, for example, we had to scroll backwards through the list to be able to find 'Test Message 2'.

When new emails have been received in the Inbox folder they have always appeared appended to the end of the list of previously received ones.

Now the presentation of these emails on your monitor screen happens to be in date/time order by default, but they do not always have to be presented so. In the next exercise we will see that we have the ability to quickly change this presentation, and we can re-order the listing of emails in a number of different ways.

There are several reasons why it may be desirable to view emails in a different order. We may, for example, be keen to see all the emails received from one particular person, so that we can track some activity with that person. We may be keen to see all the emails that have been 'flagged' appear together in one continuous block, so that we can work our way through the outstanding tasks left to do. We may wish to see emails listed in subject title order. All of these different ways of presenting the lists of emails are possible, and simple enough to do. And we can make these presentations for any of the folders that we can identify.

Let us now see these different ways of 'ordering' the lists of emails in action.

Exercise 25 – Ordering lists

We begin this exercise with **Outlook Express** open and running. You can operate either on-line or off-line. Make sure that the **Folders** and **Contacts sub-windows** are visible as before.

First we will change the order of the **Inbox folder** to be reverse date/time, that is, the most recent will appear at the top of the list, and the oldest at the bottom.

Click on the **Inbox folder** over on the left side of the screen to highlight it. You should then be able to see emails that you have received in the upper section of the main window, over on the right. Carefully move the tip of the mouse pointer over the top button of the small scroll bar in the upper section, and in similar manner to the last two exercises, click to scroll backwards until you can see the email with the subject Title line 'Test Message 1'. It is apparent from your scrolling action that the most recent email is located towards the 'bottom' of the monitor screen, and the oldest email is located at the 'top'. This is, if you like, considered the natural order.

Now carefully position the tip of mouse pointer over the 'header' for the 'Received' column. The header is the grey bar at the top of the upper section area and has the wording 'Received' labelled on it. In order to see this column actually on the screen, you way have to use the 'horizontal' scroll bar to slide it over a bit towards the left. As soon as you are positioned over the header it changes its appearance, as in the next picture.

Subject	Received /	
Test Message 1	15/07/2002 11:25	
Test Message 2	15/07/2002 11:32	
Test Message 3	15/07/2002 11:38	

Now with the tip pointing still on the header, make a click action. Suddenly the order of presentation of the emails changes, as shown in the following picture.

Subject	Received	
Fw: Test Message 8	15/07/2002 12:20	
Test Message 8	15/07/2002 12:18	
Re: Test Message 7	15/07/2002 12:15	

Compare these last two pictures. Notice that the date and time for each email in the first is progressing later in time as you go down the screen, whereas the date and time for each in the second progresses later in time as you go up the screen.

This re-ordering has changed the complete list of emails for the whole of the Inbox folder. Later, when you have accumulated more of your own private emails, you will see the effect that I have just described much more pronounced.

Okay. To change the order back again to how it was when we started, click another time with the mouse pointer on the 'Received' header. The date and time order is now restored back to the 'natural' order.

Now you can do this trick of clicking on the header to re-order the appearance of emails in the list with any of the other 'headers'. Try yourself to click on each of the headers in turn. You can do this for 'Subject' and 'From'. You can even do it for the headers with icons showing, such as 'Priority' (the exclamation symbol), 'Attachments' (the paper-clip symbol) or 'Flags'.

When you have finished trying out each of the different types of header, click finally on the 'Received' header and repeat the click until you have date and time restored back to the default 'natural' order of most recent towards the bottom of the screen, as shown in the last picture.

We will leave this exercise on presentation ordering at this point.

This concludes exercise 25.

Before we leave this section, it is worth pointing out that, when you close down the Outlook Express program, the order that you leave a folder in will be remembered when you start it running again. If things appear strange, then click once or twice on the 'Received' header until you have the ordering back to its normal appearance.

8.6 Searching for something

We end this chapter on managing email with an exercise that you will probably find very useful one day – how to find one particular email in the middle of hosts of others. Quite often when working with email, you will find yourself wanting to search back through the **Inbox** or **Sent Items** folders for a particular email from or to a particular person, but you only have some vague recollection when it was received or sent. There may be just one word that sticks out in your mind about this particular email, and that word can be very useful to help you find it quickly, without having to read through dozens and dozens of other emails trying to find the one that you want.

In this next exercise, we will search for the word 'Monday', which you may remember was used in the correspondence concerning the Bowls Club meetings.

Exercise 26 – Searching for an email

We begin this exercise with **Outlook Express** open and running. You can operate either on line or off line. Make sure that the **Folders** and **Contacts sub-windows** are visible as before. Move the tip of the mouse pointer over the label 'Outlook Express', just above 'Local folders' in the Folders sub-window, and click to highlight it as shown in the next picture.

Then click on the **Find** button on the toolbar at the top of the main window, as in the following picture.

This pops up a fairly large **Find Message box** that is a very powerful search tool, and deserves a bit of further discussion...

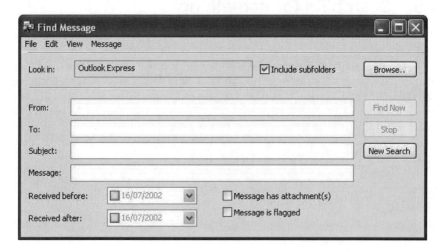

Now the reason why we first clicked on the 'Outlook Express' label at the start of this exercise is to be found in the first textbox above labelled 'Look in:'. This textbox tells the program whereabouts to make its search. Here, the program will search **all** of 'Outlook Express'. If we had highlighted one of the folders first – say the Inbox folder – then when we clicked the Find button on the toolbar, it would have said the word 'Inbox' in the 'Look in:' textbox and restricted the search to within just that one folder. Notice also that there is a check box to the right of it labelled 'Include subfolders'. If this check box is ticked, then not only will the program search inside the specified location, but it will also search inside any folders that are sub-folders of that folder.

The three white textboxes labelled 'From:' 'To:' and 'Subject:' can be left blank, or a word can be put into them. If a word is specified, then the search will look for that word in the corresponding part of the email header. The same is true for the fourth white textbox labelled 'Message:' but instead of searching in the email header, the program will search through the message contents part. Shortly, we will use this 'Message:' textbox to search for the word 'Monday'.

The two controls labelled 'Received before:' and 'Received after:' can be used to narrow down the search to a given date period, but they are only effective if the associated check boxes are first activated with a click, to put a tick inside them. You can tick one and not the other if you wish to, and the search will be made accordingly.

The two check boxes labelled 'Message has attachment(s)' and 'Message is flagged' do a similar job to restrict the searching to only those emails that fit these criteria, if they are activated with a click and a tick symbol. Remember that you click once to set the tick, and click again to reset it if you change your mind (or make a mistake).

Finally, there are four buttons on the right-hand side:

- The **Browse..** button is another method of changing the '**Look in:**' folder. Test this out yourself later when you have time.
- The **Find Now** and **Stop** buttons are shown 'greyed out' and only become active when they have a proper job to do. For example, until there is something to actually go searching for, then the Find button will not be available. But as soon as you specify any sort of criteria, then it will become available. This is the button that sets off the searching mechanism, and we will use this in a moment.
- The **Stop** button allows you to stop a search that may be underway. If you have a long list of emails that you are searching through, then you may find that it is taking forever to do the searching. Pressing the **Stop** button will bring the search to a halt, and leave you to view the results that it has already found for you before you stopped it.
- The **New Search** button is a bit of a misnomer. It doesn't really conduct a new search, it simply clears all the controls on the **Find Message** box so that you can enter new criteria and then make a new search. If you use this then you need to press the **Find** button again to actually conduct the next search.

Okay. With that discussion of the **Find Message** box completed, let us try it out and see if we can find all the emails that have the word 'Monday' contained within their message contents.

Move the mouse pointer over the white area of the **Message: textbox** and click to show a flashing cursor inside it. Now type the word 'Monday', as shown in the next picture.

Although I have shown 'Monday' with a capital letter, it does not really matter, for the program will find all occurrences of the word, in whatever form it finds it.

When you have finished typing the word, press the **Find** button as shown in the last picture. (Notice that the button is active once you have something to find.)

The program will now make its search according to the criteria that we specified. After a short while, a list of email Title lines appears in a new list box that joins itself on to the bottom of the Find box. The next picture shows the results of the search.

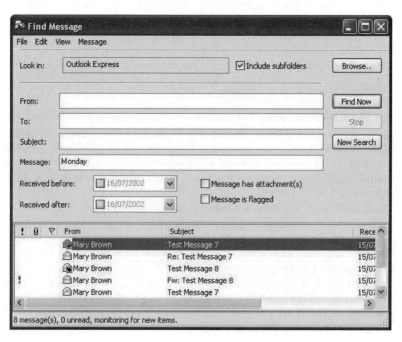

This picture is a classic case of information not fitting into the space provided, so two scroll bars are added to the new list box to allow you to move the 'viewing area' about and see the hidden information if you want to.

If we now double-click on any of the Title lines shown in the list (or right-click and then select the 'Open' option, if you find that easier to do) then the email will be opened up into a new window so that you can see its details. The following picture illustrates this for the first one…

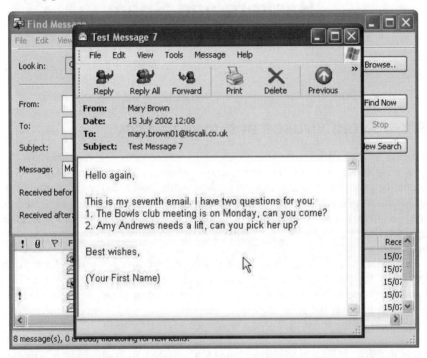

So there we are. We have found one email containing this keyword 'Monday' in the message contents section. There are more and if you care to have a quick look then close this window with the 'X' button in the top right-hand corner, select another from the list and open it in the same way.

This concludes exercise 26.

9

Protecting Against Viruses, Hackers and Spam

9.1 Avoid viruses and stay healthy

There is a lot of concern these days about computer viruses. Every now and then you hear about them on the news, and read about them in the papers. Such publicity gives them a notoriety that they justly deserve, for the damage that they can do is immeasurable. They are definitely something that all 'first-time' users of email need to be aware of, and must take suitable measures to guard against. Email is probably the biggest way that computer viruses are transmitted around the world.

In order to know what measures are suitable, we first need to understand the nature of the problem. Once you understand the character of a computer virus and understand how they are transmitted from place to place, then you are better placed to know if the measures that you personally are taking are sufficient to guard against the threat that these unwanted inventions pose.

We begin our discussion with a simple statement that a computer virus is a special form of computer program. That is what it really is – a computer program – and usually a program with a malicious intention. Straightaway, we can appreciate that if it is a computer program, then it is 'software' and we know that software is a man-made invention. It is not therefore anything biological and we don't need to worry about a computer virus creeping up and getting into the computer when it is switched off! Computer viruses can only do their damage when a computer is actually operating. It needs to be operating in order to carry out the actions of the virus program.

So, if computer viruses are programs, how do they differ from other types of program and why are they to be feared? The main difference between an ordinary program and a computer virus is that an ordinary program only runs when you want and ask it to, whereas a computer virus hides itself, usually within other programs, and runs without your knowledge or permission. Viruses also differ from ordinary programs in that they are designed to do things that you do not want them to do. Whereas an ordinary program is designed to be under your control, to help you and be constructive – a computer virus is designed to be out of control, to interfere with your work and to be destructive. An ordinary program will, in general, not interfere with any of your files unless you want them to. A computer virus will, in general, corrupt and distort the information in your files, or maybe even delete files altogether.

Once a computer virus has been running on your computer, it will not normally be sufficient to simply remove the original source of the virus. Many virus programs are written to make several secret copies of themselves hidden inside other files, so to get rid of the virus completely you need to remove all copies of it from everywhere within your computer system. To do this, you need to use other special computer programs called virus checkers designed specifically to search diligently through all your files and look for the virus program. When they find a copy of the virus, the checker will then offer the option to remove the code or destroy the file holding it. The checker will then proceed to look through the remaining files. Only when it has completed the search, will your computer system then be restored back to health. Once you have removed a computer virus from your system you must be very careful not to do anything that will 're-infect' your system and we will discuss the precautions you need to observe shortly.

Even when you have found all such copies of the virus and removed them from your system, this may not be the end of your problems. If ordinary files have been damaged, then the Windows operating system may itself not work properly. It will then have to be repaired and this is not usually a job that 'first timers' will have the necessary skills for.

If the situation with a virus comes to the worst, an expert can re-construct your computer software from the beginning. They do this by wiping out all of the information contained on the hard disk, and then reload each piece of software, program by program. This may prove to be the only enduring way of getting free from the effects of the virus once again. However, this will be a very time consuming task and has to be done carefully from backup copies of files that have not been affected by the work of the virus program. It is certainly not a job that I would recommend a 'first-timer' to attempt. Even an expert may run into trouble, for they will require certain specific files that work with your own particular pieces of 'hardware'. If you have been careful to save and store these away following the initial purchase of your computer, then it should be possible for them to do it. But if you cannot find these specific files then you may end up having to buy new pieces of hardware – for which the required files are available.

The subject of rebuilding a computer system leads us to the first important measure that you should take to protect yourself from computer viruses...

1. Make regular backup copies of your work files.

The reason for this is that you can always buy a new copy of the Windows operating system files if need be. You will not be able to replace your work files so easily.

Now you might think that if a computer virus is simply a program then why not avoid running that program and everything will be all right? This is a good idea in theory. If we can avoid running the program containing a virus then a virus cannot do its nasty work. However, the major problem is that most of the time you will be unaware that the virus program is running until well after the event. Virus programs do not usually exist as separate programs on their own, they usually are hidden inside other programs, either deliberately concealed or masquerading as something else.

This point gives us another measure that you can take to avoid being affected...

2. Never run programs on your computer whose origin or integrity you cannot be one hundred per cent sure of.

Unfortunately, many 'first-timers' are not really aware of the damage that a virus can do, until they are forced to learn the hard way. This leads to the next measure that you can take to keep yourself out of trouble...

3. Install a special virus-checking program on your computer and making sure that this special program is always running as a 'background' program, for all of the time that your computer is switched on.

My own personal favourite virus-checking program is Norton's Anti-virus. This program is owned by the Symantec Corporation and you can find out more details from their website at **www.symantec.com**. These reason why I like the program is the ease with which it continuously upgrades itself to keep abreast of the latest virus threats. This is a very important consideration. Let us be sure we understand why this is important.

The way that a virus checker program works is as follows. Because a virus is a computer program, then like all other programs, it consists of a sequential string of coded numbers. If you could examine a portion of the code sequence – say the first fifty codes – then for a particular virus program, this sequence would be the same no matter where on a Hard Drive the virus was stored. By diligently inspecting all code sequences in every file upon the Hard Drive, a virus checker program can recognise where a virus exists. There are literally thousands of different viruses that have been maliciously created, so the virus checker program needs to keep a complete and up-to-date list of these code patterns, if it is going to be successful at detecting every virus that it may come across. This list is held in a file called the virus definitions file, and has to be updated almost daily if the virus checker program is to keep on top of the problem.

Getting back to my reason for liking the Norton Anti-virus program, I am very impressed by the way it makes these updates from the Internet automatically, without me having to worry about it. Not only will it update the virus definitions file, but it will also update the checker program itself and so the program designers can also make changes to the way the program works if need be.

Okay. Why is Email particularly vulnerable to viruses? The answer is in the similarity between the sequence of codes illustrated in our 'How are you?' example (given in section 1.2) and the sequence for a virus program. If an email can contain codes for a text message, there is no reason why someone could not clandestinely insert codes for a virus program. Should they be part of the normal message contents then you would quickly spot them as a garbled message when you received it. But if they are added into an attachment, then they may not be detected until it is too late.

There is also another way in which virus coding can be associated with an email. In exercise 18 (section 7.2), we demonstrated how the message body of an email can be 'livened up' using stationery. These 'fancy' emails are possible because the email body can contain other 'objects' besides simple text. You may indeed come across some very clever emails that contain all kinds of fancy flashing objects that have a cute appearance. Now these objects can behave in the manner of the classic 'Trojan horse'. Unknown to you, in addition to the code for the fancy 'flashing' appearance, they may contain virus code directly themselves, or they can link up to virus code that is somewhere else within the Internet – the code doesn't even have to be located upon your computer! Good heavens – how can you protect yourself against this type of menace?

Fortunately, an answer to this 'linking up elsewhere in the Internet' problem has been developed. It uses another new form of computer program referred to as a Firewall. We discuss the subject of the Firewall type of program in depth in the next section, so I will not repeat that information here. I will simply say that a Firewall acts as a 'blocking' program between your computer and the Internet to stop any information or action from the Internet-side of the 'firewall' interfering with your computer-side. A Firewall program can either run on a single computer installation – such as your home computer – or it may run on a separate computer, as you might find on an office network like those we met in section 2.7. This brings us to the next measure that you should observe...

4. Always use a Firewall program when you connect to the Internet.

Now the good news for those of you who have Windows XP is that there is a Firewall program included as part of the standard set of Windows programs. Those readers using earlier versions of Windows will have to purchase and install third party software. Another very good program that I can recommend is Norton Personal Firewall, which is part of a set of programs collectively known as Norton Internet Security.

9.2   I never knew they could do that!

The last section was about computer viruses and the precautions that you should take to protect your computer against malicious intent. This section is about 'hackers' and their malicious intent to your computer.

For those readers who may have heard the term but are not quite sure what a 'hacker' is and what they attempt to do, let us clarify the meaning. A hacker usually refers to a person who attempts to gain unauthorised access to a computer system. Now the traditional picture painted by the TV and film industry of a hacker is someone who sits glued to a keyboard for hours on end, often late at night or into the wee small hours of the morning, attempting to second guess a password to get access to highly secret information stored in a government or military computer. Yes, that is the traditional image, and yes, there are such people about. But the real threat to ninety-nine point nine per cent of computer systems in the world is not to a government or military computer. The most commonplace threat today is to your little humble home computer sat there in your bedroom or study, or that humble little office computer sat on a desk at work! How so? Let us investigate...

In the days before the Internet was invented, computer networks existed in isolation. The older fashioned design was for a centralised big computer located in a special air-conditioned room, and linked by private cables to human operators sat at 'terminals' (combined keyboard and monitor screens). These people would access the information held on the central machine. To do so, operators would first type in a username and password. If these were correct and currently valid, then they were allowed access and merrily away they would go, typing ten to the dozen.

As such computer systems became more widespread and stored more useful information inside them, so the need arose to gain remote access to this information. More often than not, this remote access was from a smaller out-lying office away from the main office block. This is where the use of the telephone network first began. Using modems twenty times the size of your current modem, and more than twenty times slower, remote terminals would dial up over the telephone system into the central computer room. Now it is using this new telephone access that the traditional image of the hacker was born – that spotty-faced youth sat at home in his bedroom, armed with a very early home computer and a second-hand modem. By guessing at the telephone number, the hacker would stumble upon a centralised computer system and try many ways to 'hack' the password.

This older fashion design was vulnerable to external hackers, but the solution employed for protection was quite simple. Instead of allowing remote users to simply dial into the system, the central office would suddenly disconnect the telephone line, and then dial them back again using a pre-determined telephone number for where the legitimate operator would be located.

Then came the Internet and suddenly the game changed. Instead of computers being centralised with remote terminals dialling into them, computers became distributed with permanently connected cables linking them together. Some of these cables are still privately owned and maintained, forming privately owned networks. But for greater access by more and more people, these private networks usually have a limited connection to the Internet network.

Take government networks for example. In order to allow the public to access government information directly, these central storage points of government information can be accessed from the Internet (via the World Wide Web service). To maintain this information as current, civil servants need access to the same computers from their desktops. Now for a limited time, some government departments tried to operate two separate computer systems. Some staff even had two computer screens and keyboards on their desks! But that proved to be short lived because information from one private system would eventually need to be transferred to another public system – and having two keyboards and screens on people's desks became a physical nightmare, not to say expensive.

To isolate the private network from the connection to the public Internet network, the **Firewall** was invented. For large office installations, this is often a separate computer that stands alone from all the others. It runs a special Firewall program, whose job is simply to connect up the two sides of the networks and provide the linking between them. It does this by interrogating information coming at it from either side and making a decision about whether this information should or should not be allowed through the link to the other side. This idea is illustrated in the next diagram.

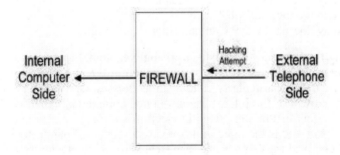

Here the diagram shows information flowing right to left. The private network is on the left, designated the Internal Computer Side. The public Internet network is on the right and designated the External Telephone Side. Information flowing into the private network has to pass through the Firewall. The same is also true of information flowing out of the private network in the opposite direction, though for clarity this is not shown in the diagram.

The Firewall program has a number of rules to determine if it should allow any piece of information to pass through it (in whichever direction that information is flowing). When a hacking attempt is made, the information comprising the attempt is tested to check for conformity with the rules. If it fails, then it is stopped dead in its tracks and entry is made in an internal log file to alert the administrator to the fact that the attempt was made.

Well you may ask, what has all this got to do with me and my humble little home computer connected to the Internet? Stay with me just for a moment longer and you will then see why.

To try and gain unauthorised access to computer systems, the hacker no longer randomly dials telephone numbers hoping to connect with a central office modem. Instead the hacker uses another principle – they try and guess the unique Internet addresses that are allocated throughout the world to individual computers. It is via these unique Internet addresses that your own computer is connected to the Internet through the ISP computer. Should the hacker accidentally stumble upon the unique address given to your system then they will attempt to hack into your computer! And this all happens without your knowledge! Seriously? Yes, seriously! If you don't believe it then you are in for a big shock.

It seems curious to me that many people are introduced to the Internet and it is never explained to them that a network is really a two-way highway. Information can normally pass in either direction. Just because you only physically witness the effects of your own actions, do not for one minute think that activity might not be going on that you cannot see and did not instigate.

When this fact is explained to many 'first timers' a few natural questions arise such as:

- Why would a hacker want to hack into my humble computer?
- Who are these people?
- Why doesn't the ISP Company stop it happening?

Answering the first question first, surprisingly enough, there are many reasons why **a hacker would want to access your computer**, not least of which is to steal information – particularly valid email addresses. One of the big problems facing the growth of the Internet is unsolicited commercial email (UCE). This is the equivalent of the 'junk mail' in electronic form. It is also known by the name of 'Spam' and is the topic of the next section. Now Spam can only be sent to a valid email address. If a hacker can steal a list of email addresses from, say, your address book, then they can use them directly themselves or sell these addresses to others.

Who are these people? This is the real eye-opener. When we connect to the Internet, we do so via an ISP Company that has its business in our own country.

It is not unnatural therefore to limit our thinking to hackers within our own society. The greatest surprise to me when I first saw the log files of hacking attempts into my own home computer was that they came from countries thousands of miles away. This is the bit that you tend to forget. When you connect to the Internet, you are connecting to a global system and it is just as easy to send information from Mogadishu to Mexico as it is from London to Leeds. The society where the hacker is based may have very different moral values to those of our own, and their economic plight may also be very different.

Why doesn't the ISP Company stop it happening? Well, the simple answer is that it is almost impossible for the ISP Company to know whether the information passing back and forth is legitimate or not. Only you yourself can really make that decision, but first you need to be aware that someone is attempting to make unauthorised access to your computer. This is where the Personal Firewall can help out, and the next diagram shows how this works.

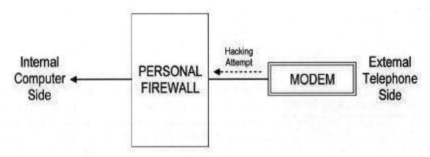

Here the Personal Firewall is another computer program running within your computer. From a theoretical point of view, it intercepts all of the information passing to or from the modem. You have control via the program of the rules governing the passage of information. Any unauthorised attempt to gain access to your computer system from outside will be flagged up for your attention.

Again for clarity, the above diagram shows information coming into the computer from the external source of the modem connection to the Internet, but the Firewall rules also govern any attempt to send information out of your computer back to the Internet. This could happen, for example, if a virus type object somehow gets deposited within your computer, and it attempts to export information clandestinely back to some other computer thousands of miles away via the Internet.

At the end of the last section, I mentioned that, if you are using Windows XP, then there is a Firewall built-in for you to use. Before we finish our discussion, it should be of interest to inspect your computer and check if this has been activated. If not then you can set it active. Users of other versions of Windows will have to install third party software such as the Norton Personal Firewall to get this form of protection.

Exercise 27 – Checking the Windows XP Firewall

This exercise can only be carried out by readers who are using the **Windows XP** operating system. However, readers who are using other versions of Windows may find it of interest to read through it for information purposes.

We start the exercise from the desktop and in the off-line state.

Click on the **Start** button and then select the **Control panel** option, as shown to the left.

You will then see the **Control Panel window** open. Search through all the icons until you find the **Network Connections icon...**

Double-click (or right-click and select '**Open**') on the Network Connections icon and you will see the **Network Connections window**, as shown on the right.

Mouse   Network Connections   Phone and Modem ...

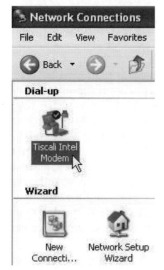

Take a little care here. You need to find the icon representing your active '**Dial-up connection**' and there may be more than one 'Dial-up' icon shown in the window. The active one is that one having a white 'tick' mark inside a small black circle placed on top of the icon picture (clearly visible in the picture to the left). Your icon will most certainly have a different label from the one shown here. When you have found it, right-click on it and select the **Properties option...** as shown here.

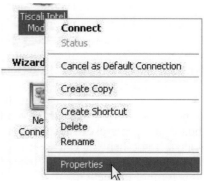

This should then open a Properties window looking similar to this next one...

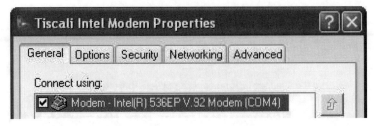

There are normally five Tab sheets for you to choose from in the Properties window. Click on the Advanced tab, as shown in the next picture.

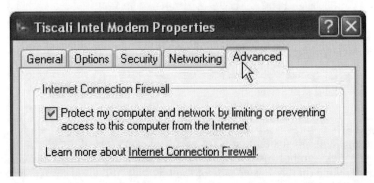

Okay. This is the place where you can inspect to see if the Firewall has been activated. If it has then you should see a 'tick' symbol inside the check box labelled 'Protect my computer and network etc.' If the **check box** is not ticked, then you are definitely at risk from a hacker and I strongly recommend that you set it now. To set it, click with the tip of the mouse pointer inside the check box.

If you would like to read more about the way that the Firewall operates, you can click on the underlined wording of 'Internet Connection Firewall', and a 'Help' window will pop up.

Now with the **Firewall** active, there are one or two further points you need to check. These concern the 'rules' that allow information to pass from one side of the Firewall to the other. At the bottom of the Properties window, press the **Settings** button...

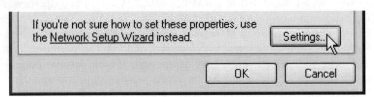

This will then show a list of the 'Services' that can be accessed from the Internet...

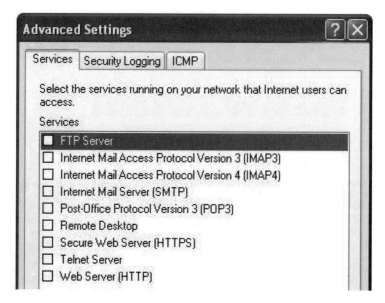

The normal and safest situation is for each and every one of the check boxes **not** to have a tick symbol inside them! This prevents any of these services being used by anyone on the remote side of the Firewall. It does not refer to your use of such services into the Internet.

If you do enable any of these services at any time then you should take great care to remember to disable them as soon as they are no longer required. For example, you may at some time be requested by a 'help line' operator (giving you support over the telephone) to enable the Remote Desktop service. They would do this to allow them to take control of your computer remotely, so that they can resolve a problem for you. When you have sorted things out with the help line, do make sure that this option gets reset back to the disabled state.

Okay. While we have the **Advanced Settings window** open, click on the **Security Logging tab**. This then reveals 'logging' (recording) controls as shown in the next picture over the page.

Essentially, what these 'logging' controls do is enable automatic recording of certain events as a line of text in a text file called '**C:\Windows\pfirewall.log**'. This file will be created for you and stored in the '**C:\Windows**' folder on your Hard Drive. The file can then be read at some later time using any normal text reader program, such as Notepad or Wordpad, and you can periodically inspect it to see if any unusual events have happened. If you do use one of these programs to look at it, make sure when you try to open the file that the '**File of type' box** is set to 'All files (*.*)'.

In the **Logging Options** control group, we see two check boxes associated with two types of events can be logged. The first one is 'Log dropped packets' and dropped packets are the 'packets' of information that will be dropped – that is, not allowed through the Firewall – originating from a sources such as hackers. By setting this check box you are only enabling the recording of any such occasions into the log file, you are not in any way enabling or disabling the ability of hackers to get through the Firewall. The second check box enables the recording of any successful connections that you may make through the Firewall in the opposite direction. For example, if you use the email program Outlook Express to connect with the Incoming mailbox of your account with the ISP Company, then the establishment of such a connection, and its later disconnection (see section 1.3 for the theory of this) is recorded in the log file. This can tell you if any software internal to your computer is performing such activity without your knowledge, as can happen if a virus program inadvertently gets deposited in your computer.

The **Size limit**: control prevents the size of this log file from growing indefinitely. If you leave this logging option running, then without a size limit the file could potentially grow to an unacceptable size. When the file reaches this size limit, then the latest events will be logged to the file whilst the earlier events are discarded. The default file size is 4096 Kilobytes (4.096 Megabytes), and is ample for normal purposes.

Let us now have a quick look at the contents of such a log file and see what kind of information it records. For most readers the details will not mean a great deal, so we will not describe it in detail. The next picture was created using the Notepad program to open the log file.

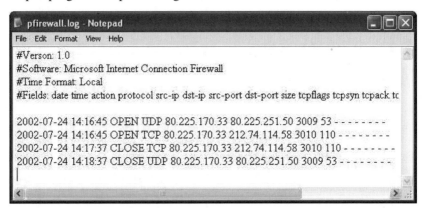

The first four lines are standard headers created once when the file is first created. Then comes a blank line, followed by the lines of text representing individual events. If we have a look at the first event line it shows us the date and time followed by an action (OPEN) then some gobbledygook that is beyond the scope of this book.

For the 'first timer', once the Firewall is activated then you are generally safe from the threats that we have discussed in this section, so you can in general ignore this information. However, if you are interested to see what a 'hacking' event looks like then you should keep an eye out for an action called 'DROP'. If you see any line in this file that shows 'DROP' after the date and time, then this is a record of an unauthorised packet of information being 'dropped' by the Firewall. The set of four numbers following the action is the Internet address of the computer responsible and you can trace the owner of this address if you want to.

Note – For those interested, the set of four numbers separated by dots (e.g. 80.225.170.45) are uniquely allocated as Internet addresses throughout the world. They are sometimes referred to as an IP address, or domain address and you can see to whom a particular address is registered to at the web site called **www.checkdomain.com**

The fact that you see an event line with the action 'DROP' does not always mean that it was sent maliciously. It can of course be an accident where someone has typed an Internet Address wrongly and you are the unfortunate individual who has received the misdirected packet of information. Remember also that if you see such an event line then you are not to worry about it. The fact that it is in the log file shows you that the Firewall is doing its job correctly!

Another point to bear in mind is that the Internet address your computer uses is given to you by the ISP Company only temporarily for a particular on-line session. The next time you go on-line you will normally be given a different Internet address, so the chances of your receiving unauthorised packets from the same would-be 'hacker' is thereby reduced.

9.3   Spam, Spam and more Spam

Spam is a curious word in the email world. It is one of those commercial words that have become synonymous with a generic object. As 'Hoover' is to vacuum cleaners, so 'Spam' is to junk email. If you care to search on the 'World Wide Web' you will discover that the reason has to do with the Monty Python comedy team and a famous sketch where a group of Vikings chant the word incessantly, at ever increasing volume, and drown out normal conversation. The analogy with junk email is that when your email address becomes known amongst some commercial organisations then you will receive large amounts of unsolicited commercial email, which can eventually 'drown' your Inbox folder with a sea of unwanted material.

To help you tackle the problem of spam, the Outlook Express program has some built-in features:

- **Blocked Sender List** – This is a list of email addresses against which senders of incoming email can be checked. Emails from persons who are on the list are automatically placed in your 'Deleted Items' folder when they arrive and never appear in your 'Inbox' folder.
- **Message Rules** – These are rules that you create yourself. Whenever incoming email matches with these rules, then some action is automatically taken.

We will have a look at the Blocked Sender List in the next exercise, and follow this with another one to show how to create a message rule.

Exercise 28 – Adding to the Blocked Sender List

We start the exercise with **Outlook Express** open and in the on-line state. As before, the **Folders sub-window** needs to be visible. Click on **Tools** from the main menu bar, and select the **Message Rules** option then the **Blocked Senders List...** option.

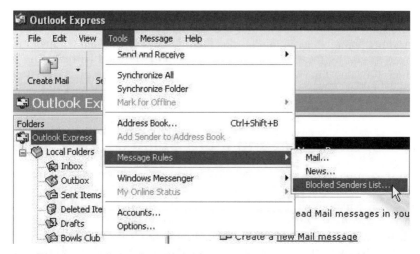

This will pop up a dialog box like this next picture. Press the **Add** button...

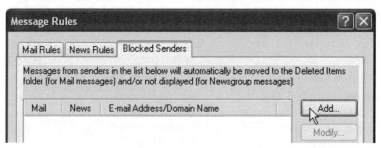

And then we see the **Add Sender window**.

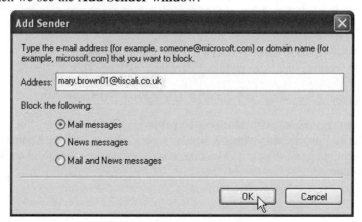

Now in the **Address: textbox** type <u>your own email address</u> then press the **OK** button. This saves the blocked sender's email address to the internal list. You will then see this list looking something like this next picture.

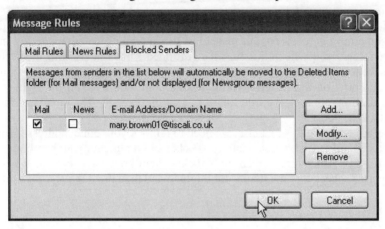

Press the **OK** button to close the window and you are back to the main window for Outlook Express.

Okay. From this moment onwards, any email that is received by you from this sender will not appear in your Inbox folder but immediately transferred to the **Deleted Items** folder. To illustrate this we will now create an email and send it to ourselves.

From the toolbar, click on the **Create Mail** button (New Mail button for users of version 5) and fill it out in the following manner but <u>use your own email address</u> in the **To: textbox**.

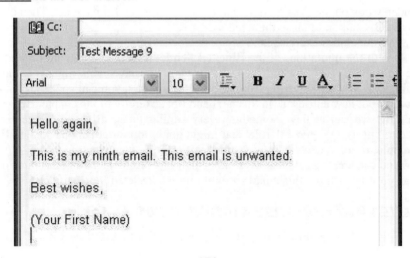

Then click on the **Send** button. The email then gets placed in the **Outbox folder** and providing you are still on-line, after a few seconds, the email will then be sent into the Internet via the ISP computer. Wait until the Outbox folder becomes empty again.

Now click on the **Send/Receive** button from the toolbar and you should see that something is received, but instead of this incoming email appearing in the Inbox folder, you will notice that it is dropped immediately into the Deleted Items folder. This is evident by the number '(1)' showing in the folder name.

Click now on the **Deleted Items folder**, and then over on the right in the upper section, click on the title line for 'Test message 9'. The email did indeed get blocked.

Before we leave this exercise, we need to remove your email address from the **Blocked Sender List**. Click again on **Tools** from the main menu bar, and select the **Message Rules** option then the **Blocked Senders List...** option. When the list appears, check that the item is highlighted and then press the **Remove** button.

You will then see a message asking if you are sure you want to remove the sender. Click on the 'Yes' button and it will be removed from the list. Then click on the **OK** button to close the window.

This concludes exercise 28.

One of the limitations of the **Blocked Sender List** is that you are limited in the total number of blocked senders that you may have. This limit is twenty-eight, so if you are suffering from a lot of 'spam' then you can soon run out of space to put new entries in. In this next and final exercise of the chapter, we will see how we can achieve something very similar to the Blocked Sender List feature but using a general 'rule' that might apply to more than one sender. For example, if you receive a lot of spam email offering you a loan for a house or a car. You can create a rule that says 'any email message content that has the word 'loan' in it then throw this email straight into the 'Deleted Items' folder'.

Exercise 29 – Creating a message rule

As with the last exercise, we start this one with **Outlook Express** open and in the on-line state. The **Folders sub-window** needs to be visible. Click on **Tools** from the main menu bar, and select the **Message Rules** option then the **Mail...** option, as in this next picture.

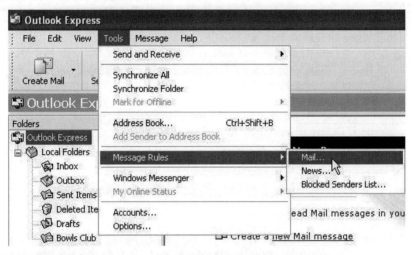

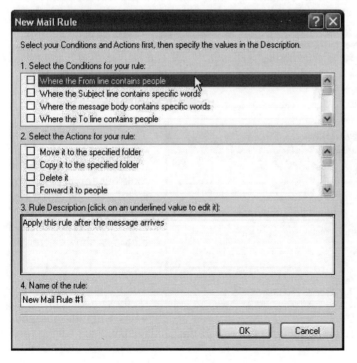

This will norm-ally bring up the **New Mail Rule window**, but only if there are no rules already set (if there are any set then press the **New** button on the **Message Rules window** that you will see appear instead).

Okay. The way that a rule is created is in three simple steps.

First we set the 'Conditions'. Move the tip of the mouse pointer over the check box labelled 'Where the message body contains specific words' and make a click...

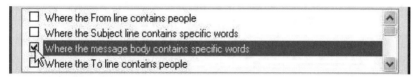

Second we set the 'Actions'. Move the tip of the mouse pointer over the check box labelled 'Delete it' and make a click...

Finally we specify the value for the 'Description'. Move the tip of the mouse pointer over the wording 'contains specific words'. Notice that the pointer icon now changes to a 'hand'. Make a click...

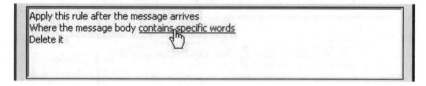

This pops up a new window where we type the word that we want to look out for in the spam email. In the first text box, type the word 'loan' and then press the Add button as shown here.

This then clears this textbox and shows the word in the second textbox.

Though we are only going to search for just the one word, you may in the future want to create rules that search for more than one word. It is at this point where you could add further words if you wanted to. You would simply type the next word and press the **Add** button again. You can do this for several words and build up a number of words, any one of which will activate the rule if they are present in the incoming email. The **Options** button allows you to then to make even more clever rules such as combinations and permutations of the words that you have entered.

We have no further words to add, so press the OK button, as shown in the next picture.

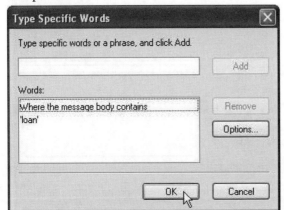

This closes the **Type Specific Words** window and returns you to the **New Mail Rule** window. Notice now that the wording in the 'Description' textbox has changed to 'contains 'loan''. In a quirky form of English, the rule description is now complete and you may read it literally to get the overall gist of what the rule is about.

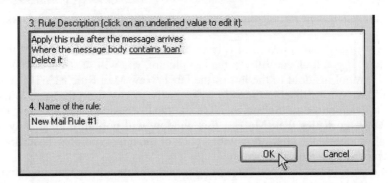

Press the **OK** button to close the **New Mail Rule window** and this then pops up the **Message Rules** window, to show you the list of all rules that are currently in force…

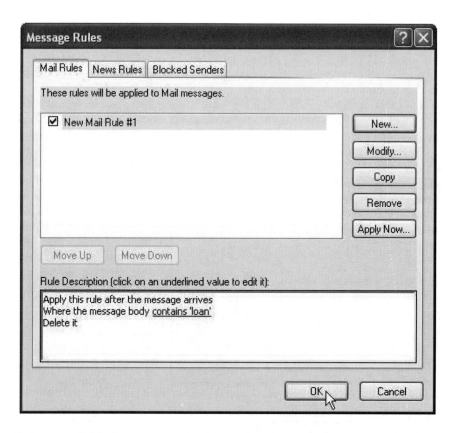

Before we finish this process of rule creation, let me point out a useful tip for the future. If you look carefully at the last picture, you will see a check box with a 'tick' symbol inside it to the left of the label 'New Mail Rule #1'. This check box allows you to disable the rule temporarily at any time that you want to without deleting the rule altogether. On the next occasion that you click **Tools** then **Message Rules** then **Mail...**, this window will pop up immediately, and you can 'uncheck' the check box with a click of the mouse pointer. To enable the rule again you do the same actions.

You can also have several rules in force at the same time. From this window, you simply press the **New** button and you can make another rule, independent of the first rule. We will keep our exercise simple and move now to the testing phase to see how it works. Click on the **OK** button at the bottom of the window, and it will return you to the Outlook Express main window.

From main window, click on the **Create Mail** button again (New Mail button for users of version 5) and fill out the new email in the manner of the next picture but <u>use your own email address</u> in the **To: textbox...**

Then click on the **Send** button. The email then gets placed in the **Outbox folder** and providing you are still on-line, after a few seconds, the email will then be sent into the Internet via the ISP computer. Wait until the Outbox folder becomes empty again.

Now click on the **Send/Receive** button from the toolbar and you should see that something is received, but instead of this incoming email appearing in the Inbox folder, you will again notice that it is dropped immediately into the **Deleted Items** folder. This is evident by the number '(1)' showing in the folder name.

Click now on the **Deleted Items** folder, and then over on the right in the upper section, click on the title line for 'Test message 10'. The email did indeed match the rule we created.

Having completed the exercise and demonstrated that the rule works fine, it is your decision now whether you want to leave this rule in operation or remove it. If you do wish to remove it, click again on **Tools** from the main menu bar, and select the **Message Rules** option then the **Mail...** option. When the list of message rules appears, check that the item is highlighted and then press the **Remove** button.

You will then see a message asking if you are sure you want to remove the rule. Click on the 'Yes' button and it will be remove from the list. Then click on the OK button to close the window.

This concludes exercise 29.

10

Using Webmail

10.1 Using email anywhere in the world

In the preceding chapters, we have been accessing the email delivery service using an email reader program – Outlook Express – running on a personal computer from our home or the office. Historically, this is the conventional way that the service first developed, and I would guess is still the most widely used method today. However, with the advent of the 'World Wide Web' service, there is a new way to use the email service known as Webmail and it has some advantages over the conventional method that are worth investigating.

Webmail does not use an email reader program. It uses a browser program (such as Internet Explorer), which is the type of program needed for viewing web pages from the 'World Wide Web' service. Now, because Webmail uses a browser program, it immediately offers two significant advantages:

- First, it is very simple to use.
- Second, you can use it from any computer (such as those in an Internet café) anywhere in the world.

The first advantage of simplicity stems from the fact that you have no specialised email set-up actions to perform with respect to your own personal computer. If your browser program is working to provide you with the 'World Wide Web' service, then you can start using email immediately.

The second advantage arises out of the first one. If there are no specialised email set-up actions to perform on the computer you are using, then you can use any computer, absolutely anywhere in the world that has a connection capability into the Internet. This could be a friend's computer, an Internet café or even a computer in a public library.

The email service that you use with Webmail is exactly the same delivery service as accessed with the conventional method using Outlook Express; it is not a different service. If you send an email to someone, then it will not be evident whether you sent it using Webmail or whether you used the conventional

181

method. You can indeed use both methods interchangeably and in some circumstances this is a good and desirable way to work.

There are differences between the two methods of using email, and whether these differences are important to you depends on other factors. We discuss these differences later in section 10.3, when we investigate how Webmail works.

Probably the most significant point about Webmail for all users of email is the fact that you can use it anywhere, even when you are on holiday. Although I am firm believer that holidays should be kept free from the normal daily grind, there are occasions when you need to keep in touch with friends or relatives. In our modern world of global travel, contact methods such as the telephone are not always convenient. Not everybody in the UK appreciates a phone call from Australia in the small hours of the morning! But email is a fantastic way of 'time-shifting' your communication, and using Webmail you can do this without having to carry a computer around with you. All you need do is walk into an Internet café, or in many places these days – a public library, and you can access your same ISP account that we discussed in chapter 1.

To learn how you use Webmail, we shall now undertake a few more exercises.

10.2 Using Webmail

In the following examples, I am going to use Webmail via the Tiscali UK ISP service. Your own ISP Company should be able to provide you with a comparable service, and if not then I would recommend that you change your ISP Company! Obviously, if you are using a different company, then the precise method of using their Webmail service will differ somewhat in presentation, and you will have to make your own interpretation for your own situation. Quite often, companies will use the words 'Mail' and 'Email' interchangeably, so if you are searching to find Webmail with a different ISP company, you may need to click on a button labelled 'Mail' rather than 'Email'.

The browser program that I am going to use is **Internet Explorer**, which is one of the standard Windows programs normally available on Windows style computers. You may use any other browser program that you have installed, and again, you will have to make your own interpretation of my instructions for your own browser program during the exercise.

Before you start the next exercises, you will need to know the home page address of your ISP Company. For those readers who are new to using a browser program, this is something that looks like '**www.tiscali.co.uk**', which is the Tiscali UK home page address.

Exercise 30 – Sending and receiving via Webmail

Start your browser program running. For Internet Explorer, you can do this with a click on icon located on the taskbar as shown in the next picture.

We need to be on-line to the Internet, so if a Dial-up Connection is not made automatically, then enter your Username and Password at the prompt and press the Connect button to get connected.

Note – For those readers who have not followed the exercises using Outlook Express, if you need help with connecting, you can read exercise 1 in section 2.3 and substitute the use of the browser program for the email program.

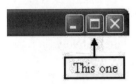

If the browser window is not maximised to fill the whole monitor screen then click on the maximise button (shown here) to make it so.

Often, the first page shown within the browser on start-up is the 'home page' for your ISP Company and this is the web page that we need to be able to view. How can you tell if it is the home page? Well, somewhere it should say so, like the browser title bar shown here...

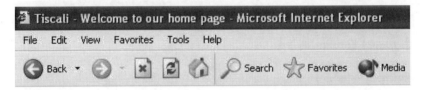

If your browser is not showing your ISP Company's home page then you will need to enter the home page address into the Address textbox and then action the browser to display it. If you are familiar with using a browser and entering a web page address then go ahead and do so now, and skip the next four paragraphs.

For those readers new to using a browser program, the complete address for a web page consists of a prefix of 'http://' then immediately followed by what I call the www wording (the bit that looks like 'www.tiscali.co.uk'). With most browsers these days, you can simply enter the www wording and the prefix will be added for you automatically, when you action the browser to display the page.

To enter an address into a browser, first click once on the existing wording shown in the Address textbox to highlight the whole of it, as shown in this next picture.

Then type exactly the www wording for the new home page address (the bit that looks like 'www.tiscali.co.uk') at the keyboard. When you type the first letter, all the previously highlighted lettering should disappear. Don't worry about typing the 'http://' bit – that should be added automatically for you in a moment. Be careful to enter the full stops, but note that there isn't one at the very end. Some new page addresses do not have 'www' at the start of the wording so don't worry if you have been given an ISP home page address that does not.

When you have finished typing, press the **ENTER** key on the keyboard in order to action the browser to display the new page, or alternatively, you can click on the **Go** button, as shown here. This button is at the right-hand edge of the **Address textbox**.

If all is well, you should then see your ISP home page appear in the browser window in similar manner to that shown here (notice how the 'http://' prefix was added automatically):

Now when you are viewing the ISP home page, you should be able to see a button somewhere on the page to click on, labelled 'Email' (or 'Mail'). When you have located it, move the tip of the mouse pointer over it and make a click, as shown in the next picture (notice how the pointer icon changes to a 'hand' symbol for buttons that you can press).

This will then automatically re-direct your browser to view the services login page for the ISP Company, as shown in the following picture.

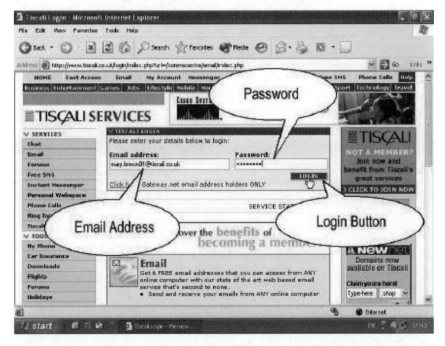

Here you simply type in your email address and password, and then press the 'Login' button. This should then bring up your email page, as shown in the picture overleaf.

Note -If you have difficulty logging in, it may be the case with your ISP Company that you only need to enter the 'Name' part of your email address, rather than the full address. Also, remember that passwords are case sensitive (use of capital or non-capital lettering) so check that the Caps Lock feature is not on (see Exercise 1, section 2.3 for more about Caps Lock).

Okay, looking at this email page, you can see a line above centre like this one.

The wording 'FOLDERS >> Inbox' on this line is telling us that we are actually looking at the Webmail Inbox folder on this page, and lower down we see…

This informs us that there are no emails waiting to be read in this folder. Your own monitor display may show an email, but if it does then for the purpose of this exercise you can ignore it for now.

Now the first thing that we are going to do is to create an email and send it. Using the mouse pointer, find and press the button labelled 'WRITE MAIL', as shown here.

This will bring up a new page to allow you to create an email. Carefully fill it out with the details shown, but use your own email address in the **To textbox …**

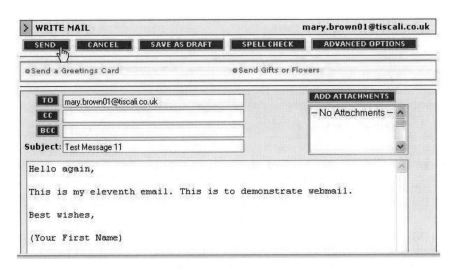

Check again that you have <u>your own email address</u> in the **To textbox**, and then press the **Send** button.

Your email is now on its way through the Internet and a confirmation message usually pops up like this next picture...

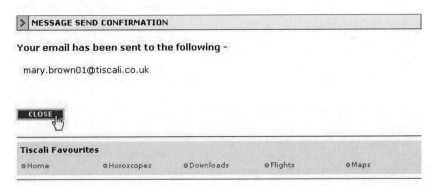

Press the **Close** button as shown and the browser will return to the Inbox folder. That is all there is to sending a simple email. It is very easy to do using Webmail.

When the browser window returns to the Inbox folder, you should see that the email has arrived and is sat there waiting for you, as in this next picture...

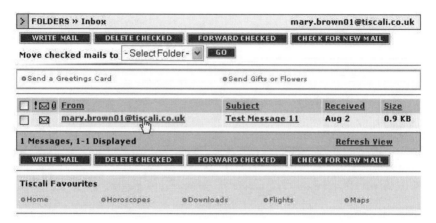

Click either the email address in the **From** column (see the 'hand' in the previous picture), or the email title in the **Subject** column and the email will be opened so that you can read it, as in the following picture...

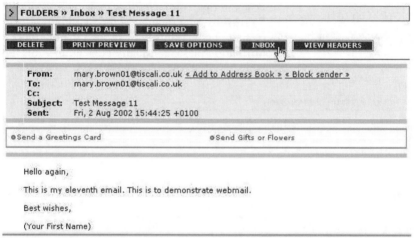

To go back to the **Inbox folder**, press the **Inbox** button as shown above.

This concludes exercise 30. If you wish to proceed immediately with the next exercise then leave your browser program open and connected on-line, or else close the browser window and press the **Disconnect Now** button on the **Autodisconnect** message box to disconnect from the Internet.

Exercise 31 – Sending and receiving attachments via Webmail

We begin this exercise with the browser program running and connected on-line to the Internet. If you have not followed on from the previous exercise, then repeat the starting procedure described for exercise 30 to become connected, until you reach the Email page and the Inbox folder.

Using the tip of the mouse pointer, press the Write Mail button...
This will bring up another new page to allow you to create an email. Now carefully fill it out with the details shown, but use your own email address in the **To textbox** ...

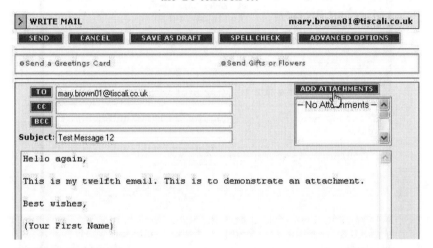

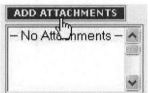

Check again that you have your own email address in the **To textbox**, and then press the **Add Attachments** button as shown here.

This will bring up a new window like the one over the page.

The first thing we see here is that there are no attachments currently attached to the email. We then see a list of four steps to follow in order to attach a file. We now carry out these steps:

Step 1. - This specifies the name and location of the file that we wish to attach. There is a **Browse** button provided to make it easy to pick out the file that we wish to select, but for convenience in this exercise we shall simply type the name and location of our attachment directly into the specifying textbox instead. Click with the tip of the mouse pointer inside the white **textbox** just to the left of the **Browse** button, and then type at the keyboard the following line exactly as shown ...

c:\windows\backgrnd.gif.
(This is a picture type file that should be available on all Windows computers.)

If you make a mistake during typing, you can use the **Delete** key or the **Backspace** key to rub out the error. The last picture shows you what your typing should look like.

Step 2. - When you have completed your typing, use the tip of the mouse pointer to press the **Attach** button (also shown in the last picture). Now there will be a slight delay here once the button has been pressed. What is happening during this delay is that the file specified for the attachment is being copied from your own Hard Drive across the dial-up connection to the ISP computer. Keep an eye on the list of attached files shown at the top of the window. When the copying process is complete, then the list will change to include the new file, like this...

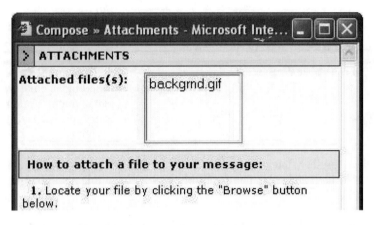

Step 3. - At this point, if you wanted to add more attachments to the created email then you could repeat steps 1 and 2 in order to do so. For this exercise, we will be content with just the one attachment.

Step 4. - Finally, press the **Done** button to close the window...

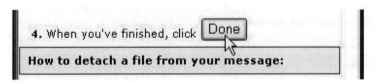

Now when we return to inspect the created email, as in the next picture, we can see that the attachment list over on the right-hand side shows the name of the file that we specified.

Press the **Send** button as shown above, and the email will now be sent to the Internet (as seen in the confirmation)...

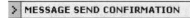

MESSAGE SEND CONFIRMATION

Your email has been sent to the following -

mary.brown01@tiscali.co.uk

Press the Close button as shown and the browser will return to the Inbox folder.

That is all there is to sending an email with an attachment. Again, it is very easy to do using Webmail.

When the browser window returns to the **Inbox folder**, you should see that the email has arrived and is sat there waiting for you, as in this next picture...

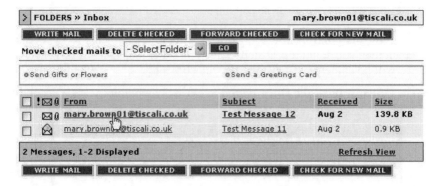

Notice in the last picture that this email has a 'paper-clip' icon in the 'paper-clip' column, indicating that it contains an attachment.

Okay. Using the mouse pointer, click on either the email address in the **From** column (see the 'hand' in the previous picture), or the email title in the **Subject** column and the email will be opened so that you can read it, as in the top picture over the page.

At the very bottom of the picture, we can see the 'paper-clip' icon again and the name and size of the file attachment. Click on the underlined name as shown and this opens the attachment so that we can view it, as in the lower picture opposite.

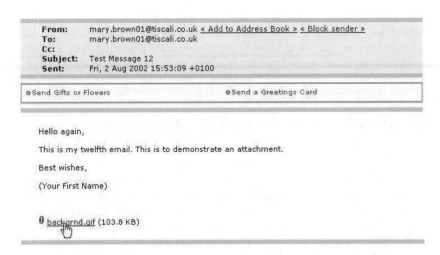

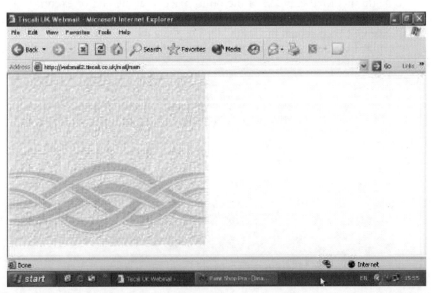

The attachment that we made is simply a pattern picture, but it demonstrates that you can view the standard picture files (those of type .gif or .jpg) inside the browser window, as well as read the text of an email message. If someone sent you a digital photograph, you would be able to immediately view it in this way.

Okay. Let us review what we have achieved so far in Webmail. We have created an email, made an attachment to it and sent it. Now we have received the email and viewed the attachment.

We will conclude exercise 31 at this point. For those readers interested in learning how to detach a Webmail attachment (saving it as a separate file stored somewhere upon your own Hard Drive) then proceed immediately to exercise 32. Otherwise, close your browser window with the **Close** button in the top right-hand corner, and press the **Disconnect Now** button on the **Autodisconnect** message box to disconnect from the Internet.

Exercise 32 – Detaching Webmail attachments

Detaching 'attachments' is a little bit of a misnomer. It does not usually take away the actual attachment from the incoming email as you might think it should. What really happens is that a copy of the attachment is made and stored somewhere else where you specify. This is not just an academic point, but an important one should you ever lose, damage or change the 'detached' copy. For then you can normally go back and 'detach it' for a second time. You will then have another copy just as it was originally received.

We begin this final exercise at the point reached at the end of exercise 31 – that is viewing the attachment. If you have not followed on immediately from the last exercise then repeat the latter steps to view the attachment.

Now place the mouse pointer anywhere over the viewed image itself and make a right-click...

From the pop-up menu, select the **Save Picture As...** option and this will bring up a dialog box to allow you to save a copy of the attachment, as shown in the next picture.

Note – With a different ISP Company, the exact wording for saving the attachment may be different from that demonstrated here. Using a right-click over the picture, there should be some option from the pop-up menu to allow you to do it.

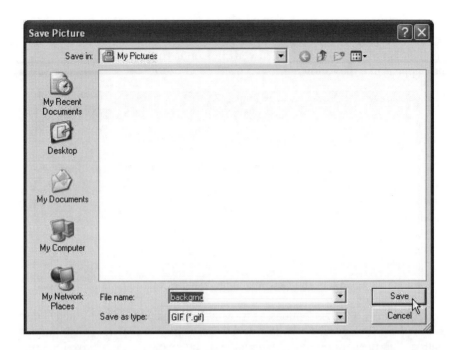

Readers using Windows XP computers will be offered the folder 'My Pictures' as the default folder in which to save the copy of the attachment. Those using earlier versions of Windows will probably see 'My Documents'. You can change the folder to be any that you wish by clicking on the 'down arrow' shown at the top of the picture in the **Save in: box**. You may also rename the copy in the **File name: box** if you choose. It is unwise to change the file type in the **Save as type:** box because your computer (and yourself) may become confused. When you are ready click on the **Save** button, and the file will be saved to the specified location. Again, there will be a delay here because the file is being copied from the ISP computer down the modem dial-up connection into your computer.

When the saving is finished, the window will close and you will view the picture image again in the browser window. You then need to use the **Back** button on the browser program's toolbar (at the top of the browser window) to return to the email message, as shown here.

When you are back at the email message, press the Inbox button to take you back to the Inbox folder.

Before we end this exercise, it may be worthwhile just mentioning how you go about detaching an attachment to an email that is not a

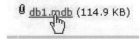

picture file. The last picture shows an attachment that is a database file as used by the Microsoft Access program, called 'db1.mdb'. If you should receive any file that is not a picture file, when you click on it you will see another message box appear like the following...

You then have different options as to what to do next. To make a copy of the attached file (in the same way that we did for the picture file) then press the **Save** button. You then are presented with a dialog box similar to the 'Save Picture...' one, and you can save the file in any folder you wish. Again, there is likely to be a delay while the file is downloaded to your computer. If you press the **Open** button instead, then your computer will attempt to open the file together with the associated program relevant to the file type. For example, with a .mdb file, then your computer will attempt to open the Microsoft Access program. It can only do this if you have this program installed on your computer.

This concludes exercise 32. Close the browser window and press the **Disconnect Now** button on the **Autodisconnect** message box to disconnect from the Internet.

10.3 How Webmail works

The previous section was concerned with the use of Webmail. In this section, we review how it actually works. You may then be clear about the difference between the Webmail and the conventional email principles. This leads us to some important security considerations about using Webmail that you should be aware of.

With conventional email – that is, using an email reader program such as **Outlook Express** – the ISP computer acts only as an intermediary in the delivery service. It is a relay in a delivery chain, and your own computer is the terminus point where incoming emails finally end up.

With Webmail, the ISP computer behaves as the terminus point and incoming emails do not travel any further. They are stored on the ISP computer. When you read Webmail with a browser program such as Internet Explorer, you are effectively using the browser computer as a viewing device with which to observe the internal content of your account on the ISP computer. You can use the browser from anywhere, such as in an Internet café in another country. Putting this another way, it is as if the browser was acting for you as a 'telescope', able to see inside the ISP computer from as far away as the other side of the world...

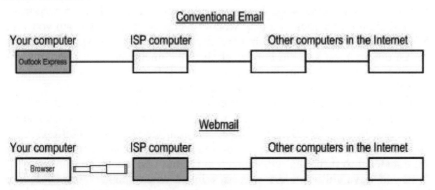

In the above diagrams, the grey shading represents the 'end-point' for incoming emails. This highlights the important difference between the two approaches – the location of where incoming emails terminate.

Now a reasonable question to ask is 'If Webmail works anywhere, then why bother at all with conventional email? Why not use it from home?' The answer is that some people do exactly that – they find it convenient to use a browser program for all their Internet activity, including email. The reason why conventional email exists is partly historical in that it was invented a long time before Webmail. But there are also the questions of performance and control that differentiate the two systems.

One of the reasons why personal computers became popular in the mid-eighties is that, as the user, you alone have use of the processor chip inside your own computer. All of the computing power inside the machine is applied to the tasks that you want to perform, and it is not shared with the tasks of others. Consequently, the response times to your mouse or keyboard are normally very short. When you are manipulating objects such as files, or folders and the like, fast response times are an important consideration. With conventional email, you get this benefit of personal computing and its rapid responses. With Webmail on the other hand, you are very much dependant on the ISP computer and the speed of your modem dial-up connection. It is likely that many others are using the ISP computer at the same time that you are, and consequently it has much more work to do. The response times therefore with Webmail can be much slower, particularly at times of peak usage.

The control aspect is another important human consideration. If email is delivered to your doorstep as with conventional email, then you make the decisions about how long to keep it before deleting it, and how backup copies are made in case of an emergency. With Webmail you are to some extent in the hands of a third party; you must trust them not to delete items before you are ready and to keep them secure.

Another aspect of Webmail that some people find confusing concerns attachments. If someone sends you an attachment to an email, say for example, a digital photograph, then you may wonder where on earth it is when you want to print it out. The important point to realise becomes obvious when you look at the last diagram – if you did not detach the attachment and save it to your own computer, then it will remain stored inside the ISP computer, so no amount of searching the Hard Drive of your own computer will ever find it!

You can save email received via Webmail to your computer should you wish to, but you have to make a conscious decision to do so. If you look back at the last picture in exercise 30, you will see a button labelled **Save Options** to the left of the **Inbox** button. You use this button in order to make a copy of the email and transfer it over the dial-up connection to your own computer.

If you have followed the exercises in previous chapters using Outlook Express, then when you next go on-line via this method (conventional email) you are in for a bit of a surprise. The two emails that we created in this chapter using Webmail will suddenly be transferred to your Outlook Express Inbox folder. To understand why this happens we need to return to the conventional email diagram.

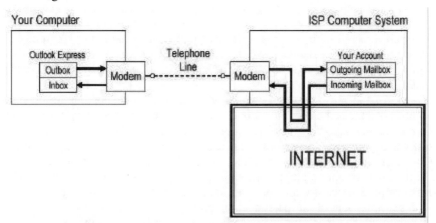

You may remember from chapter 1 that in order to use the email delivery service, you need to subscribe to an ISP company (the Internet Service

Provider). In exchange for your subscription payment, the ISP Company will provide you with an account on their computer system that consists of **Incoming** and **Outgoing Mailboxes** and we see these in the diagram. In particular, the Incoming Mailbox acts as a temporary storage place for your incoming emails when you are not connected on-line to the Internet.

Now, when you are using Webmail, you are using a web page service via a browser on your computer. The web page service uses the same **Incoming Mailbox** as its **Inbox** folder. Consequently, if you can see mail sat in the Webmail Inbox folder, you are actually viewing the internal contents of the Incoming Mailbox, and the conventional email service will transfer these to **Outlook Express** in the normal way if you are running this program and connected on-line.

After you have used Outlook Express, you can then close the program down and start up a browser program. When you then view the Webmail service for a second time, you will discover that the Inbox folder is empty! The reason simply being that it was automatically deleted from there when you made contact using Outlook Express.

This point now brings us to the issue of using these two services collaboratively. It matters not whether you read your email in the conventional way, or with Webmail service. You are going to see exactly the same incoming emails whichever way you do it. If you are at home or in the office, you can use conventional email and get the benefits of personal computing together with storing your emails on your own Hard Drive. If you are away from your computer on holiday or on business, then you can use the Webmail service, and you can do this from anywhere in the world!

10.4 Be careful with your password

The Webmail service is a brilliant concept, and a major step forward in the utility value of the email delivery service. But its simplicity of operation carries with it a potential risk that you would be wise to keep in mind – even if you yourself do not use the service.

If you can access your email account anywhere in the world – knowing only your username and password – then so can anyone else. Therefore it is important your password remains confidential and is not disclosed to anyone else. If you suspect that it has been compromised then change it as soon as possible.

There are some measures you can take yourself to help protect your account from unauthorised use. When you choose a password, the longer that you can make it, the better. Most systems have limits on these items, so obviously there are choices that you will not be allowed to use. We have stressed throughout this book that passwords are normally case-sensitive, that is, there is a difference between capital and non-capital letters. One way that you can make it more difficult for someone to get unauthorised access to your account would be to mix them up. For example, if you want to use 'tarantula' as a password, why not decide on some letters to be capitals 'tarAntuLa'. Then even if someone learns your password name, it would take a lot of guesswork to figure out which letters are to be entered as capitals and which are not.

Now the problem with all these ideas, particularly for older folk like myself, is that one's memory cannot be trusted. Some information technology experts will warn you not to write these down on paper. My answer to them is simply 'Wait until you become a pensioner, and then try tell me not to write things down!' A very simple idea you can use to overcome the worries of writing a password down is to write your password on paper and use a sealed envelope to enclose it. Then write your signature over the flap, so that you can tell if someone else has opened it. Place the sealed envelope in a safe place. If you run a business and have an office safe, then store it in the safe. If you need to remind yourself of the password, tear it open, read it and destroy it. Then create a new sealed envelope.

There are many other ideas that you can use to disguise your password, and I am sure that you can think of some of your own.

Now one other point that is not so obvious when entering a password on someone else's computer, is that it is possible to include software running on a computer that memorises the keystrokes that are entered at the keyboard. Now I don't wish to raise un-necessary alarm, but be aware that this is technically possible. As electronic information becomes more and more valuable, there are unscrupulous organisations that may gain commercial advantage by recording information that they should not. My advice is simply to always be careful and watch out for the small signs that usually tell you something out of the ordinary has happened.

10.5 Concluding remarks

I should like to end this chapter, and the book itself, by recanting a few personal thoughts and experiences to you about using email.

The power of email as a tool in the 21st century is beginning to make itself apparent all over the world. It is without doubt a very powerful tool and as with any powerful tool, you must be careful how you use it. I read recently some advice on the subject that advocated never saying anything in an email that you would not want to say to someone face to face. I endorse that sentiment entirely, but I would also go one stage further. There are some things that you should say face to face, and not use email. If you have an unpleasant conversation that you must conduct with someone, then I do not recommend using email as a substitute.

You must also be careful not to convey a wrong idea unintentionally using email. It is very easy for someone reading your email to misinterpret the feelings and sentiment that you had when you wrote it. Remember that you don't always have to send an email at the instant when you write it. If you are using Outlook Express, then you can always save a composition to the drafts folder, and sleep on the idea overnight before finally sending it.

In writing this book, I have used it extensively to make contacts that I never expected to make when I first had the idea to write it. Some weeks ago, I made contact with a person in the USA, from my base within the UK. Before I sent my email, I never knew that this person existed – I did not know the person's name or anything about him. By being polite and courteous, I gained the trust of the individual and kindly received help with some technical enquiries. Now it may be argued that I could have done the same thing by telephone. I do not believe that this is true. One of the big benefits of email is that you can 'time-shift' communication, and I am not just talking about the clock in different parts of the world, although this is certainly a big help. I mean that if you ask for information, people can postpone responding to you when it is inconvenient for them to do so promptly. If they are busy with other important issues, then you can communicate with them without getting in the way. At a later time, when they have a bit more time to help you with your information, then they can respond in a much more positive manner.

I have also met a number of celebrities and personalities using email. Not everyone will respond to you, for considering the mountains of email that some people must receive, it surely would be impractical for them to reply to each and every one. But if they find your email interesting, and they have the will to send you a reply, then it is surprising who you can actually converse with.

Sadly, we have now reached the end of the second book in this 'First Time' series. Whichever direction you now care to take with your new skills and knowledge of email, I hope that you gain a great deal of fun and enjoyment from it. I have certainly enjoyed writing this book for you to learn from.

Appendix I

The Internet – what is it?

This is a simple question that deserves a simple answer. The Internet is a global mixture of long distance cables and computers connected together in such a way that computerised information can travel from anywhere to anywhere.

One of the best comparisons that can be made to understand the Internet is with the Telephone Network. As the Telephone Network is to voice, so the Internet is to computer information. The point of the Telephone Network is to allow public transmission of voice from any one place to any other place. The point of the Internet is to allow public transmission of computer information from any one place to any other place.

Not all of the cables within the Internet are of the same type and not all of the computers within the Internet are of the same type. Some may argue that radio waves should also be included in the mixture of cables and computers, and I would agree.

The word 'Internet' itself is a shortening of the words 'Inter Network', meaning between networks. The networks being referred to were originally computer networks owned by companies or organisations, and the idea was to link them together to share information. Many books on the subject of the Internet will tell you of its origins, beginning with the American Government Defense Department. I think that the basis of today's public Internet really began with the universities throughout the world, and their need to exchange information.

The comparison with the Telephone Network is particularly apt because we use a series of numbers (the 'phone number') to specify all of the destination places that we want to reach via telephone, and so it is with the Internet where we again use a series of numbers (the 'IP address' - pronounced 'eye-pee') to specify the destination places of the computers that we want to reach. To try and make life easier for humans, we don't normally think of the destination computer as a series of numbers. Instead we try and code these numbers with more meaningful combinations of letters, but that is purely for our own convenience. Ultimately, all of these letter codes have to be converted back to the series of numbers for the Internet to operate with.

There are two forms of coding that you may often see today, but these forms are changing fairly quickly and if we attempted to define these forms absolutely then we would be out of date before we even got started. However, because these two forms are widely used at the present time, it is worth pointing them out and describing them. I hope that the purists amongst us will forgive me for the liberties that I shall take in the description, but my wish is to get the commonly held viewpoints across rather than being one hundred per cent academically accurate.

The two forms I want to emphasise are the two forms that you may commonly see painted on the side of a van or lorry these days. The first form of coding is what I call the 'www' wording or 'World-Wide-Web' wording. Not too long ago, the www wording would appear, for example, as 'www.brandname.com' but now you will see 'www.brandname.co.uk' or even 'www.brandname.co.de' and many other similar expressions. The second form of coding is the 'something@brandname.com', which is an email wording. This second form is discussed in detail in section 1.4.

The 'World-Wide-Web' service is a source of confusion for many people today. The reason for the confusion is that most people are not technical, and many find the new words, terms and services bewildering because they have never been properly introduced. The biggest confusion seems to be with the Internet itself and the 'World-Wide-Web'. And it is not hard to see why the confusion arises, because in terms of plain English they seem to refer to something very similar.

To try and make life simple, always think of the Internet in terms of the definition I gave at the start of this appendix – the Internet is the mixture of cables and computers – it is the infrastructure that lies at the fundamental heart of the invention. There are many different services that can be provided over the infrastructure, but you need the basic structure in place first before you can have the services provided over it. That structure is the Internet.

What is the 'World-Wide-Web'? The web is really a service provided over the Internet, just like email is a service, but a service of viewable 'pages'. To view web pages, you use a 'browser' program and you type in the 'www' wording in the address textbox of the browser window. Internet Explorer is a browser program provided by the Microsoft Corporation and is a standard part of the Windows software system. Originally, these pages were simple combinations of text and fixed graphics, supplying information much as a book page supplies it. However, they were designed with one important feature that made them very different from book pages, and also made them a huge success. This feature is called a 'hyperlink' and for the reader it is a method of jumping from a place on one 'page', to another place on a very different 'page' instantly. This jumping is the 'link' bit, and the instant jumping to maybe a very different page is the 'hyper' bit.

... taste the Colombian coffee beans ...

To illustrate this point about a hyperlink, let us take a practical example. Suppose we are using our browser program to view a page showing a company's product advertisement on coffee beans...In the text, there is information telling us the country of origin of the beans, and there is a 'hyperlink' on the word 'Colombian'. This is indicated by underlining and showing the word in a different colour. By moving the tip of the mouse pointer over this hyperlink, the pointer symbol changes to a hand. If you then click the mouse on this hyperlink, the page displayed in the browser changes to a different page about the country 'Colombia'...

COLOMBIA - A South American country producing coffee beans.

Now this second page may be held on a completely different computer system from the first page. It may not even belong to the company who owns the first page. It may even be held on a computer system at the other side of the world. The hyperlink allows you, the page viewer, to make this instant jump from one page to another, without having to know anything about where the second page is, or what its 'www' wording is. Shown in the picture of the second page is yet another hyperlink that can make an instant jump back to the first.

The World-Wide-Web service has developed considerably in terms of its features since it began. Moving coloured graphics and sounds are now commonplace in addition to text and fixed graphics. However, the hyperlink feature is still one of its most powerful.

There are many other services provided over the Internet besides the 'World-Wide-Web' service. The email delivery service is obviously another. These two services seem to be the most prominent ones from a commercial point of view.

Another service that you may use without realising it is the 'FTP' service (File Transfer Protocol service). This allows you to transfer a copy of a file from a remote computer to your own computer. The most common encounter people make with the FTP service is when they make a click with the mouse pointer on the name of a file appearing in a web page. Automatically, this click invokes the FTP service and the file transfer begins. This file transfer is also known as 'down-loading'.

Appendix II

Setting up a Modem for Use on a Computer

Setting up a modem for use on a computer can be a little tricky because there are different types of modems and many different manufacturers, some having their own installation procedures. If you can get an expert to install it for you then my advice is to do so. However, if you have no one at hand to help you, then this appendix will give you some guidance on the general procedure.

There are two important points to understand and observe before we begin:

1. **Always make sure that mains power is switched off at the wall socket before you start work on physically connecting the modem. Keep it switched off whenever the processor case is removed.**

2. **Be aware that static electricity from your body can damage either the modem or you computer. When physically installing it, try to 'earth' yourself by touching a large metal surface before you begin (for example, the rear of the processor case frame), and avoid shuffling your feet on the carpet or body movement on a chair (both of these can generate static). Also, be very careful not to touch the electronic components of an internal modem, or the connector strip on the bottom. Handle it by the metal faceplate and the top rear corner edge.**

With these two important points made, we are ready to begin our discussion. The first thing you should now do is read the Modem Installation Guide that came with the modem. Often a manufacturer will stipulate that actions must be performed in a certain order to get their modem working in the way that they intended. Their instructions take precedence over any advice given in this appendix. Having said this, sometimes you will receive a guide booklet that covers several models of modem that can be quite different. You then have the problem of deciding which model you have actually purchased, and this is not always obvious. If you have a problem, don't be afraid to ring the supplier and ask them to find out.

Today, there are two types of internal modem. One is known as a conventional or standard modem, having its own microcontroller on the modem card. The other is a cheaper variety known as a 'Win' modem ('Win meaning 'Windows'), relying on the computer's own processor chip to do the 'microcontroller function'. I have seen some other peculiar terminology used to describe these two types. You may see the conventional type referred to as 'controllerless' and the 'Win' type as 'host controlled'. What the manufacturers are trying to get at here is that a conventional modem has its own controller, so it is 'controllerless' in the sense that it does not need any help from the computer acting as a controller; and a 'host controlled' type is referring to the computer as the host, meaning that the computer is acting as a controller. The reason why I mention these facts is that the installation procedure can vary between these two types. My preference is to use a conventional modem and pay the extra cost. My experience is that they can both be easy to install, but if you have a problem to resolve then usually it is easier to sort out a conventional modem than it is for a 'Win' type modem.

All modems require 'driver' software to work with the Windows operating system. This is software that usually comes on a CD-ROM and has to be installed and configured on the computer before you can use the modem. The confusing bit is generally that the manufacturer supplies more than one CD, and you have to fathom out which one has the driver software on it. This software can vary for different versions of Windows, and in particular, the Windows XP system is different from earlier versions of Windows in that 'driver' software that works with other versions often does not work satisfactorily with Windows XP. This is an important point to check. If your computer uses XP, then read the box cover or instruction guides, and look specifically for confirmation that the modem driver software 'supports Windows XP'.

When a modem (internal or external) is successfully installed, it generally uses a resource within the computer known as a serial port or 'COM port'. There are several different COM Ports (often numbered 1 to 4) that can be used and it is a good idea for problem resolving to know which number COM Port has been finally allocated to the modem. These days, allocating the COM port is done automatically, but with older computers it was a manual selection process. Sharing the COM Port resource between a modem and another device can be successfully achieved, but only if both of these devices were originally designed to work in a sharing manner. This is another point to be aware of if you experience a problem with installation.

It would be impossible in this appendix to cover installing all types of modems that you may come across. We will therefore limit discussion to the procedures for a typical conventional PCI internal modem, using the Windows XP and Windows 98 operating systems. A PCI modem is a modem designed to fit the newer (smaller) PCI-bus slots inside the computer processor unit, as opposed to the older (larger) ISA-bus slots. These procedures should give you some idea of what is involved, and if your situation is different then you may have to modify your approach accordingly. The important point I would like to stress is <u>do follow the detailed instructions</u> given in the modem installation guide and take those instructions as having precedence over any discussion we have here. It is possible that your modem manufacturer may have created their own installation program for you to run from their CD, and this would make the procedures described in this appendix redundant. With that caveat in mind, we now come to the installation process itself.

Installing internal modem hardware

Remembering the first point given at the beginning of this appendix, make sure that mains power is turned off at the wall socket.

Remove the case from the processor unit. Gently lower the unit onto one side (if need be) so that you can see down onto the top of the main motherboard, and other existing cards appear vertical in their PCI slots.

Select a free PCI slot to use for the modem and prepare it by removing the blanking plate at the rear of the processor unit. Some have a retaining screw at the top of the blanking plate, but many now are attached 'semi-permanently' by a thin metal strip and you bend the blanking plate back and forth to break the strip to free the blanking plate from the chassis frame. Be careful with sharp metal edges that can cut your finger.

Remembering the second point, 'Earth' yourself by touching the metal chassis frame. Now carefully remove the modem from the anti-static plastic bag, handling it by the metal faceplate at one end, and the rear top corner at the other end. Align the modem card inside the chassis frame over the selected PCI slot connector, so that the faceplate is ready to go into the space vacated by the blanking plate.

Now here is the tricky part. Install the internal modem card into the PCI socket, taking care to locate the faceplate in the hole provide at the base of the chassis. Carefully push down firmly on the modem card, and observe its seating as it enters the socket to be sure that it is aligned correctly. When the card is installed properly, the modem card edge connectors should have almost disappeared completely into the socket, and they should appear level at either end (not one end sticking up more than the other). You normally need some reasonable force to push down on the modem to seat it correctly. When it is fully home, the faceplate should be in the place of the former blanking plate and the top just about flush with the other PCI cards (if it doesn't appear to be fully home then it won't be). You then need a correct size screw to fasten the card in permanently at the top of the faceplate to the chassis proper.

WARNING – If you drop any screws or washers inside the processor unit, make sure you recover them all immediately. Leaving such items inside when you eventually re-apply mains power can be a very expensive mistake!

When your modem is properly inserted in the PCI slot, it should look something like this next picture.

If you lowered the processor unit onto its side, restore it to its normal upright position. Replace the processor case and retaining screws. If you disconnected any leads, connect them back again.

Now apply mains power to the computer once again and watch the power up sequence on the monitor. If it begins to power back up as normal, then this is a reassuring sign that all is well. If anything appears unusual, then you may want to switch off quickly and investigate. Your nose is often a good indicator when something is not right!

During the power-up sequence, you will probably get some new messages telling you that 'New Hardware has been found'. At this point you are ready to install the software and we discuss the procedures for Windows XP and Windows 98 in the next sections.

Procedure for installing modem driver software with Windows XP

With Windows XP, as soon as the computer reaches the normal desktop stage, you will see the 'Found New Hardware Wizard' appear as shown in the next picture.

Here we can see that not only has it detected that a new modem has been installed, but it has automatically recognised the modem model type as 'Intel® 536EP V.92'.

At this point, you can put the manufacturer's CD into your CD drive. When you close the drive door, you need to wait a few seconds for the drive to reach operating speed. You should then witness the wizard move automatically to the next stage. This will be indicated by a message saying, 'Please wait while the wizard searches'. If it does not move on automatically, you can click on the **Next** button.

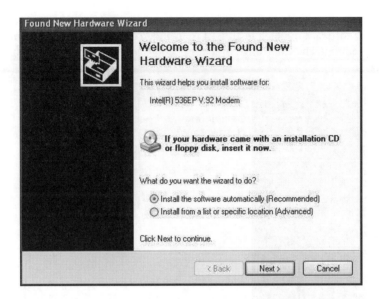

The wizard will then search automatically for the required driver. If the correct driver software cannot be found, then the automatic routine will terminate, and you have to 'Install from a list or specific location' (the other option on the previous picture) - basically you have to find the location of the driver software yourself.

If the correct modem driver software has been found, then there will normally be some indication. The following picture is quite commonly seen and does indicate that the driver has been found.

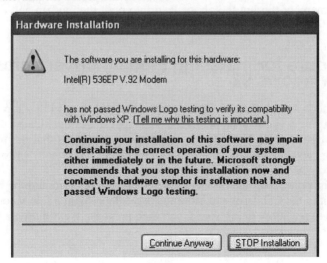

Don't worry about this because it is quite common for manufacturer's not to enter their software for such testing (it is an added expense). Press the **Continue Anyway** button. The final stage of the procedure arrives when you see this next message...

Press the **Finish** button and your modem is then fully installed. If you want confidence that it is functioning okay, then read and follow the appropriate part in Appendix IV.

Do remember to plug the phone lead into both the modem and a telephone socket before you try to use it in earnest.

Procedure for installing modem driver software with Windows 98

With Windows 98, before the computer reaches the normal desktop stage, you will see a 'New Hardware Found' message appear. Automatically, this will be followed by the 'Add New Hardware Wizard' telling you that the wizard will search for new drivers for the 'PCI Communication Device'. Press the **Next** button and you will then see the next picture.

At this point, put the modem manufacturer's CD containing the driver software into the CD drive and close the drive door. Wait a few seconds for the CD drive to reach operating speed, and then press the **Next** button again.

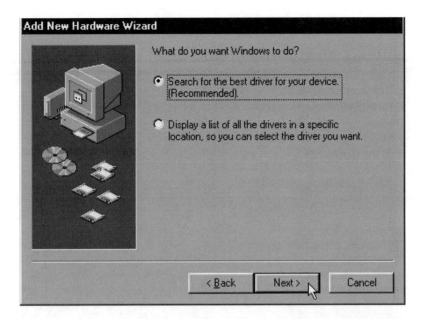

This pops up yet another screen message showing four checkboxes, as shown in the following picture. The checkbox for the CD-ROM drive is normally already checked for you. Now we have reached the tricky stage of modem installation with Windows 98! In theory, it should be sufficient to let the computer search the CD for the driver it requires, but my experience is that this rarely works automatically. If you want to try an automatic search on the CD then press the **Next** button yet again now and wait to see what happens. If it is successful then the subsequent messages will tell you so. If it is unsuccessful, then the next message in the sequence will tell you that it has been unable to locate a driver – and you should then press the **Back** button to go back one step and follow the procedure I will now outline.

More often than not, you will have to specify a location (that is a folder) where the driver software is located. One reason why the automatic search of the CD can fail is that there are several versions of driver software on the same CD-ROM; each version is for different models of modem. Your problem now may be to decide on the model of modem you are trying to install, and then deciding which folder on the CD contains the correct version of driver software. Unfortunately, in our discussion here, it is impossible to guide you accurately. However, there is a technique using the Browse button that may help, and we will now describe it.

First click with the mouse pointer on the '**Specify a location checkbox**'. Then press the **Browse** button as shown above. This will then pop up a hierarchical list box like this one...

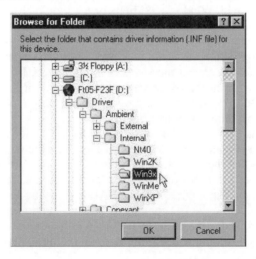

When you first see this box, most of the folders will be closed. You open them by using a click with the mouse on the '+' symbol in the little squares (and close them with a click on the '-' symbol).

Your task now is to find the folder where the correct driver is located. A good tip is to look for folders that have the word 'driver' in the folder name. If you find it, you make need to select a folder for a model type and then the last folder should be referring to the version of Windows that you are using. In the example shown in the last picture I have located the correct driver for my modem as follows:

- First, I opened the D: drive which is the CD-ROM drive. The CD is in the drive and you can see the CD label is 'Ft05-F23F'. If the CD was not in the drive then there would not be a label shown.
- Second, I opened the sub-folder called 'Driver'.
- Third, I opened the modem model type, which in my case is an 'Ambient'.
- Fourth, I noted that there are folders for both External and Internal modems. My model is an Internal one so I open this folder.
- Fifth, I am using the Windows 98 operating system, so I opened the folder called Win9x (the '9x' here means either '95' or '98').
- There are no more sub-folders so I stopped at this point.

Now press the **OK** button. This closes the hierarchy list box, and automatically puts the full pathname for the final selected sub-folder into the combo box for you, as shown in the next picture.

At this point, press the **Next** button again.

If your selection of folder contained a driver file, the screen next to show will confirm the folder path and filename it is going to install, as shown in the next picture.

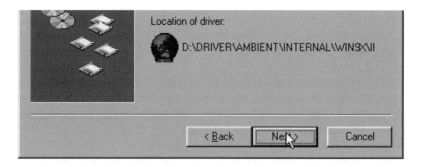

Press the **Next** button again, and the computer will search for the specified driver file. When it finds it, it will then copy the file (and any related ones) from the CD into the correct place on your hard drive...

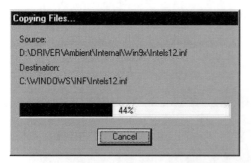

When the process has been completed, you should then see the final message screen like the one below ...

If another 'modem preferences' dialog box shows, then ignore it and close it with the **OK** button. Finally, close the wizard by pressing the **Finish** button. The modem is now installed.

Appendix III
Setting up an ISP Account

Included at the rear of this book is a CD from the ISP Company, Tiscali, to make it easy for you to set up an ISP account. There are a few points you may want to think about before you start. The first of these is a choice of username and password that you will need to register, and the second is the type of ISP account you want to use.

The username will also become the first part of your full email address (see section 1.4). You should therefore give this a bit of thought because once your email address has been decided you may keep it for some time. Like your personal telephone number, you can include your email address on letterheads and such like.

In considering a username, the ISP Company will allow you to make a personal choice within limits. In making your choice, the name can only be accepted provided that it is not already in use by another person, and it meets the company's guidelines. It may be prudent therefore to have a second choice ready in case your first is not acceptable. The username does not have to be related to your real name (though for many it is), and some choose to use a pseudonym. In considering a password, your choice is fairly flexible, but most ISP companies have a minimum and maximum length restriction (for example, between 5 and 16 letters or numbers – but this varies from one ISP to another).

The second consideration is the type of ISP account you want to use. There are several alternative types of ISP account available for you to select from, depending on your preferred use of the system. You will be asked to choose the type of account you wish to operate as part of the registration procedure.

One type of account is the 'Pay As You Go' type, where you pay for the service by call charges on your telephone bill. For the duration of the time that you are on-line to the ISP account then call charging at local rate applies, and part of this call cost is automatically forwarded by the telephone company to the ISP Company in payment of the account. Therefore, you only need to settle the billing with the telephone company in the normal way.

Another type of account is the 'Anytime' account, where you pay a fixed monthly fee to the ISP Company directly. There are no separate telephone charges applied to this type of account, so you can use the service more or less as you want to, as often as you want to. You do not have any separate charges made to you by the telephone company, for this use of the phone line. The ISP

Company pays for this use of the phone line out of the fixed monthly fee.

There are other types of account that are 'intermediate' between the two just described. You will see details of these during the set up procedure. The choice you make will depend on the time of day that you think you might want to use the service, and how heavily you might want to use it.

All accounts are subject to the Terms and Conditions set out by the ISP Company, and at the time of writing for the fixed fee type, many require you to be using a BT line. You do not usually need a BT line for the 'Pay As You Go' type.

A. Setting up an ISP account automatically

At the rear of this book you will find a CD from the Internet Service Provider – Tiscali. You can set up an ISP account automatically with this company simply by inserting the CD into the CD Drive and closing the drive door. Follow the on-screen instructions, and at the end of the procedure, an account will be set up for you.

B. Setting up an ISP account manually

If for any reason you prefer not to set up an account automatically, then this section will guide you through setting it up manually.

There are three stages in setting up an ISP account and getting it working manually:

- The first stage is to register with an ISP company and they will then create an account for you on their ISP computer system. You can do this from some other computer that has Internet access (for example, from a friend's computer system or an Internet café).
- The second stage is to set up the Dial-up Networking 'program' mentioned in sections 2.5 and 5.1 to use the ISP account. You will often hear this referred to as a 'connection' rather than a program (but it is software that we are setting up).
- The third stage is to set up Outlook Express to use the ISP account, and to use Dial-up Networking from the second stage.

In this section, we will follow an example of setting up a 'Pay As You Go' type of account and Outlook Express from the beginning, as an example of stage 1. We will then look at setting up Dial-up Networking and Outlook Express for both Windows XP and Windows 98.

Stage 1 - Registering with an ISP Company

Using a friend's computer, start a web browser program such as **Internet Explorer** running, and connect on-line to the Internet...

Enter the web page address 'www.tiscali.co.uk' into the **Address textbox** as shown in the previous picture (the 'http://' bit will be added automatically). Then press the **Email** button using the mouse pointer.

At the Email page, click anywhere on the 'Click to Join Now' button...

Now select the service that you want to subscribe to. In our example, we will use the 'Pay As You Go' type of account, as shown below...

You may then get a message warning you that you are about to view pages over a secure connection. This is a good alert because when you have accepted it, the information that you then supply over the Internet cannot be intercepted from the telephone line (it is specially encoded). If your friend has had this kind of alert previously and ticked the little 'In the future' box, then you won't see this warning, but you will still be using a secure connection. Press the OK button if you see it...

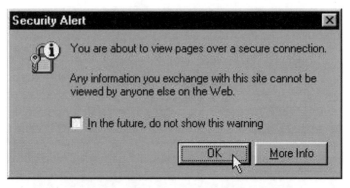

Next comes the registration classification. For home access, check that the 'Consumer' option is selected and then press the Next button, as illustrated in the following picture.

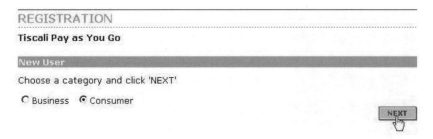

After this comes the personal details section. Now all of the textboxes which have a '*' symbol marked against them are compulsory pieces of information, and like it or not, you must enter your details (sorry ladies, even the age one!). If you don't enter information into these textboxes then your application will be rejected automatically – remember, this is an automated system. The next picture shows a typical set of detail entries.

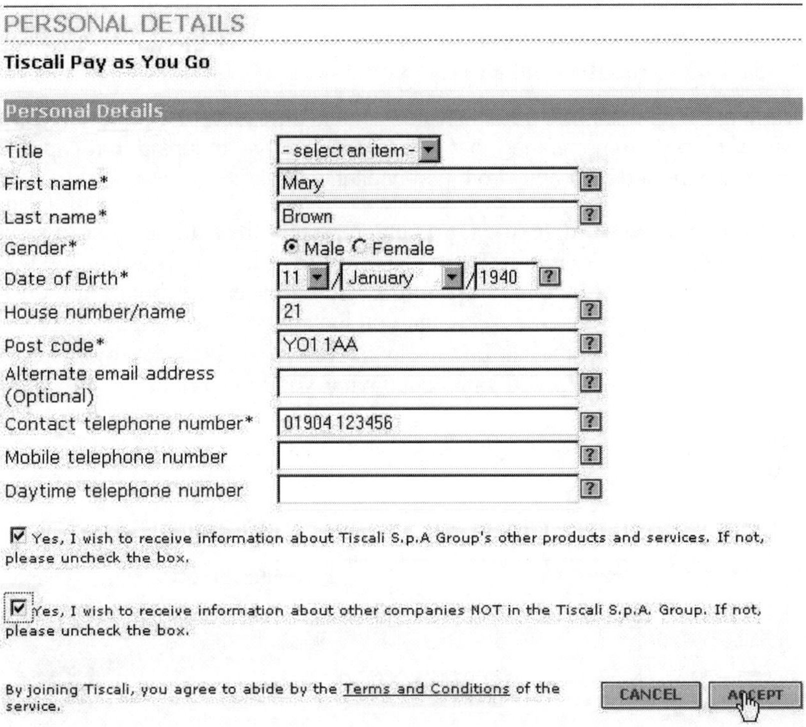

PERSONAL DETAILS

Tiscali Pay as You Go

Personal Details	
Title	- select an item - ▾
First name*	Mary [?]
Last name*	Brown [?]
Gender*	⦿ Male ○ Female
Date of Birth*	11 ▾ / January ▾ / 1940 [?]
House number/name	21 [?]
Post code*	YO1 1AA [?]
Alternate email address (Optional)	[?]
Contact telephone number*	01904 123456 [?]
Mobile telephone number	[?]
Daytime telephone number	[?]

☑ Yes, I wish to receive information about Tiscali S.p.A Group's other products and services. If not, please uncheck the box.

☑ Yes, I wish to receive information about other companies NOT in the Tiscali S.p.A. Group. If not, please uncheck the box.

By joining Tiscali, you agree to abide by the Terms and Conditions of the service. [CANCEL] [ACCEPT]

If you don't wish to receive future information about products and services, you have the choice to 'un-tick' the lower two checkboxes. When you have finished then press the Accept button.

The next screen will show you a summary of the details that you entered previously – just as a check to make sure that they are correct. At the bottom part of the summary screen, press the Continue button...

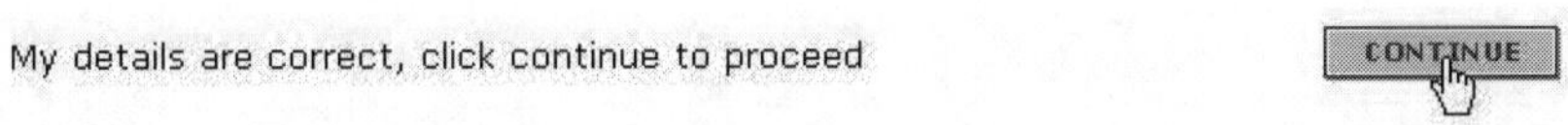

My details are correct, click continue to proceed [CONTINUE]

Now comes the step where you enter your desired username and password, and this can be just a little tricky. If your first choice is already taken by another subscriber then it won't be accepted. Be prepared with an alternative choice as a backup, just in case.

Be aware also that the term 'username' can be confusing because it is used by different people to mean different things! In this book, we will use it to mean the first part of the full email address – the part before the '@' symbol (see also section 1.4). When taken together with the '@' symbol and the second part after it, it then forms the full email address.

Go ahead now and type the three entries required. If you make a mistake, don't be afraid to rub it all out and re-type.

Warning – I he password you enter now should be exactly the form that you want it to take, remembering that it is 'case-sensitive' meaning that capital letters are treated differently from non-capital letters.

In the 'Confirm Password' textbox, you enter exactly the same password as you have just done for the 'Password' box. The purpose of this duplication is to make sure that you have not inadvertently fumbled an adjacent keyboard key during the typing, because you cannot see what you have typed. As each key is pressed it will be represented in the textbox as an asterisk. This is a security feature so that any person sat next to you cannot see what you have typed!

EMAIL ADDRESS AND PASSWORD

Tiscali Pay as You Go

Choose your email address and password

Email address* mary.brown @tiscali.co.uk [?]

Password* ******** [?]

Confirm Password* ******** [?]

REGISTER

When you have finished making the entries, then press the Register button.

Now it is at this point where you find out whether your choice of username entered in the first textbox is a good one. If someone else has already registered this name then you will see a subsequent message like this next picture.

Sorry, an error has occurred

Username not available

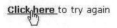

Click here to try again

If you do see this message, then click to try again.

In this next picture, we see a modified username formed by adding the numbers

'01' on to the end of our desired username. If this too has already been allocated then you may have to go round this loop several times.

EMAIL ADDRESS AND PASSWORD

Tiscali Pay as You Go

Choose your email address and password

Email address*	mary.brown01	@tiscali.co.uk [?]
Password*	✱✱✱✱✱✱	[?]
Confirm Password*	✱✱✱✱✱✱	[?]

REGISTER

A successful choice of username will then get you to the next step (that is beyond the 'Sorry, an error has occurred' step). If you scroll to the top of the web page now showing, it should say something like 'Congratulations – Tiscali Pay As You Go'.

Warning – Now here you have to be careful. Don't click anything until you have read this next piece of advice.

This last step assumes that the computer you are using is your own computer, and that you are at liberty to make changes to it. The chances are that this may not be true. If you are using a friend's computer, they will not thank you for messing up their own computer settings by continuing in the way that the web page is now suggesting to you. If you take care to follow what I now advise, then you can 'gracefully' complete your registration of the ISP account without falling out with your friend!

First of all, scroll down the web page and you will see a complete listing of all of your account details. Effectively, you have now been registered at this point, but the information that is shown here is going to be needed for setting up the Dial-up Networking of the second stage. You may also need it in the future should your computer system get into difficulties and you have to set things up for a second time. If you have a printer connected to the computer you are using then the best thing to do is to print it out in the following way. Down near the bottom of the web page, you should see a Print button like that shown in the next picture.

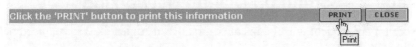

Press the Print button to get paper copies of your account details. If you don't have a printer, then you need to record the following information by writing this down on paper, <u>exactly as it appears on the web page (being careful about</u>

capital and non-capital lettering) - and take care not to let your password details be seen by others:

Customer Account Code
Customer Account Password

Dial up Username
Dial up Password
Dial up Number

Email Address
Email Password
Webmail

Outgoing Mail Server
Incoming Mail Server
IMAP Server

The other information given may be needed, so record it if you can. The above listed information is essential information for setting up Email on your own computer.

Finally, just above the start of the 'Customer Account Details', you should see a Close button. Press this button as shown in the following picture...

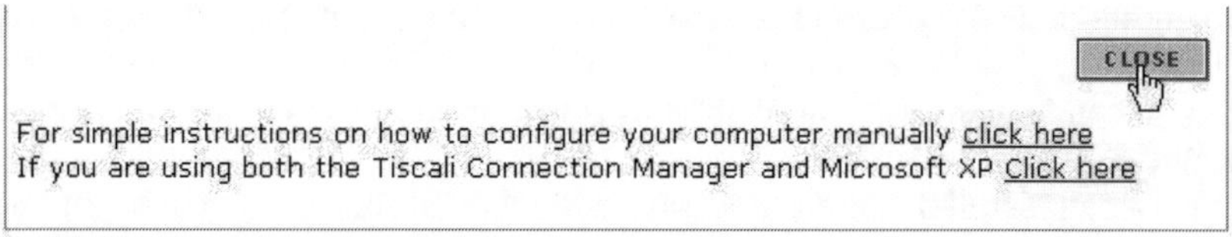

CLOSE

For simple instructions on how to configure your computer manually click here
If you are using both the Tiscali Connection Manager and Microsoft XP Click here

The browser will now stop running and the Internet connection will be terminated. If you cannot find this button, then close the browser program in any case.

Your ISP account has now been created. We are ready to proceed to the second stage.

Stage 2 - Setting up Dial-up Networking

(Note – Your modem must be installed first. Read Appendix II if you need help on how to do this).

Setting up Dial-up Networking manually with Windows XP
From the Desktop, press the **Start** button and select **Control Panel**...

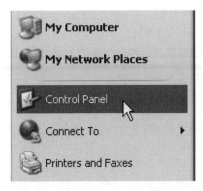

From the **Control Panel window**, double-click (or right-click and select **Open**) on the **Network Connections icon...**

From the **Network Connections window**, double-click (or right-click and select **Open**) on the **New Connection Wizard...**
This will start the **New Connections Wizard** running...

Press the **Next** button. You are then asked which type of connection you want. Make sure the '**Connect to the Internet**' option is selected, as shown in this next picture.

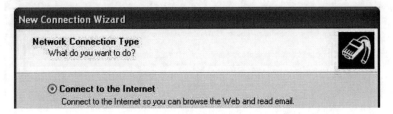

Press the Next button. You are then asked how do you want to connect. Change the selected option to **'Set up my connection manually'**...

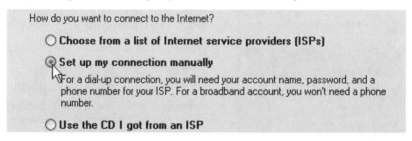

Press the **Next** button. You are then offered three options. Make sure the **'Connect using a dial-up modem'** option is selected...

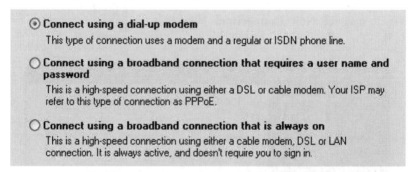

Press the Next button. What you then see depends on whether you have more than one modem device installed on your computer. If you have only one modem installed, the procedure will skip over this next paragraph.

Should you have more than one modem, you will be shown a list of devices, as in the next picture. Select the device that you want to use for this Dial-up Networking set up by making sure that there is a 'tick' symbol in the checkbox at the left-hand side of the selected modem. Press the Next button.

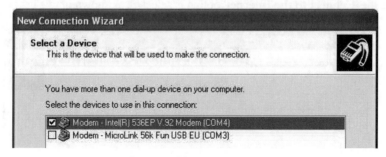

You are now invited to type in the name of your ISP Company. The name is only a label for this particular 'Dial-up networking' setup (you can set up more than one if you have a need to) and you are free to choose any text that you care to. In the following example, I have chosen an ISP Company name combined with the modem type as 'Tiscali Intel Modem'...

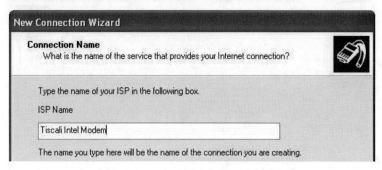

When you have completed the name press the **Next** button. You are then invited to type in the telephone number that you need to dial in order to access the ISP computer system (the Dial-up Number from stage 1). In the example illustrated in the following picture, there is a prefix of '1470' and then a comma separating it from the main number. This prefix ensures that 'Caller Line ID' is released for this one call, which is a requirement for some ISP companies.

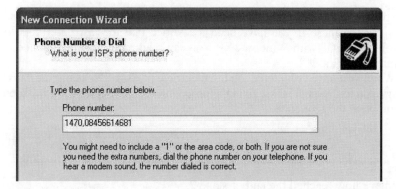

When you have completed the telephone number press the **Next** button. You are now invited to enter your ISP account username and password, and confirm the password. If you refer back to the information recorded at the end of stage 1, you will see that the 'Dial-up Username' is not just the username that you selected but the full email address. Some ISP companies require this, but some others specifically require that you do not do this. You must check the precise text needed to access their system, or you will fail to gain entry. For security reasons, many ISP computer systems will not send an error message if you get it wrong – they just keep dropping their end of the telephone call.

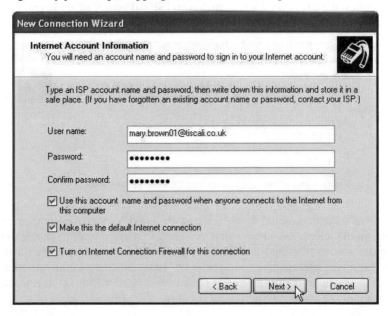

The three checkboxes in the lower part of the entry form are 'ticked' as standard. Only change these if you have need to. Notice that the last one refers to the built-in 'Firewall' with Windows XP. You can read more information about this feature in section 9.2.

When you have completed the three entries, press the **Next** button. This then brings you to the final message in the procedure. Simply press the **Finish** button to complete the sequence...

You have now reached the end of stage 2.

Setting up Dial-up Networking manually with Windows 98

With Windows 98, there are two important considerations for Dial-up Networking. One is obviously the settings for Dial-up Networking itself; the other is 'Telephony' settings. We need to check the Telephony settings first.

From the Desktop, press the **Start** button and select Settings and Control Panel...

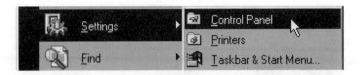

Telephony

From the **Control Panel window**, double-click (or right-click and select **Open**) on the **Telephony icon**...

This pops up the **Dialing properties** box. Make sure that the correct country/region is selected, and that 'Dial using' has the Tone dial option selected.

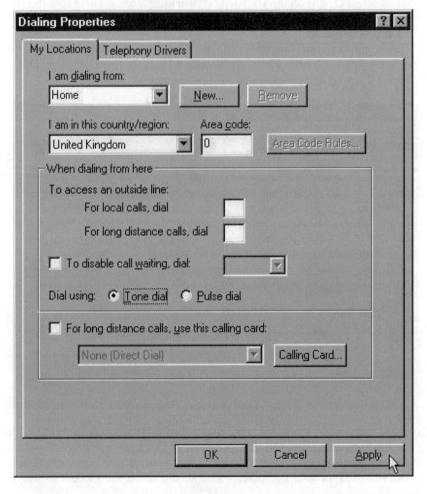

If you have changed a setting you need then press the Apply button. Press the OK button to close the box. Now close the Control Panel window to return to the Desktop.

(i) From the Desktop, double-click (or right-click and select **Open**) on the **My Computer icon...** (ii) From the My Computer window, double-click (or right-click and select **Open**) on the **Dial-Up Networking icon**... (iii) From the Dial-Up Networking, double-click (or right-click and select **Open**) on the **Make New Connection icon...**

This begins a wizard sequence. You are then invited to 'Type a name for the computer you are dialing'. The name is only a label for this particular 'Dial-up networking' set-up and you are free to choose any text that you care to.

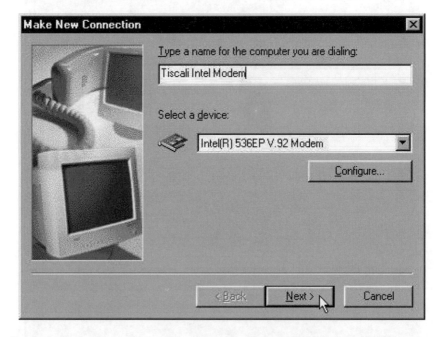

Go ahead and type in a suitable name to use for this Dial-Up networking set-up. In the illustrated example, I have chosen an ISP Company name combined with the modem type as 'Tiscali Intel Modem'. Then – only if you have more than one modem installed on your computer – you should select the modem using your

mouse and the arrow at the right-hand side of the 'Select a device' combo box.
   When you are ready, press the **Next** button. You are now invited to type in the telephone number that you need to dial in order to access the ISP computer system (the Dial-up Number from stage 1). In the example illustrated in the following picture, there is a prefix of '1470' and then a comma separating it from the main number. This prefix ensures that 'Caller Line ID' is released for this one call, which is a requirement for some ISP companies. I have also deliberately not used the 'Area code' box and I advise you to do the same. Because we are using the '1470,' prefix, we need this prefix to be the first thing that the computer dials when establishing the on-line connection into the Internet. If you use the 'Area code' box, the prefix will not be dialled correctly ahead of the required local call Dial Up Number, and when you attempt to contact the ISP computer system it will fail.

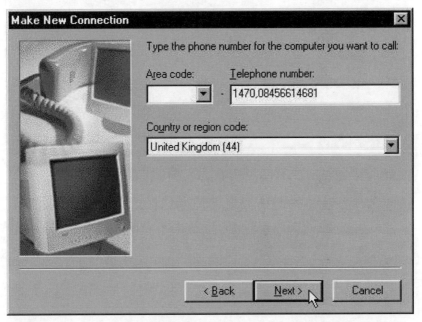

Note – When you do eventually attempt to contact the ISP computer system, you can observe the telephone number that is being automatically dialled (see exercise 1, section 2.3) as part of the text shown in the on screen messages. If you are having problems in establishing a good connection, check that the number is what you are expecting and if not, then you will need to return and adjust either these 'Dial-up Networking settings, or the 'Telephony' settings accordingly.

When you have completed the entry details press the **Next** button. This brings you to the final message, as shown in the next picture...

Press the **Finish** button to complete the wizard sequence.

Make New Connection   Tiscali Intel Modem

There is one last task to do now. When the wizard sequence ends, you should see your new **Dial-up Networking icon** in the Dial-Up networking window, as shown here on the left ...

Right-click on the new modem icon, and select the Properties option, as shown in this next picture.

Make New Connection

This will then pop up the **properties window** for your new Dial-up Networking set up, as illustrated on the next page.

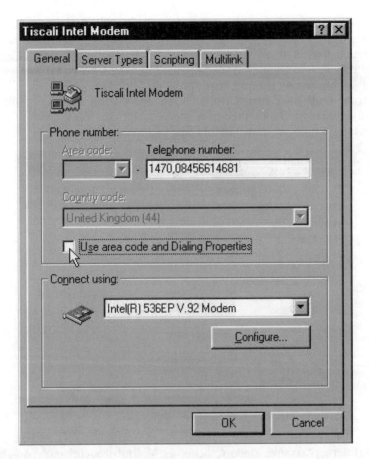

The task is to remove the 'tick' symbol from the 'Use area code and Dialing Properties' checkbox. Simply click on the checkbox as shown above, and then press the **OK** button. The **Properties window** now closes.

Close the **Dial-Up Networking window** in the normal way. You have now reached the end of stage 2.

Stage 3 - Setting up Outlook Express to use the ISP Account

The procedure illustrated here uses Outlook Express version 6, running on Windows XP. The same procedure should be fine for users of Windows 98 and versions 5 and later of Outlook Express.

From the Desktop, start the **Outlook Express** program running.

If the program has not been set up previously, then the **Internet Connection Wizard** will begin running straight away. In this case, you can jump ahead to the relevant step... Otherwise, the program window will open and you may be asked if you wish to connect to the Internet. Choose to '**Work Offline**' or press '**Cancel**'. If you see an error message, press the Hide button.

With the **Outlook Express** window now opened and working off-line, we are ready to begin. From the main menu, click on '**Tools**' and select the '**Accounts...**' option, as shown in this next picture.

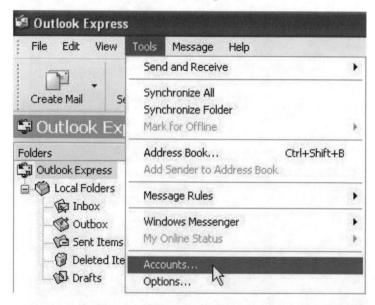

From the **Internet Accounts window**, click on the **Mail tab** then click on the **Add** button. Select the **Mail... option** from the pop-up menu, as shown in the following picture.

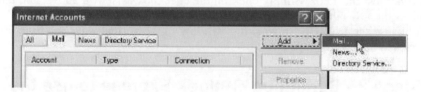

This will then start the **Internet Connection Wizard**. You are then invited to type in your name. The entry that you decide to make here is a matter of personal choice and you are almost free to enter anything you like. However, this name will be appended to the emails that you send out, and if you have chosen a pseudonym for your email address then you probably do not want to enter your real name. Type in the name that you wish others to see.

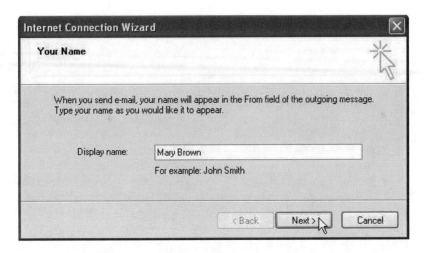

When you have made your entry press the Next button. You are then asked to enter your full email address, and this should be exactly as shown in the Email Address details recorded in stage 2.

When you have completed the entry, press the Next button. You are then requested to enter the Email server names. The first textbox on this form specifies the type of incoming mail server, and the setting of 'POP3' is correct for home users using Dial-up Networking. The second textbox entry should be exactly as shown in the recorded details during stage 2 for Incoming mail Server. Likewise, the entry for the third and final textbox should be exactly as recorded during stage 2 for Outgoing Mail Server.

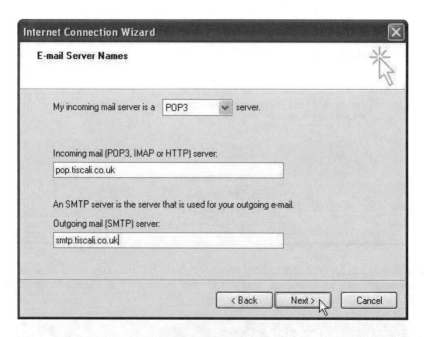

When you have made the relevant entries press the **Next** button. The next form in the sequence concerns the Internet mail Logon details. Now this is often where mistakes can be made, and the reason is the different interpretations of the terms 'Account name' and 'Username'. You need to enter here exactly the details recorded during stage 2 for **Dial Up Username** and **Dial Up Password**. Some ISP companies want you to enter just the first part of your full email address, others insist on it in full. (See picture opposite.)

If you have any doubts then you can check with your ISP Company using their telephone helpline, but maybe a faster method is to first try it one way and, if it works okay, then that's fine. If not, then repeat this whole procedure (you can remove your first attempt at the Internet Accounts window when you reach that step) and try it the other way. You may find the 'try it and see approach' is faster than trying to get through on a helpline!

Be careful when you enter your password – unfortunately there is no 'confirm password' textbox and as you cannot see what you have typed its easy to make a mistake. A very common mistake is to accidentally catch the **Caps Lock** key, so that you are typing capital letters when you think you are typing non-capitals. Remember also to enter the password exactly as it is recorded during stage 2, for capital letters are not the same as non-capitals for passwords! It is also a good idea to ensure that the 'Remember password' checkbox is 'ticked' (click on it with the mouse if it isn't). Then you will find that the procedure for going on-line is much easier.

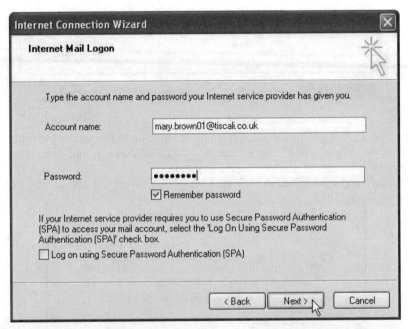

When you have completed the form, press the **Next** button. You will then see the 'Congratulations' message...

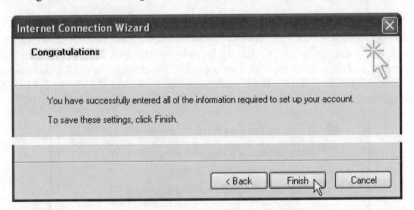

Press the **Finish** button to complete the wizard sequence. This will return you to the **Internet Accounts window**. Notice that you now have a mail account set up.

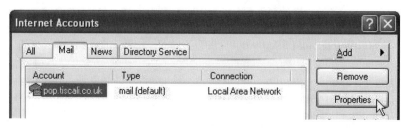

There is one last job now to do. Click on the wording of the account to highlight it (the wording in our example here is 'pop.tiscali.co.uk'), and then press the **Properties** button, as shown in the last picture.

In the **Properties window**, click the **Connection** tab as shown in the next picture.

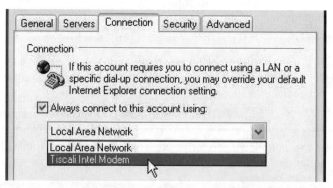

Click the checkbox labelled 'Always connect to this account using:' and then click the down pointing arrow to the right side of the box below it. Select the appropriate choice from the list with a click. This choice should be the relevant name of the 'Dial-up Networking' modem connection created in Stage 2. Once the appropriate connection choice is shown in the box, then press the **Apply** button...

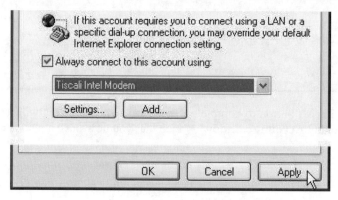

Finally, press the Close button to complete the procedure. Your ISP account should now be ready to use. This concludes stage 3.

Appendix IV

How to Check that Your Modem and ISP Account Are Ready for Use

If you are not sure whether your computer has been set up to use a modem and an ISP account, then the checks described here may be used to find out. The procedures vary slightly depending on the version of Windows you are using. In this appendix, we will demonstrate the procedures for users of Windows XP and Windows 98.

A. How to check that a modem has been set up

For users of Windows XP

Click on the **Start** button and from the **Start menu** select the **Control Panel** option, as shown in the next picture.

When the Control Panel window opens, either double-click (or right-click and select **Open**) on the **Phone and Modem Options** icon.

Then click on the Modems tab, as shown in the following picture.

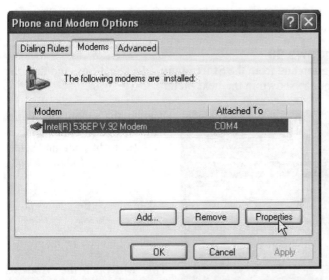

This window will show any modem that has been set up on the computer, and you may see more than one entry. This picture illustrates that an Intel model 536EP has been set up. To be sure that the modem is presently connected (internally or externally) to the computer, you can press the Properties button.

On the **General** tab, the central **Device Status** box is telling us that this device is working properly. Therefore, de facto, it must be c u r r e n t l y connected.

Note – With most modems, you can change the volume of the internal speaker inside the modem from the **Modem tab** of the **P r o p e r t i e s window**.

Press the **Cancel** button to close the Properties window, and then press the

Cancel button to close the Phone and Modem Options window. Close the Control Panel window using the Close button in the top right-hand corner.

For users of Windows 98

Click on the **Start** button and from the **Start menu** select **Settings**, and then the **Control Panel** option, as shown in the next picture.

When the Control Panel window opens, either double-click (or right-click and select Open) on the Modems icon.

Mail   Modems   Mouse

This will open the **Modems Properties** window...

This window will show any modem that has been set up on the computer, and you may see more than one entry. The picture here illustrates that a Creatix model V.90 HaM has been set up. To be sure that the modem is presently connected, you can press the **Properties** button. Then select the **Diagnostics** tab...

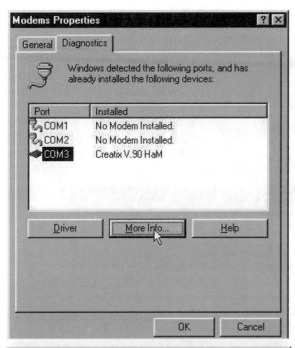

Now click on the **Port** appropriate to the modem (COM3 in this picture) and then press the **More Info...** button. A brief message will show informing you that the computer is communicating with the modem. If all is well then you will see a further window showing you the results of the communication, as in the following picture.

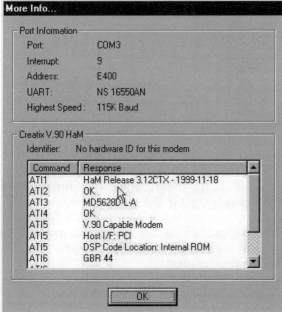

Press the **OK** button, then the **Cancel** button. Then close the **Control Panel window** using the **Close** button in the top right-hand corner.

Note – With most modems, you can change the volume of the internal speaker inside the modem from the **General** tab of the **Properties window**, which is reached by highlighting the modem listed on the **General** tab of the **Modem Properties window**.

B. How to check that an ISP Account has been set up

For users of Windows XP

Network
Connections

Phone and
Modem ...

Power Options

Click on the **Start** button and from the **Start menu** select the **Control Panel** option (as with the modem check). Now double-click (or right-click and select **Open**) on the **Network Connections** icon.

The Network Connections window now opens...

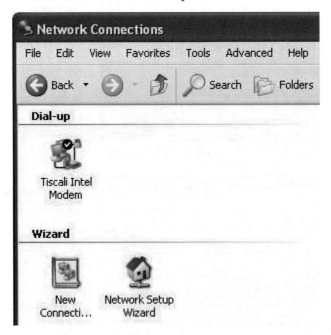

If an ISP Account has been set up, then you will see an icon for that account in the **Dial-up section** of this window. In the above picture we illustrate an ISP Account with the Tiscali ISP Company, using the Intel modem connection, called 'Tiscali Intel Modem'.

The small white 'tick' symbol with a black circular background indicates the account that will be used by default when either the **Outlook Express** program or **Internet Explorer** program are first set running.

Close the **Network Connections window** using the **Close** button in the top right-hand corner. Close the **Control Panel** window in the same way.

For users of Windows 98

From the Desktop, double-click (or right-click and select **Open**) on the **My Computer icon**.
This will open the **My Computer** window, as shown in the next picture.

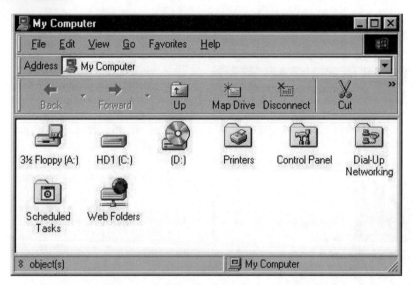

Now double-click (or right-click and select Open) on the Dial-Up Networking icon. This will bring up the Dial-Up Networking window, as shown in following picture.

If an ISP Account has been set up, then in addition to the **Make New Connection** icon, there should be another icon showing two small monitor screens linked by a telephone (there may be more than one if more than one account has been set up). In the above picture we illustrate an ISP Account with the Tiscali ISP Company, using the Creatix modem connection.

Close the **Dial-Up Networking window** using the **Close** button in the top right-hand corner. Close the **Control Panel window** in the same way.

Appendix V

Showing Sub-windows in Outlook Express

In a number of the exercises, you need to be able to see the Folders and Contacts sub-windows. If the view you have on your monitor screen of the main window for Outlook Express does not show these sub-windows, then you can make them visible in the following way.

From the main menu bar, click on View and select the **Layout...** option, as shown on the left.

This will pop up a dialog box like the one below...

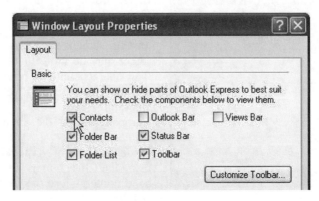

Using the tip of the mouse pointer, click on the **Contacts** checkbox to make the 'tick' symbol visible and also on the **Folder List checkbox**. Then press the **Apply** button at the bottom of the dialog box, as shown in the following picture...

And then press the **OK** button. When the dialog box closes, you will then be able to see the **Folders** and **Contacts sub-windows**.

If the dividing line between the **Folders** and **Contacts sub-windows** is low down on the screen, you can adjust its position by placing the tip of the mouse pointer over it and making a 'drag' action, as in the next picture.

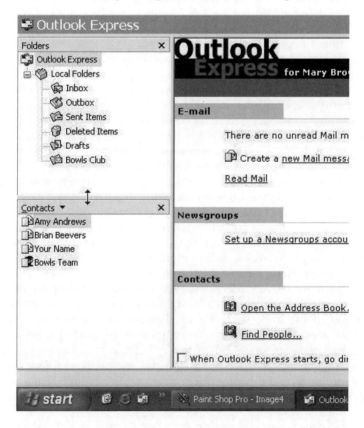

Ideally, the two sub-windows should appear about the same size.

Appendix VI
Using Different Identities and Accounts

The email reader program **Outlook Express** is often used by just one person to work simply with his or her own ISP account. For many people this arrangement is fine because they have nobody else to worry about. For families, however, there may be two or more people who want to share the use of the computer, but they don't want to share the same email folders or contact lists. Horror of all horrors – they definitely do not want to let other members of the family read their email. If Mum or Dad could read Sunny Jim's or Sunny Janet's email 'willy-nilly' things might prove too embarrassing!

This problem of sharing use of the Outlook Express program with others is solved using a technique called '**identities**'.

When individuals are working on their own, they do not realise it but they are using an identity every time that they start Outlook Express running. It is called the 'Main Identity' and because there is no one else to consider, it never changes, so it remains fairly invisible. The folders they are using for the Inbox, Outbox, Sent Items and such like – and the contact list – all belong to the 'Main Identity'.

To provide a second person with personal folders and a contact list, you need to create a new identity. The act of creating the new identity automatically creates a new set of folders and a new contact list. These are 'owned' by the new identity, and are separate from the folders and contact list of the Main Identity.

Each new identity that is created is added to a list of identities held within the Outlook Express program. It is then possible to switch between identities to allow different people to work with the program at different times. On switching the identity, the previous set of folders and contact list are stored away, and those appropriate for the next identity are made visible in the sub-windows.

In the process of creating a new identity, you can also create a password for it, should you choose to do so. If anyone then attempts to switch to that new identity, they must first enter the correct password before the switching is permitted. This prevents Sunny Jim or Sunny Janet from casually switching to Mum's or Dad's identity and vice versa. However, such password security is not absolutely foolproof, and if Sunny Jim or Janet acquire enough technical skills at school or college, it is theoretically possible to 'hack' the password protection. Mum and Dad's be warned!

As well as having private contacts in contact lists, it is also possible to have shared contacts. Shared contacts appear in the contact lists of all identities, so everyone has access to them. Any identity can create a shared contact, and as soon as it has been created, it will subsequently appear in all the contact lists automatically.

How does this technique of identities work with your ISP account? Well, there are two ways that they can work together:

- The first way is for all identities to use the same ISP account, but to set up different email addresses within it. Most ISP companies will offer you the option of setting up a limited number of additional email addresses over and above the main email address on the one ISP account. Each email address effectively has its own incoming mailbox on the ISP computer system, storing mail separately and keeping it ready to be transferred to the Inbox of a particular identity at the right time. The advantage for Sunny Jim and Sunny Janet is that they can use Dad's 'Anytime' ISP account whenever they want to, and leave Dad with the pleasure of paying for it.
- The second way is to have completely separate ISP accounts, either with the same company or with different companies, but this can prove more expensive.

When considering the word 'Account', there are really different aspects to the word with Outlook Express that can be confusing. To avoid this confusion, let me spell things out clearly:

- ❖ In one way, we refer to an Account as that allocation on the ISP computer of an incoming and outgoing mailbox, and you pay for this through your subscription to the ISP Company. When this account is first set up, it is known as the 'Primary Account' and there is a specific email address associated with it. When you set up a new email address on that same account – as part of the additional email addresses offered – it is known as a 'Secondary Account', and additional mailboxes are created for it on the ISP computer system.
- ❖ We also refer to an Account in another way as 'something' (an item) that is created inside the Outlook Express program. It relates to the first use of the word in that it holds the display name, email address and password, server names and such like, so that when you want to go on-line this item can arrange it for you automatically. But it has to be set up separately, inside Outlook Express, for each identity that you create. When you create the identity and switch to it for the first time, then you will be prompted by the computer to set this 'item' up. This is illustrated later, in the pictures for section A of this appendix.

To create a new identity over and above the Main Identity and get it working properly, you have three things to do:

1. You must access the Primary Account on the ISP computer system, using a browser program, and then set up the Secondary Account – specifying the new email address and password for it.

2. You must create the new identity within Outlook Express, so that you can switch to it away from the Main Identity.
3. You must set up the 'item' aspect of the Account within Outlook Express. This is normally done when you switch to the new identity for the first time. The Internet Connection Wizard will begin running to prompt you for all the information needed.

In the following sections A, B and C, we will illustrate how to do each of these things, and discuss some advice along the way. In section D, there are a few comments concerning changes you may want to make to the Main Identity and its password.

A. Adding a Secondary Account to the ISP computer system

Start a web browser program such as **Internet Explorer** running, and connect on-line to the Internet using the Primary Account email address and password.

Enter the home web page address for the ISP Company, such as 'www.tiscali.co.uk', into the Address textbox. From the home page, then press the **My Account** button, as shown in the following picture.

Then press the **Click Here To Enter** button...

This may activate the Security Alert message, which is a good thing, telling you that all information entered on web pages from hereon will be encoded. If you see this alert, then press the OK button. (If the 'In future...' checkbox has previously been 'ticked' then you may not see it, but you should see the little Lock symbol appear near the bottom of your browser window.)

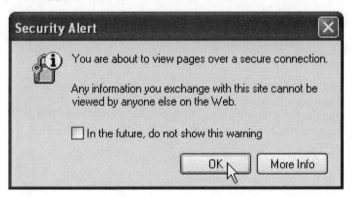

At the next web page, enter your **Customer Account Code** and **Customer Account Password** as shown in the following picture. This information was recorded (or should have been!) when the ISP Account was first set up (see section B, stage1 in Appendix IV). If you are struggling to find these details, you should look back through the emails that you have received for the Main Identity (that is the email address on the Primary Account). Providing that you have not deleted it, then you should see an email with something like 'Welcome to Tiscali' in the subject title. It was probably one of the very first emails that you received on the Main Identity (see exercise 26 in section 8.6 if you need some help on searching). If you can find this email, then the details will be in the message content section.

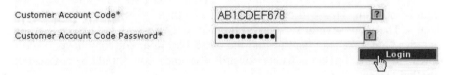

If you make a mistake during entering the details, you can use the **Rubout** or **Delete** keys and then re-type. Press the **Login** button on the web page when you are ready.

Once you have been logged in to your 'My Account', then you will see the list of available services...

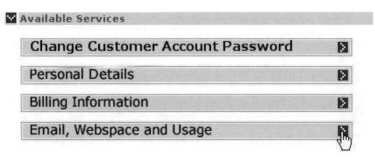

Press the '**Email, Webspace and Usage**' button as shown above. This then takes you to the 'Package information' aspect of your account. In the next picture, we can see typical details for a 'Pay As You Go' account. Towards the right-hand side of the web page, press the **Go** button underneath the 'Details and Services' column…

You should then see the 'Account Details' page, listing details about the 'Primary Account' and the full email address associated with it…

Account Type	Userid	Status	Request Date	Activation Date	Action View Details
Primary	mary.brown01@tiscali.co.uk	Active	06/26/2002	06/26/2002	GO

On the line of the primary Account, press another **Go** button, under the 'View Details' column. This will bring up a new web page showing the 'Service List' details. There are several sections to this list, one of which is labelled 'Service Details'. Now take care here to find the correct section. You may have to scroll down the page, but somewhere towards the end, you should see a section labelled 'Tiscali 10.0'…

Web Space / ftp

   mary.brown01@tiscali.co.uk   06/26/2002   GO

Tiscali 10.0

   mary.brown01@tiscali.co.uk   06/26/2002   Active   GO

Press the **Go** button again. On the next web page showing you the details for

'Tiscali 10.0', at the very bottom of the page, there is a button called 'Add Account'. Again, you may have to scroll down the page to find it. When you can see it, press this button, as shown in the next picture.

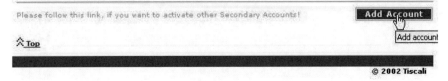

Finally we reach the page that allows us to enter the details of the Secondary Account. Now the same restrictions that were applicable to setting up the 'Username' and 'Password' for the Primary Account are applicable here (read section B, Appendix IV to get more help about Usernames and Passwords). Enter these details carefully, remembering to be extra vigilant about the choice of capitals and non-capitals for the password. Remember also that if you want to use a pseudonym for the account, then you should use it here because it will form part of the full email address...

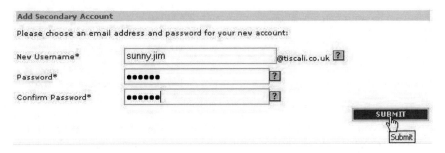

When you are sure that you have entered these details exactly as you really want them to be, then press the **Submit** button at the right-hand side.

If the details just entered are acceptable, then you should see a message like the next picture. If not, then you can go back and try again.

Press the **Main Menu** button. This returns you to the 'Account Details' page, and you should now see that a Secondary Account line has appeared below the Primary Account line...

Account Type	Userid	Status	Request Date	Activation Date	Action View Details
Primary	mary.brown01@tiscali.co.uk	Active	06/26/2002	06/26/2002	GO
Secondary	sunny.jim@tiscali.co.uk	Provisioning Request	--	--	GO

Accounts Information

Look carefully under the column labelled 'Status' and you will probably see the words 'Provisioning Request' - basically telling you that your Secondary Account is not quite ready yet. If you wait a few minutes and then press the **Refresh** button on the browser's toolbar (at the top of the browser window) ... you should see the status for your Secondary Account change to 'Active', as shown in the next picture.

Accounts Information

Account Type	Userid	Status	Request Date	Activation Date	Action View Details
Primary	mary.brown01@tiscali.co.uk	Active	06/26/2002	06/26/2002	GO
Secondary	sunny.jim@tiscali.co.uk	Active	08/18/2002	08/18/2002	GO

Only when you see this 'Active' status is the Secondary Account ready for use.

Having created the Secondary Account successfully, and confirmed its status as 'Active', you can now close the browser window and disconnect from the Internet.

B.Adding a new Identity to Outlook Express

From the Desktop, start the **Outlook Express** program running. We need to work off-line, so if you are asked if you wish to connect to the Internet, choose to '**Work Offline**' or press '**Cancel**'. If you see an error message, press the **Hide** button.

With the Outlook Express window now opened and working off-line, we are ready to begin. From the main menu click on '**File**' and select '**Identities**' then '**Add New Identity...**' as shown in the next picture.

When the **New identity window** pops up, type the name for the new identity. This is only a display name to label it, so you are free to enter it more or less as you like. In the worked example here we will set a password for the new identity. This is optional; skip over this part if you don't wish to set one. Click on the '**Require a password' checkbox**...

If a password is requested, you then see the **'Enter Password' window**, as in the following picture. Now be careful here. You need to remember the password that you choose exactly in the form it is entered (use of capital and non-capital lettering), so that you can pass the details on to the user of the new identity. They in turn will be able to change it later so that it is completely private, but they will first have to enter the password that you choose now in order to gain access. An easy approach is to make the password here the same as their identity name. Check that the Caps Lock indicator is not on, and then enter the password in both textboxes in turn.

Press the **OK** button when you are ready. The **Enter Password window** then closes and you are back to the **New Identity window**. Notice now that the 'Change Password' button is now active (it was 'greyed-out' previously)...

Press the **OK** button for this window when you are ready. The window will then close and you should see this next message...

At this point, the new identity has now been created. Press the **Yes** button. This will automatically start the **Internet Connection Wizard** to allow you to set up the Account information within Outlook Express, which is the 'item' aspect of the Account that we talked about at the beginning of this appendix. We continue with this item set up in the next section.

C. Setting up the Account within Outlook Express for the new Identity

Following on from the previous section, the **Internet Connection Wizard** should now be running. Enter the display name that you would like to appear on all outgoing emails that the new identity creates. If the new identity wishes to use a pseudonym in the email address, then you wouldn't want to put anything in this display name that relates to their real name...

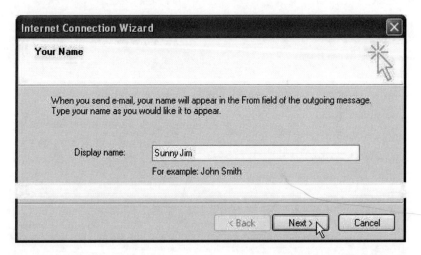

Press the **Next** button when you are ready. Then enter the full email address for the new identity (this is the email address for the ISP Secondary Account)...

Press the **Next** button. At the next window, leave the first box set to 'POP3'. Enter the **Incoming Mail Server** and **Outgoing Mail Server** details exactly as recorded when the Primary Account was first set up (as in stage1, section B, Appendix IV)...

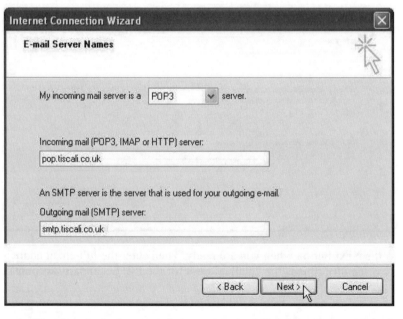

Press the **Next** button. At the next window, enter the full email address and password for the Secondary Account. Also, click the **'Remember Password' checkbox**...

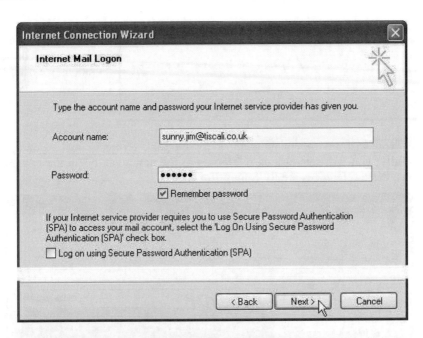

Press the **Next** button. Finally, you will see the 'Congratulations' message...

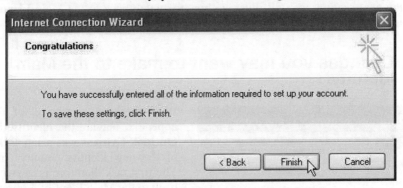

Press the **Finish** button. This is the end of the **Internet Connection Wizard** sequence.

The next message that you will see reflects the fact that you have now fully prepared the new identity and that you have switched to this new identity. In consequence, the computer will ask you if you want to go on-line now...

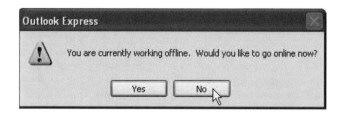

Press the **No** button, because there are some other considerations we need to make.

Now you will see the main window for Outlook Express, but if you look carefully, you will see various references to the new identity (in the example shown these references are to 'Sunny Jim')...

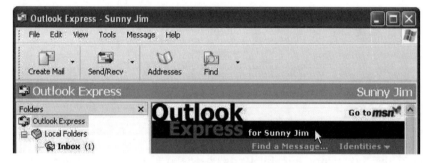

In the next section, we will illustrate how to switch back to the Main Identity, so that we can discuss a few changes to it that you may want to make.

D. Changes you may want to make to the Main Identity

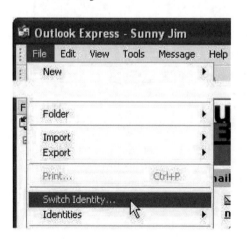

We completed section C of this appendix, leaving the identity that **Outlook Express** was using as that of the new identity 'Sunny Jim'. The first task therefore is to switch back to the Main Identity. From the main menu, click on '**File**' and select the '**Switch Identity...**' option...

On the Switch Identities window, click to select 'Main Identity'...

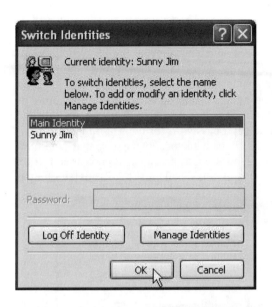

Then press the **OK** button. The whole **Outlook Express** program will then automatically close, and it will re-open with the identity switched back to the 'Main Identity'. If prompted with the 'You are currently working off-line. Would you like to go on-line?' message, press the **No** button, or press '**Cancel**' if it is automatically attempting to go on-line – so that we are then working off-line.

At this point, you are back to the situation you started from at the beginning of this appendix, with the exception that you have the new identity set up and ready to use.

Now if you have other members of the family accessing the computer and using email, it might be prudent to set a password for the Main Identity (assuming you don't have one already). Then when Sunny Jim comes to use the computer, he won't get access to all your email as well! You can also arrange for the Outlook Express program not to automatically start up each time to the Main Identity each time you set it running, but instead to pop up a small menu – and let whoever is currently using the computer make a decision of which identity to start with. If you decide not to change these things, then you can quit now.

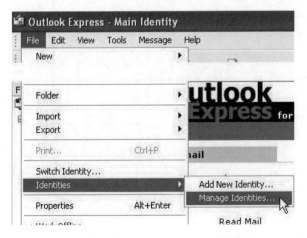

From the main menu, 'click' on '**Identities**' and select the '**Manage Identities...**' option...

This pops up the **Manage Identities window**, as shown in the next picture. In the centre of the window is a checkbox marked 'Use this identity when starting a program' and in the list box just below it you see that the entry is normally 'Main Identity'. Simply click once on the checkbox to 'un-tick' it, and you will then observe that the list box below is 'greyed-out'. From now on, when the Outlook Express program starts running, a pop-up menu will first appear to allow you to select the identity to use for that email session. We will see this happen shortly, but first we need to set a password for the Main Identity.

On the same screen as shown in the next picture, make sure that within the large white box, the Main Identity is now highlighted (as demonstrated in the picture) - if it isn't then click on it to make it so. Then press the **Properties** button.

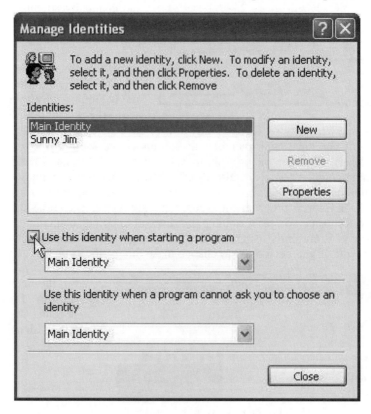

Pressing the Properties button will pop up the Identity Properties window...

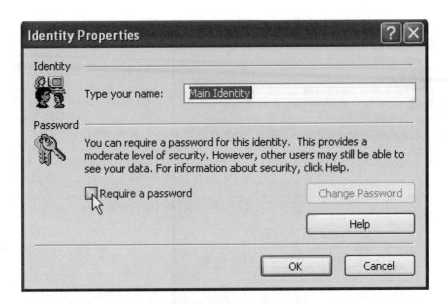

Click the '**Require a password**' **checkbox** and the Password window appears...

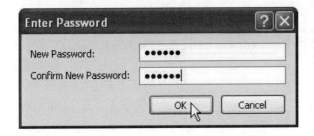

Fill in the password of your choice in the first textbox (remembering all the precautions that we have previously mentioned about passwords!) and repeat it again in the second textbox. Then press the **OK** button.

Press the **OK** button to close the **Properties window**, and press the **OK** button to close the **Manage Identities window.** You should now be back at the main window for Outlook Express. Close down the program with the **Close** button in the top right-hand corner, in the usual way.

Now we are ready to test the changes we have made.

Start up the **Outlook Express** program once again. This time you will first see the **Identity Login window** appear, to allow you to select the identity that you want to use...

The change we made to the password for the Main Identity is now effective. Check that the Main Identity is highlighted (if it isn't then click on it to make it so), and then enter the new password for it in the **Password textbox**. Finally press the **OK** button. The Outlook Express program will now start running as normal.

When someone else wishes to start the program with an alternative identity (such as 'Sunny Jim') they should first click their choice to highlight it, enter the appropriate password if requested, and then press the **OK** button.

Appendix VII

Setting Up Accounts for Dial-up Connections

If a mail 'account' within Outlook Express is not set up to use a dial-up networking connection, then the dialog box seen when the program starts running may be different from that shown here. Worse still, it may not show itself at all.

Users of Windows XP Professional may even get a different set of starting dialog boxes to users of Windows XP Home Edition, as shown in these next two pictures.

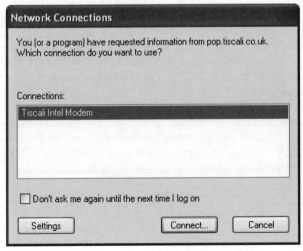

Although computers set up as in these last two pictures will still dial up correctly, you will probably find that the **Auto-Disconnect dialog box** (as shown in Exercise 3, section 2.6) does not appear when you close the Outlook Express program.

You can adjust all editions of Windows XP (and other versions of Windows) to give the same Dial-up Connection dialog box, and make the Auto-Disconnect dialog box becomes visible, by using the following method. Start the Outlook Express program running off-line. From the main menu click 'Tools' and select the Accounts... option as shown in the following picture.

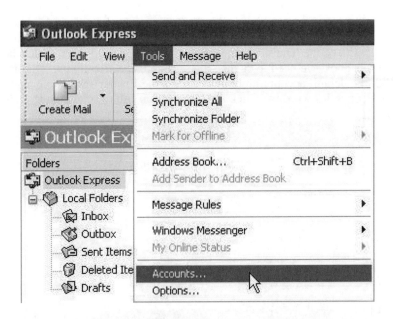

When the Internet Accounts window pops up, click on the **'Mail' tab** to see only the mail accounts. Make sure that the account is highlighted, as shown in the next picture (if you have more than one account, you can choose one as the 'default' account – that is the one that you normally wish to use – by then pressing the **'Set as Default'** button when it has been highlighted).

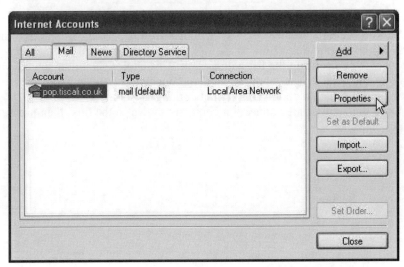

Notice in the above picture that under the 'Connection' column, it does not say 'Dial-up' (there are a few different wordings that you might see). To make sure that you will see the 'Dial-up Connection' and 'Auto-Disconnect' dialog boxes used in this book, we need to change the setting to specifically use 'Dial-up'.

With the default account highlighted, press the **Properties** button. You then see the **Properties window**. Click the **Connection tab** to see the next picture.

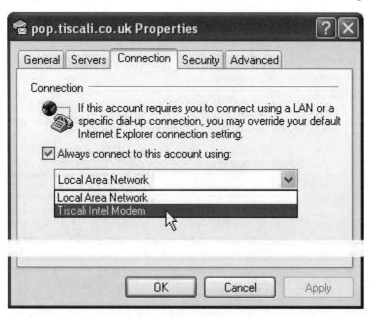

Click the checkbox labelled 'Always connect to this account using:' and then click the down pointing arrow to the right side of the box below it. Select the appropriate choice from the list with a click. This choice should be the relevant name of the 'Dial-up Networking' modem connection (Appendix III, Stage 2, has more information about 'Dial-up networking' if you need it).

Once the appropriate connection choice is shown in the box, then press the Apply button...

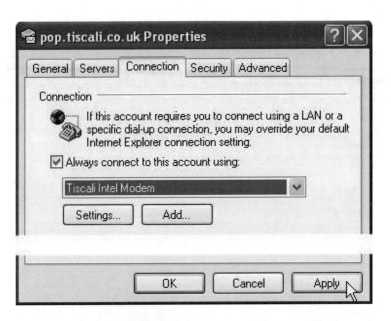

When you are ready, press the **OK** button. This will close the window and show you the Internet Accounts window again. This time you will notice that the wording in the 'Connections' column has altered to say 'Dial-up:' as in the next picture.

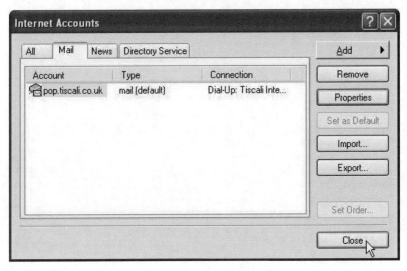

Press the **Close** button and the necessary setting changes are completed.

Note – If someone has ticked the 'Don't use Auto Disconnect' checkbox on the Auto-Disconnect message then you may have a problem resetting it. Even if you delete the Dial-up Networking connection and recreate it (as in Stage 2 of Appendix III) then the computer may pick up the old settings where it had been turned off! The best thing to do in this circumstance is to create a new Dial-up Networking connection with a slightly different name. Then the use of Auto-Disconnect will return, however you need to make sure that the 'Internet Account' described in this appendix uses the new name and not the old name.

Index

1470 code, 229

Adding a new identity, 252
  a secondary account, 248
Address book, 98, 103, 106
Addressing an electronic letter, 25
Adobe Acrobat, 75
ADSL (Broadband), 52
'Anytime' account, 215
ASCII, 16
Attach button, 78
Attaching an image file, 76
Attachments, 27, 73
  via Webmail, 188
Auto-disconnect, 50
  dialog box, 264
Automatic disconnection, 35

Backup copies, 160
Bitmap, 85
Blocked sender list, 171
.bmp, 75
Breaking up a file, 85

Caller ID, 41
Caller Line ID, 229
Call-waiting, 91
Cc: textbox, 69
Changes to main identity, 258
checkdomain.com, 170
Closing Outlook Express, 49
COM port, 34
Connect automatically check box, 96
Connecting to the Internet, 32
Contacts, 55
Customer Account Code, 222, 249
Customer Account Details, 222

Customer Account Password, 222, 249

Default email, 101
Delete key, 143
Deleted items folder, 144
Deleting in the address book, 108
  unwanted email, 142
Delivery Trigger Action, 22, 30
Desktop, 36
Detaching Webmail attachments, 194
Dial Up password, 234
  username, 222, 234
  connections, 263
  networking, 88, 222
Disconnecting, 49
'Douglas Bader' method, 145
Drafts folder, 66
Driver software, 206

Editing an email, 64
  in the address book 106
Electronic letter 15
  post office, 26
Email address, 57, 98
Email anywhere in the world, 181
Email body, 18
  header, 18
  tail, 18
External modem, 33

File Transfer Protocol, 204
File types, 73
Filing to a new folder, 145
Firewall, 161, 163
Flag Message option, 150
Flagging an email, 149
Folders, 55

Forwarding, 116, 135
FTP, 204

.gif, 75
Go button, 184
GPRS, 52
Group of addresses, 109

Hackers, 162
HTML, 29
Hyperlink, 203

Identities, 246
Inbox folder, 22, 141
Incoming Mail Server, 222
  Mailbox, 23
Internal modem, 33
Internet, 202
Internet Connection Sharing, 90
Internet Explorer, 182
IP address, 202
ISA-bus slots, 206
ISDN, 51
ISP Account, 238

.jpg, 75, 85

Kilobytes, 84

LAN, 53
Logging options, 169

Main identity, 247
Managing email, 141
Manually checking for mail, 46
Mary Brown, 104
Megabytes, 84
Megapixels, 84
Message rules, 171
MIME, 28, 124
Miniature monitors icon, 51
Mobile telephone ,52
Modem, 19, 32

Modem hardware, 207
My Documents, 195
My Pictures, 195

New hardware wizard, 209
New message window, 57, 66
Norton's Anti-virus, 160

Office Local Area Network, 53
On-line and off-line, 88
On-line connection, 48
Ordering the lists, 151
Outbox folder, 22, 60
Outgoing Mail Server, 222
Outgoing Mailbox, 23
Outlook Express, 21, 32, 244

Paper clip icon, 79
Password, 20, 199
Pay As You Go, 215
PCI-bus slots, 206
.pdf, 75
Pixel, 84
Plain Text, 124
POP3, 24
Primary account, 247
Priority setting, 137

Read, 64
Read Receipts, 116, 118
Receiving an attachment, 80
Registering with an ISP Company, 217
Replying, 128
Rich Text, 124

Save password' feature, 96
Saving an email, 65
Searching, 153
Secondary account, 247
Security logging tab, 168
Send/Receive, 62
Sending an attachment, 73
  an email, 54

Sent Items folder, 61
Setting up a modem, 205
  an ISP Account, 215
SMTP, 24
Spam, 171
Stamp, 19
Starting Outlook Express, 36
Stationery, 122
Stationery option, 124
Subject, 57
Sub-windows, 244
System tray, 51

TCP/IP, 21
Time shift, 71
Tiscali UK ISP, 182
Trojan horse, 161

Unread, 64
USB, 34
Username, 20, 25
Username@ComputerNetwork, 25

V.92 modem, 91
Viruses, 158

Webmail, 181
Windows XP Firewall, 166
Wizard, 209
Working off-line, 88
World-Wide-Web, 203
www' wording, 203